A History of Gordon Road School

1907–1974

Walter Rose

Walter Rose

W Rose
109 Harvey's Nurseries
Reading RG4 8TW

ISBN 0 9534798 0 3

Produced by MRM Associates Ltd., Unit C4, Weldale St.,
Reading, Berkshire RG1 7BX

Contents

1
Preface

The name Gordon Road School became a legend to Maidonians before, during and after the Second World War and was automatically considered as the next choice if a child failed to gain a place at the County Boys' School (now Desborough) or County Girls' School (now Newlands).

Its reputation was held with high esteem in the town, its standard of education synonymous, its staff trusted and respected. Of the thousands of pupils who passed through its doors many went on to achieve creditability not only for themselves but for the name of the School.

In its sixty seven year history the first two Headmaster's dedicated sixty years to the School and three of the first day teachers remained until their retirement.

And yet up until now nothing has been done to record these achievements. This book is just about that – recording the true and simple facts which made Gordon Road the popular School of its time.

I, like many pupils of my age, did not possibly see the School at its best. The war years portrayed hard times, shortage of supplies, rationing, shortage of men teachers due to call-up for military service, older teachers coming out of retirement to 'help out', sometimes no teacher at all with the member of staff in the next class room keeping an eye on both classes. Beside this many of the staff were engaged in war work, Red Cross and St. John, Home Guard, Air Raid Precautions, Auxiliary Fire Service, Fire

Watchers, assisting with evacuees, clothing coupons, national savings, ration books, all tasks essential for the war effort. They did not always have the time to teach as they would have wished, but I am sure I speak for most of my generation, every effort was made to turn scholars into first class citizens.

Much of the information contained in the text has been compiled from School Log Books, Headteacher's Reports and Governors' Minutes. My thanks are due to Dr. Peter Durrant, Berkshire County Archivist for reading the typescript and his staff in the Record Office (Archives) at Shire Hall for their invaluable help and encouragement in enabling me to complete this project.

While every care has been taken to ensure the accuracy of dates and names the author cannot accept responsibility for any omissions or misspellings.

The copyright of two or three photographs were untraceable but I would like to thank Maidenhead Library for letting me choose from their collection.

The Maidenhead Advertiser supplied the photographs of Mr. Jeavons and John Rimmer and gave their consent to the publication of the School building and the 1911 Relay Team.

My special thanks also to Luke Over for his help and advice.

2
Education in Maidenhead at the Turn of the Century

Although an Art Class began in 1881 and eventually became an Art School 'Technical Instruction' in Maidenhead dates back to December 14, 1894 when the Technical Instruction School Building Committee consisting of members of the whole Council met to invite estimates from three firms – Messrs. Cooper & Sons, Maidenhead, Doulton & Co., Lambeth and King and Co., Stourbridge. An advertisement for tenders for terra cotta was placed in 'The Builder', 'The Maidenhead Advertiser', 'The Reading Mercury' and 'Building News' in January 1895. Eight firms submitted estimates, the tender going to the lowest, the Measham Terra Cotta Co. of £250.

A contract with Mr. Martin the builder was drawn up by mid January for the entire completion within twelve months or 'might be speedily proceeded with and finished if possible within nine months'.

By January 28 three candidates had been interviewed for the post of Clerk of Works, Mr. W. Peart being appointed as from February 4 at a weekly salary of £2. 12s. 6d.

The foundation stone reads 'This stone was laid on the 13th day of May, 1895 by John Budgen Esq, Mayor'.

The opening ceremony was performed by the Mayoress, Mrs. Grenfell on August 20, 1896 who was presented with a silver key obtained through Mr. Biggs. Capt. Serocold, 1st Volunteer Battalion of the Royal Berkshire Regt. was asked to allow his Company and the Band to parade on the occasion and the

Gordon Road School Building.

Maidenhead Volunteer Fire Brigade formed in 1866 also attended.

From an Art Class to a Technical Institute now comprising a science lecture room, class room, laboratory, modelling room, carpenters' shop and cookery class.

Under the Education Act, 1902 a sub-committee consisting of seven members (four at least members of the Council) was appointed for the purpose of administering the Institute.

The first meeting of the Education Committee for the Borough of Maidenhead constituted in accordance with the scheme made by Council under Section 17 (1) (a) of the Education Act 1902 and approved by the Board of Education with respect to Higher Education, Elementary Education and Technology was held on June 26, 1903.

The School Management Committee of sixteen members met on July 7, 1903 to:-

Consider and approve all appointments, transfers, dismissals of teachers made by Managers

Consider all matters affecting teachers salaries
Consider reports from Board of Education and to make recommendations thereon
Consider all complaints made by or against teachers
To enquire as to the sufficiency of staff and general efficiency and suitability of the secular instruction given in schools
Arrange for appointment and training of pupil teachers and establishment of scholarships
To conduct the examinations of any examining Board
To receive and consider all requisitions made by the Managers and to prepare estimates and obtain tenders for school furniture, books, materials, fuel and other school necessaries
Report generally to the Education Committee.

A Sub-Committee called 'The School Attendance Committee' of eight members would:-

Report upon questions touching and take all necessary steps for securing school attendance
Have the superintendence of School Attendance Officers
Deal with all business relating to the Elementary Education (Blind and Deaf Children) Act 1893, the Elementary Education (Defective and Epileptic Children) Act 1899 and the Industrial Schools Acts
Visit and inspect Certified Industrials Schools and other schools in which children from the Borough are maintained
Report generally to the Education Committee.

A letter from the Hon. Sec to the Managers of the British Schools and Maidenhead Congregational Church dated July 3, 1903 stated that the deacons of the Church let school rooms for British School purposes to either a British School Committee or the Town Council as the Education Committee at a rent of £20 per annum.

At a meeting of the Managers of the British Schools on March 2, 1903, a resolution was passed 'The Managers of the British Schools decide to request the Education Authority of the Town to take over the schools and conduct them as provided schools'. The deacons of the Congregational Church to which the building belong were willing to let them to Maidenhead Education Authority at the normal rent of £20. All British School Managers would hand over to the Education Authority the balance in hand and all the school fittings and plant without payment. The British School originates from the Congregationalists and dates back to the late 1840s.

By July 20 British Schools would become 'provided', correspondents having been duly appointed for the following – Boyn Hill, British, National, Wesleyan (became Municipal 1907), St. Mary's Roman Catholic and Braywick. The requisition from all the schools was approved (subject to minor details in some cases).

A letter from the Board of Education urging an arrangement between the County Council and the Corporation for the combination to jointly maintain Braywick and North Town Schools was dated September 8, 1903 and on the 28th the Managers of British Schools had applied to the Board of Education for an order to appoint Foundation Managers.

A scheme was prepared by the Town Clerk for the establishment of a Higher Education Committee which, when complete, would consist of:-

Members of Maidenhead Town Council	16
Nominated by Maidenhead Town Council	2
	18

and would be responsible for secondary education of boys and girls in its higher and lower grades; technical instruction; commercial and industrial education; training of teachers.

Details of schools in 1903 –		*No. on Books*
1. National Schools, Boys, Girls & Infants East Street		833
2. Wesleyan Schools Mixed & Infants King Street		472
3. Boyn Hill Boys	)	
4. Boyn Hill Girls & Infants Boyn Hill Avenue	)	791
5. New Boyn Hill Girls Rutland Road	)	
6. St. Paul's Infants Albert Street		82
7. British Schools, Mixed & Infants West Street		350
8. Braywick School, Girls & Infants Braywick		81
9. Roman Catholic, Mixed & Infants Cookham Road		179
		2788

The Boyn Hill Evening Continuation School opened in 1903 and for the quarter ending Christmas 1903 recorded:-

Commercial Arithmetic	40
Book keeping (elementary)	36

Book keeping (advance)	8
Carving	10
Cookery	18
French (E1)	26
French (Adv)	10
German	7
Manual Instruction	19
Shorthand (E1)	35
Shorthand (Adv)	28
Shorthand (Speed)	16
Chemistry (Theory)	21
Chemistry (Practical)	16
Building Construction	14
Geometry	12
	316

The fitting up of a Brock Lane School as an overflow from British Schools was discussed in 1904 and on July 5 the Mayor opened Brock Lane Infant School and West Street Mixed School as Council Schools, to be named 'West Street and Brock Lane Council Schools'.

In June 1905 the Education Department declined to give further grants to the Maidenhead Modern School until the buildings were brought up to standard. The County Council was the Authority for carrying out the Education Department's suggestions but could not do so because the School was owned by a Board of Governors, (being established as a limited liability company in 1894). If the County Council carried out alterations to the buildings and the Board of Education and the County Council made full grants for the maintenance of the School, the Town Council would acquire freehold of the site if reasonable terms could be arranged. It was taken over on April 1, 1906, the repayment of an existing mortgage of £855 would be cleared in 1933 by annual payments (1906 being £68 including interest of 4 per cent).

The Managers intended to close the Wesleyan (Day) School as from March 31, 1907, the number of infants attending

Albert Street	71
Wesleyan	140

Council	95
	306

Figures for 1907 show

National	Boys	28
	Girls	11
	Infants	20
Wesleyan	Mixed	21
	Infants	6
Boyn Hill	Boys	81
	Girls	103
	Infants	87
Braywick		78
St. Mary's	Mixed	9
St. Mary's		3
Council	Mixed	54
	Infants	12
		513

A Joint Committee of six members of the Town Council and five from Berkshire Education Committee was formed in March 1908 and was known as the Governors of the Technical Institute.

At a special committee re Secondary Education on June 12, 1908, particulars had not been given to the nature and cost of the proposed new school for boys and of the charge proposed to be made upon Maidenhead for secondary education, and also of the representation on the Governing Body to be given to Maidenhead by the scheme in connection with the Boys' School. A deputation was appointed and had an interview with the Assistant Secretary, Board of Education to enquire the position of the Town Council in regard to the representation on the Governing Body of Secondary Schools.

A conference between representatives of Windsor and Maidenhead Town Councils took place on August 5 and resolved that the two councils were of the opinion that each should have adequate representation on Governing Bodies of Secondary Schools in their districts such to be in proportion to the amount contributed by such districts towards the cost of such schools.

3
Loan Sanctions

The Board of Education approved the site purchased by Maidenhead Borough Council and the Local Government Board sanctioned a loan of £750 (Common Seal of Council affixed to the Indenture of Mortgage March 20, 1905), the repayment being extended over a period of sixty years. Application was made to the Public Works Loan Commissioners for the advance referred to be made within a period of thirty years, the Council being informed that the maximum period for which the Board would lend is fifty years. The rate of interest would be £4. 10s. 0d. per cent but if the loan was taken up for a period of thirty years, the interest would be £3. 15s. 0d. per cent. The half-yearly payment of principal and interest would be £20. 18s. 7d.

The minutes dated July 31, 1905 show the Education Committee made an application to the Local Government Board for sanction to a loan not exceeding £10,000 (approved August 17, 1905) for the purpose of erecting and furnishing of schools on land recently purchased.

Minutes dated October 1, 1906 show the Public Works Loan Commissioners agreed and would be taken up in January 1907. It was resolved on December 3, 1906 'That the Common Seal be affixed to an Indenture of Mortgage to the P.W.L.C. for securing the repayment of the sum of £8,350 and interest at the rate of £3. 15s. 0d. per centum per annum repayable by half-yearly payments by way of annuity within a period of thirty years and of the sum of £670 and interest at the rate of £3. 10s. 0d. per centum per annum repayable by half-yearly payments by way of annuity within a period of ten years'.

		£	s	d	
Purchase of land	J. Budgen	500	0	0	August 20, 1904
Purchase of land	W. Creed	190	0	0	August 20, 1904
Vendors' Solicitors Costs		19	17	10	August 20, 1904
Purchasers Solicitors Costs		17	1	0	August 20, 1904
Solicitor P.W.L.C.		9	10	6*	March 30, 1905
		£736	9	4	

	£	s	d
* Stamps on mortgage	1	2	6
* Solicitor's fee	8	8	0
	9	10	6

NOTE	£750	0	0
Less	736	9	4
	13	10	8

As this amount was less than the application the sum of £14 (fractions of pounds not included) was paid back on August 18, 1906.

	£	s	d		£	s	d
Builders estimate	7,920	0	0	Expenditure loan	8,350	0	0
Total cost of building	7,883	11	10	Total cost (inc furnishing)	8,297	11	10
Credit balance	36	8	2	Credit balance	52	8	2

	£	s	d
Ex loan	670	0	0
Less	650	14	9
Credit balance	19	5	3

4

First Day Pupils

Two hundred and twenty nine boys were due to be admitted on the first school day – April 8 1907. For record purposes these have been listed in admission number order (not alphabetical or class). The first on the list was PANNIERS, Edward, who lived in Wellington Road and transferred from Boyn Hill.

BLICK Charles Abram
FRYER James Clarence
SMITH Harold
BROOKER Arthur
CORNELIUS Reginald
CORNELIUS Frank
DUNN Henry
GOODALL Alfred
SMITH Cyril George
WILSON Harold
COXALL Arthur John
STURT Albert John
RANDALL Edward David
GIBBONS Albert
VEVERS Montague
VEVERS Harold
POWELL Ernest Edgar
WHEELER William Job
HARRIS Harry John
WILDER John Malcolm
WILDER Christopher
CASTLE John
GIBBS Harry
WHEELER John
POOLE Stanley James
** AYLIFFE Neil
BUGDEN Harry
BUGDEN Stanley Edward
STOKES Henry
LORD Harry
PRICE Owen
HARMSWORTH Frank
Hazel
AYRES George
PYM Frank
MEAD James
GRINSTED George
WATSON Arthur
WATSON Charles
EDEN William
COOPER Horace
HUGHES William Albert
MAZEY Thomas
WALTON Leonard
BATTEN William
WAIZENEKER Clarence
WAIZENEKER Bertie
GIBBONS Ben
RANCE Cecil Andrew
SOUTHGATE Leonard
LARBEY George
EVANS Harry
HALL Philip
JONES Frank
STONE Alvery
STEVENS Fred
CARTER William Frederick
BATES Ronald
HOLLAND Frederick
BURNS Herbert
COTTON James
COTTON Reginald
WARREN Wm. Stephen
IVERMEE Wm. Alfred
SALMON James Henry
SALMON Wm. Frederick
PREECE Arthur
JENNINGS Howard
HUMPHREYS Augustus

BROWN John
EDWARDS William
HOOPER George
SAINSBURY Edward Victor
FISHER Victor George
LAKER Cyril
BROWN Victor
HALL Edwin
EDWARDS Rowland
Edmund
GEORGE Sidney Alexander
GEORGE Thomas
CHOULES Shirley
WINGRAVE Norman
SWIFT Leonard
WEST Richard
HABBIN Arthur Leonard
HARRIS Robert
HARRIS Stephen
SELLWOOD Percy
GREENHARD Leonard
Charles
WHITMILL George
SIMPSON Ernest
POOLE Harry
CHOULES Jack
DEVERALL Henry
DEVERALL William
COX Leonard Cyril
ALLEN William
COLMAN Oliver
JACKSON Bernard William
JACKSON John Cyril
JACKSON Rowland George
HAYES Harold James
HAYES Lewis Minter
BOND Ernest Walter
BOND Frederick George
GAINES Alfred
GAINES Lawrence
CORBIN Ernest Reginald
COLSELL William Thos.
ORAM Jack
ORAM Arthur
PICKMAN Harry
PICKMAN Ernest
SHORTER Harold

LINDSEY Donald Victor
EDWARDS Arthur
DIXON Horace
COURTNEY Horace
ROWSELL Alfred George
MEADE Cecil
BROCKS Harry
WRIGHT Maurice
COOKE Frederic Telfer
COOKE Frank Hugh
HOBBS Wilfred Charles
BOORE Albert Edward
NURSE Leslie Henri
SMITH Frederick
SMITH Robert James
PHILLIPS Alexander Hovell
WEST Major
COLE Aubrey Hatterley
GRAY Norman Arthur
KEATS Frederick.
BOLTON Charles
FITZGERALD Thomas
DANCE Percy William
MARKS Reginald
BROWN Frank
ILES Frederick William
HARRIS Jack
WHITE Albert
POORE Reginald Charles
HAMBLIN Charles Robert
EDWARDS Alec
BLAY Eric
BOORE Fred
TAYLOR Fred
STANTON Matthew
WILSON Ernest Arthur
NORCUTT Arthur (1)
BOORE George
RAVEN Arthur
KEELEY Harry
HERMON Sidney
STACEY William
BALDWIN Harry John
GRESWELL Thomas
GRESWELL Henry
BAYLEY Richard
DYSON George

HUSKINSON Horace
MUGGRIDGE Fred
BELCHER Jesse
JACKSON Reginald
FOLLEY Walter
RACKSTRAW Percy
SAUNDERS Thomas
ALDRIDGE Charles
COCKER Sidney
NORCUTT William
SUCKLING Cyril
GRINSTED Joe
AUSTIN Harold
CAMPBELL George
ROE Arthur
BROWN Leonard
HIGGINS Albert
COURTNEY Arthur Thomas
FRANKLIN Arthur
FRANKLIN George
FRANKLIN Albert
CAMPBELL Henry
SEYMOUR Cecil
GEMMEL Arthur
COUSINS Leslie
CARTER Benjamin
CARTER Leslie
QUAIN William
BRAXTON William
DREWITT Edgar
ROGERS Charles
WOOD John Henry
GRIFFITHS Arthur
DOMONEY Cyril
SANDS Arthur
COOPER Charles
BRIDGE Samuel
KEMPTON Dan
KEMPTON Herbert
BELCHER Sidney
ANDERSON Victor
MEAD William
MEAD Horace
GASCOYNE William
ROGERS Frank
ROGERS Arthur
HARRIS Clifford

BROMLEY Arthur
HAINES Fred
HIGGS Herbert
WHITE Thomas
ROE Albert
NORCUTT Arthur (2)
ELLIOTT Arthur
GROVES William
REED Alfred
WESTCOTT Maurice
SMITH Ronald
MARCHAM Frederick
BELCHER Ernest
JOHNSON Albert
HAINES Walter
JOHNSON Victor
STINTON Fred
FISHER James
CRASWELL William
WOOLFORD Harry

** Made no attendance

Although the official number on roll for the first day was recorded as 229 this should read 228 as one pupil had been registered twice.

Two hundred and seventeen girls were listed to be admitted on the first school day – April 8 1907. Again these appear in admission number order (not alphabetical or class). The first was COWARD, Nancy who lived at The Cottage, Oldfield Road and transferred from a 'Council' school.

SMITH Gladys Nina
PANNIERS Olive
WEST Winifred
WEST Lily
HAZELDINE Minnie
WHITLOCK Hilda
BLICK Ellen
BEALE Dorothy
BARNSHAW Ethel
BURROWS Gladys
LOHMER Mary M.
WEBB Ellen A.
RANCE Frances C.
CASTLE Ethel
COXALL Elizabeth
ALLEN Frances
STEVENS Minnie
LEGG Doris M.
GIBBONS Elsie
LANE Clara
DEACON Kathleen
HILL Doris
WHEELER Ida D.
WHEELER May
GURNEY Emily M.
HOLEYMAN Rose Mary
HOLEYMAN Margaret
GRINSTED Daisy
PITHERS Lydia
PITHERS Milly
MILES Lily R.
MILES Violet J.
AYLFFIE Dora
FITZGERALD Gertrude
MARTIN Florence E.
MARTIN Beatrice
MILLIN Dorothy
FOWLER Emily
TAYLOR Frances
SALMON Elsie
HOLLIS Doris
CARTER Agnes
CARTER Annie
BUGDEN Evelyn
CARTER Winifred
MORLEY Edith Ella
MORLEY Beatrix
WAY Ruth
GREEN Doris
GILDING Ruth
BAILEY Cecelia B.
BAILEY Amy
BAILEY Winifred
BLICK Annie
BUXTON Nellie
ALEXANDER Ivy
CARTER Lily
ALMOND Elsie E.
SNOW Constance
HUGHES Maud H.
HEARN May V.
DENHAM Kathleen
DAVIS May
SWALLOW Gladys
HARMSWORTH Gertrude
WOODBRIDGE Doris
WOODBRIDGE Eva
WEIZENEKER Nora
LINEY May
JENNINGS Doris
LOWMAN May
LOWMAN Edith
SOUTHGATE Ada
CRAYTHORNE Dorothy
MAZEY May

MAZEY Annie
HOLLAND Agnes
HOLLAND Hilda
STONE Evelyn
STONE Ruby
SAMMONS Bessie
CARTER Winifred
SOUTHGATE Dora
CHALLIS Florence
ROBINSON Bessie L.
LARBEY Annie
CRAYTHORNE Ada
VAISEY Amy
VAISEY Jessie
STINTON Nellie
WINGROVE Nellie
CAINES Hilda
HAINES Florence
REES Ella
EDEN Violet
TRIPP Violet
GRACE Hilda
JAMES Elizabeth
GEMMEL Kathleen
HARRIS Flora Kathleen
HARRIS Amy Louise
CHANDLER Edith A.
CHALLIS Gladys H.
SAINSBURY Mabel R.
PIGG Ella
PIGG Hilda
FISHER Lydia
FISHER Tamar
KNIBBS Mary
PAVEY Florence
YOUNG Nellie
BARNEY Lilian F.
HOILES Edith E.
ALLEN Ivy
SIMMONDS Florence E.
LEE Edith
HAZELDINE Kathleen
SIMPSON Mabel
DENHAM Frances
MINES Elsie M.
JACKSON Margery
SHERVELL Florence
BAKER Nellie
NORCUTT Ella
NORCUTT Phoebe
HUMPHREYS Phyllis
ROBINSON Sophia
CORBIN Stella
BALDWIN Nora T.
BELCHER Milner
STEVENS Dorothy
STEVENS Lily
COLEMAN Elsie B.
TUCKER Dorothy
THOMAS Elsie
MESSENGER Lily
BOND Annie V.
ROWSELL Kathleen
BERRISS Elizabeth
ELLIOTT Annie D.
PHILIPS Clara L.
FEWTRELL Sarah Annie
KEATS Amelia
BELCHER Beatrice
WEST Doris
BLAY Dorothy
COURTNEY Violet
PRICE Ina
PRICE Jessie
BENNETT Alice
BARTLETT Mabel
GRAY Mabel E.
HIGGINS Annie
TAYLOR Lilian
GILDER Edith A.
SPOONER Frances H.
WALTON Agnes E.
FOUNTAIN Mary
WORTH Daisy
BARRETT Mabel
BOULTER Dorothy
GARDNER Hilda
MULLARD Kathleen
WALL Gladys L.
GOLBY Rose
SPILLETT Edith
ROBEY Evelyn
BROWN Gladys
WORTH Edith
NASH Dorothy
MEADE Emily
MESSENGER May
EGGLETON Florence N.
EGGLETON Doris
NORCUTT Ada
HIGGINS Mervyn
HERMON Rose
MARTIN Ivy
NORSWORTHY Edith
WOOD Florence
PHILIPS Ada
BADCOCK Florence I.
WHITE Lily
MARKS Lola
GRIFFITHS Rose
GRIFFITHS Agnes
STREET Amy
CHAMBERLAIN Mabel
GENTLE Lilian
GENTLE Bertha
BROWN Dorothy L.
HARRIS Elsie
BOLTON Dorothy
WOODS Grace
BAILEY Clara
STEVENS Annie
WISE Elizabeth
CLEMENTS Florence
WILSON Alice
HARRIS Louise A.
HIGGINS Ellen
READ Edith
HARRIS Florence
GIBBONS Florence
ILES Florence E.
LORD Elsie
HAYNES Dorothy
WALL Violet
POPE Lily L.
TAYLOR Ada
BLICK Mabel
BARKER Olive
BRADLEY Emily
WALDER Eva
FANCOURT Rose
O'LEARY Grace

5
Synopsis

Under the Elementary Education Act 1870 (Forster's Act)* School Boards provided elementary schooling where voluntary provision was insufficient. Attendance was made compulsory around 1880 school fees being abolished in 1891.

The Education Act 1902 (Balfour Act)** transferred control of elementary education from School Boards to local authorities, every large town forming an Education Committee with country areas doing the same for urban and rural districts. Therefore for the first thirty eight years of its existence Gordon Road was governed by its 'Managers', Maidenhead Borough Council Education Committee. The demands made by this Act was the result of the school being built.

* William Edward Forster, Liberal M.P. for Bradford 1861–86.
** Arthur James Balfour (1st Earl of), Prime Minister 1902–05.

A special meeting was held on April 28, 1905 to consider the number of places to be provided at the school and a provisional figure of 950 children was quoted. This was, however, amended to 300 boys and 300 girls by March 1906. Boys and girls would be separate departments each with their own staff and Head. Tenders for the construction of the school were invited in July 1905 from builders within a three mile radius of the Town Hall, but it was not until another special meeting on May 29, 1906 that they were considered. Six were received and the Council was recommended to accept the lowest tender of £7,920 from F. Bissley. The foundation stone was laid by the Mayor, J. Wesley Walker, on July 12, 1906.

The school was designed by Mr. E.J. Shrewsbury already well-known for his designs of the Technical Institute in Marlow Road, St. Paul's Church in High Town Road (now demolished) and St. Peter's at Furze Platt.

On December 3, 1906 the managers recommended the immediate appointment of a committee to advertise for teaching staff. This consisted of the Council School Managers with the Rev. Canon Drummond and Councillors Upson and Hewitt deputed to formulate proposals for the consideration of the Committee.

On December 17, three teachers from the Wesleyan School, Miss G.M. Evans, Miss A.B. Goody and Miss L. Brett and Miss B.F. Freeman from the West Street School were appointed to the girls section. Mr. R.W. Murray, Miss R.A. Fielder and Miss E.J. Maddison from the West Street School and Mr. J.E. Cluff from the Wesleyan School were appointed to the boys side.

It was proposed that the posts for Headmaster and Headmistress should be advertised in 'The Schoolmaster' and that applicants should not be less than 30 years of age. One hundred and fifty-eight applications were received for the post of Headmaster, five shortlisted, the successful candidate being Alfred Bell. Sixty-one applications were received for the post of Headmistress, three shortlisted, Bertha Partlo being appointed.

Forty-four applications were received for the post of the schools' first caretaker. Three were shortlisted and Mr. Albert Neeve commenced his duties on March 25, 1907.

The school was publicly opened on April 4.

6
Boys' Department

1907

126 children were admitted on Friday April 5, 103 on Monday April 8, making a total of 229. Most had been attending the West Street Council and Wesleyan Schools.

Staff:-
Edwin Alfred Bell (Headmaster)
Robert William Murray
John Ernest Cluff
Rose Amelia Fielder
Elizabeth Jane Maddison (ceased duties April 12)
John Bolton (a pupil teacher from the Maidenhead Modern School, later the County Boys, now Desborough).

The average attendance for the first week was 222.7. Mary Florence Cripps commenced duties on April 15 together with another 7 boys (236).

A scheme of work for the year ending March 31st 1908 had already been compiled.

ENGLISH

Reading, recitation of poetry, oral and written composition (essays and substance of stories told by teacher), word-law grammar, copywriting from blackboard, transcription.
Standard 6 & 7 only. Writing letters and addressing envelopes.

ARITHMETIC

Standard 2.	4 simple rules, 4 rules in money (amounts not over £10), multipliers and divisors up to 12. Measuring and weighing.
Standard 3.	As above but up to £100 and up to 100. Reductions of money. Measuring and weighing.
Standard 4.	Numeration and notation to millions, simple multiplication by numbers over 100, 4 rules and reduction in avoirdupois weight, long measure, measure of capacity, time measure, principles of decimal system and vulgar fractions, Roman numerals.
Standard 5.	g.c.m. (Greatest common measure), l.c.m. (Least common multiple) vulgar fractions (4 rules), concrete fractions, simple and compound practice, bills of parcels, weights and measures, metric system.
Standard 6.	Weights and measures, decimals, metric system, simple proportion, simple interest, mensuration of rectangles and rectangular solids.
Standard 7.	Vulgar and decimal fractions, averages, percentages, profit and loss, investments, use of literal symbols, graphs, mensuration of plane surfaces and solids.

GEOGRAPHY

Standard 2.	The school and its neighbourhood, geographical terms introduced by stories of travel, talks about the continent and oceans, Maidenhead, Berkshire and Bucks.
Standard 3.	England.
Standard 4.	Scotland and Ireland, the earth as a planet, size, shape, motions including day and night, things which influence climate.
Standard 5.	Europe, Upper Thames Valley, map drawing.
Standard 6 & 7.	Asia and Africa (special attention to British possessions), Industrial England, map drawing.

HISTORY

Standard 2 & 3.	Stories from English History.
Standard 4.	Stories from English History (especially dealing with relations of England, Scotland and Ireland).
Standard 5.	Stories from European History (including English).
Standard 6 & 7.	(a) Constitutional events in English History

(b) Parts of English History dealing with the countries taken in Geography.

ELEMENTARY SCIENCE

Lessons in nature study and on common things (Standard 6 and 7 chiefly on physiology and hygiene).

DRAWING

Ruler and freehand drawing, common objects, brush drawing (nature forms and design), memory drawing. Standard 2 claymodelling, Standard 4 scale-drawing, Standard 5 plane geometry, Standard 6 & 7 geometry and geometrical design.

SINGING

Tonic Sol-fa and old notation.

DRILL

Model course.

It was customary for the Mayor, Councillors or the Education Secretary to make regular visits to schools, call and check registers, count heads, in the effort to make sure all was correct and in good order.

Empire Day officially recognised in 1904 was on May 24, the birthday of Queen Victoria. It was always celebrated on that day unless the 24th fell at the week-end or during the Whitsun holidays. In 1907 this took place on May 17, children assembling in the playground and singing, being addressed by the Mayor (C. W. Cox) and Councillors Walker and Bidmead and afterwards each child being presented with a bun. School closed after the morning session to begin the Whitsun holiday.

Only 124 children out of a total of 233 was accounted for on May 30. 62 attended the Agricultural Show leaving 62 in school. Mrs Hill, a supply teacher, began on this day until the end of term August 2.

Many children of this era attended Sunday School and Sunday School 'Treats' accounted for many absences usually during July. They normally took place on a Thursday presumably because it was early closing day for shops in the town. The first year saw:-

		absent
June 20	Wesleyan	65
July 4	3 more treats	
July 11	Boyn Hill	
July 18	St. Mary's and Congregational	46
July 25	2 more treats	51
August 1	Wesleyan Sunday School Bazaar	44

A whole day's holiday was granted on July 8 owing to a fete at Taplow Court.

When the new term began on September 2 Mr. W.F. Spratt became the teacher of Standard 5. Attendance was poor for the first week as children had not returned from holiday. Some elder boys were occasionally allowed to play football from 3.45pm under the charge of a teacher. On September 19 in a race for the Schoolboys Swimming Championship at Maidenhead and the first contest for the Curtis Shield, Arthur Gemmel gained 2nd prize (a medal). All boys were taken to the Chrysanthemum Show on November 1 having previously received lessons on the subject. Mr. Bolton returned to the Modern School on November 11. The term ended on December 20 with entertainment in each classroom for the children given by the boys themselves. It was Mr. Spratt's last day.

1908

The new term commenced on January 6 with poor attendance owing to measles and unsatisfactory heating arrangements. Temperatures only reached 45°F. Mr. J.F. Whitby joined the staff on the 28th, Oliver Colman was awarded a 'Cherry' Scholarship tenable at the Modern School on the 30th and Standards 6 and 7 visited Cookham Paper Mills on the 31st.

The first report was issued by His Majesty's Inspectors on March 10. It stated that 'Improvements could be made in drawing exercises, drill, English and arithmetic, most teaching was skilfully given and work of boys generally creditable. Tone and discipline are very good and the future is most promising. The town is to be congratulated upon the possession of such excellent school buildings.'

Anyone for Domestic Science? Boys ironing *(see p 103).*

Anyone for Domestic Science? Boys at cookery *(see p 103).*

On April 1 the number on roll was 248. There was poor attendance on the 30th through floods.

Rehearsals for Empire Day this year to be held on May 21 took place on the 4th, 7th, 11th, 13th and 18th. The whole school visited Kidwells Park on the 20th. This all resulted in a procession, drill display and sports in the Park on the 21st.

There were many absences on July 2 owing to a Fire Display in the town and a whole day's holiday was granted for the 6th for the Fete at Taplow Court. Sunday School Treats again on July 9, 16th and 23rd.

Four boys were successful in gaining scholarships to the Maidenhead Modern School.

Special lessons were given on December 9 to celebrate the tercentenary (300 years) of John Milton's birth.

Medical inspections were held on December 16, 17 and 21, term ending on the 23rd. Entertainment was given in each classroom by the boys.

1909

School resumed on January 11.

Another H.M.I. Report was issued on March 31. It read 'Considerable improvement has taken place in the general condition of the school since the last inspection. The teaching is vigorous and intelligent, the boys are industrious and make sound progress, the discipline is of the best'.

The school year commenced on April 1. N.O.R. 251.

Staff 1909–10.

	Mr. E.A Bell (Headmaster)
Standard 6 & 7	Mr. J.E. Cluff
Standard 5	Mr. J.F. Whitby
Standard 4	Mr R.W. Murray
Standard 3	Miss M.F. Cripps
Standard 2	Miss R. Fielder.

Mr. Murray accompanied 14 boys of the shooting class to a Naval and Military tournament on May 12. The school visited Kidwells

Park for the Empire Day celebrations on the 26th. Standard 5 were accompanied on nature study walks throughout the year.

Chris Wilder (13), Harry Pickman (14), Victor Anderson (12) and Herbert Hine (12) were selected for the Perambulation of the Borough Boundaries Ceremony on September 16, each being provided with a flag with which to 'beat the bounds'.

At the Town Council monthly meeting held on September 28, it was proposed to erect an Infants' School to accommodate 300 children on the site. The motion was declared to be lost as only the mover and seconder voted in favour.

Boys visited the Chrysanthemum Show at the Guildhall on November 12, school closing for the Christmas holidays on December 23.

1910

The new term commenced on January 10.

The heating apparatus had to be inspected by the Borough Surveyor on February 9, radiators in rooms 1–4 having to be enlarged.

Everyone was familiar with the 'Mayor's Poor Box Fund' but on February 11 the Mayor (F.W. Porter) and Deputy Mayor (D. Bidmead) visited the school in connection with the 'Mayor's Boot Fund'.

When school resumed after the Easter holidays on April 4 numbers had risen to 257. Further medical inspections took place on April 13, 15, 18 concluding on the 20th.

Extra drill lessons started on May 2 for Standards 4–7 to continue for the ensuing fortnight in preparation for Empire Day. On the 9th boys attended Grenfell Park in the afternoon to hear the Proclamation of King George V.

Miss Cripps resigned on June 30 and was replaced by Miss Maud White on July 4. Frank Cooke was awarded a Cherry Scholarship to the Modern School on July 21. Victor Denham, Frank Harmsworth and Owen Price were awarded free places to the school on September 5. Standard 5 were taken on six nature study walks during the year, the Chrysanthemum Show was on November 4 and a further medical inspection on the 30th. Teachers were granted the use of the schools on the evening of November 15 for a social in aid of the Mayor's Poor Box Fund, but had to pay the cost of the lighting and heating of the building for the evening.

1911

Re-open January 9. A considerable number of backward children were admitted to the lower part of the school on February 10, the Headmaster giving special attention to these. Time-table had to be varied. The Mayor (Alderman Good) and Deputy Mayor (Alderman Truscott) visited on the 15th in connection with the distribution of boots to poor children. An epidemic of measles resulted in poor attendance on March 3, an address given by the Rev. S. Welwyn of the Imperial Sunday Alliance was given on the 10th, and lessons on the 'Census' given to all classes during the week of the 20th.

At the beginning of the new school year on April 3 the N.O.R.

Relay Team 1911.

was 259, the highest since its opening.

Nature study walks for Standard 6 and 7 on May 12 and a state visit by the Mayor and Deputy Mayor on Empire Day, the 24th.

King George V expressed the hope that the children attending all elementary schools would receive a week's holiday in honour of the Coronation. This commenced at the end of lessons on June 16. Local festivities which included river sports and a Venetian Fete were planned to be held in the Borough on June 22 (Coronation Day) and June 23, but owing to inclement weather, the sports were postponed, the Thanksgiving Service and Variety Entertainments held in the Drill Hall in Marlow Road, the Dinner in the Skating Rink, the Baby Show in the Town Hall and the tea to the school children served in the various schools.

Three boys were awarded free places to the County Boys' School in July. School opened and closed a quarter-of-an-hour earlier on August 3 to allow pupils to attend the Schools' Swimming Championships. Summer holidays began on the 4th, until September 4.

By September 19 the school held the following trophies:-

*Upson Shield	)	
Pitcher Shield	)	for running
Joicey Cup	)	
Mason-MacFarlane Cup	)	
Maidenhead Rifle Club Shield	)	for shooting

*First presented by Councillor Arthur Upson in the year of his mayoralty 1907.

Miss White resigned on October 20 and Miss E.G.K. Nash was appointed on November 7. After a visit by His Majesty's Inspector (Drawing) on November 21 all classes took drawing after 11 a.m.

A 'terminal' exam was always held before the end of a term and although the time-table was adhered to as far as possible it did become necessary to vary it at times.

November 21, December 4 and 5 saw a further H.M.I. inspection of the school.

1912

The new term commenced on January 8. The H.M.I. Report was issued on January 19. This time it dealt with Boys and Girls. It read 'These departments are working under excellent discipline and are ably conducted generally. Children are alert and responsive to the effective teaching which prevails. Very good progress is being made in all subjects. English is very well treated and good books in prose and poetry are read. Girls read and recite with first-rate expression and fluency, boys have less expression, a fact commonly noted in schools. Composition shows careful and methodical teaching and is very creditable. The oral side is particularly strong. Arithmetic is well cared for, sums suitable, statements clear, working accurate. History and Geography are taught side by side wherever possible. Standard II classes contain but a small portion of children who have passed through the Infants School. The lack of a direct 'feeder' was felt to be a hindrance to their work'.

Referring to the BOYS SCHOOL it said 'Cardboard and clay-modelling was a very valuable means for hand and eye training. It was a pity it was not continued in the woodwork shop. The scheme of work had been prepared with considerable care in pencil drawing and covers various sections of the subject'.

40 children were admitted on April 1 making a total of 269. Mr. Whitby resigned on April 26, Mr. F.G.W. Hammond commencing on May 1. On the 17th owing to the illness of Miss Nash there were six classes with only five teachers (including the Headmaster). No two classes could be put in one room owing to their size. Rooms hold 50 and no two classes combined were less than 80. Visitors on Empire Day, the 24th, included the Mayor, Deputy Mayor, four Managers and the Education Secretary.

June 10 presented a problem. Three brothers named Edgington and two named Roper were admitted. All by their attainments should have been in an infants school, but as they were too old for that, had to be placed in Standard 2.

Mr. Murray was absent with boys entering for the Joicey Cup on July 10 and the school had the whole of the outside repainted on September 2.

1913

Miss Nash resigned on January 4 and Miss Eleanor S. Morley replaced her on the 6th. Empire Day celebrations on May 23 followed a similar pattern to last year. A violent rainstorm just before 2 p.m. on July 10 resulted in six boys who were wet through having to be sent home. On July 16 the School Running Team took part in the Windsor Forest Sports and on the 24th, 83 were absent due to Sunday School treats and choir outings. Again a thunderstorm just before 2 p.m. on October 2 was the cause of 65 absentees, 11 being sent home wet through. The school closed for the Christmas holidays on December 19.

The year saw improvements to the north entrance of the Boys' School. An estimated cost of £5. 17s. 6d. (£5.87p) was needed for the provision of two steps and a gulley and iron grating to intercept the storm water.

1914

School began on January 5 but without Mr. Murray who was serving as a juror at Reading for the first two days.

Registers were frequently checked by the Town Clerk, Managers and the Education Secretary and to show how seriously this was taken, an entry in the School Log Book for February 4 reads 'Examined Registers Nos. 2, 3, 4, 5, 6 and found same correct. Children on Register 1 could not be checked as a number were absent at Handcraft Class. (signed) H.E. Davies, Correspondent'.

As many older Maidonians will remember, Mr. Murray was involved with the Technical Institute in Marlow Road and on occasions was absent in order to attend the audit of their accounts.

April 1, N.O.R. 251. Usual proceedings for Empire Day, May 22; the School Running Team was at the Windsor Forest Sports on July 8; the Headmaster recommended that the schools should be closed on the 16th as the Wesleyan, St. Mary's and Congregational Sunday School treats would affect the attendance of some 191 scholars; poor attendance with Sunday School treats and Police

Sports on the 23rd. Two pupils gained free places to the County Boys on the 31st. The H.M.I. Inspection was on July 13.

The playground had been tarred when school returned on August 31.

The H.M.I.'s Report was available on September 11 and read 'BOYS the school is organised with much care and skill, the schemes are ably drawn up and the class teachers carry them into effect with industry and thoroughness. The large proportion of boys in the highest classes deserves favourable mention. The children read with readiness and good expression and show a good understanding of the subject matter. The exercises in written composition are satisfactory on the whole. Arithmetic is rather disappointing in the lower classes but the work of the upper divisions is on good lines and very creditable in its results. The boys have a very good knowledge of Geography and History and show much interest in these subjects. The upper classes are very properly trained to get information for themselves and to make notes. A good feature of the school is the prominence given to oral expression; as a result the boys are unusually well able to give an account of what they have learnt'.

BOYS & GIRLS 'It is suggested that arrangements might well be made for the teachers to specialise in several of the subjects of instruction'.

On November 30, owing to illness of staff, Mr. Murray was taking Standard 6, 7 and Ex 7 together; the Headmaster Standard 3 with singing being taken in Standard 3 on Tuesday morning and Thursday afternoon.

The school was used by Capt. Carey of the Durham Light Infantry on the morning of December 4 to pay his men and in the afternoon to pay his billets. On the 10th to pay soldiers, on the 11th, billets, and on the 17th, lecture to soldiers at 4.30pm. Christmas holidays began on the 23rd.

Under the Finance Act (1909–10) the provisional valuation of the Gordon Road Schools' site was fixed at £935.

1915

School resumed on January 12. It was being used a great deal both in and out of school hours by the troops billeted in the town for lectures, payment of soldiers and billets etc. This affected the organisation of the school resulting in variations to the time-table.

The new school year commenced in April, N.O.R. 251. As the top division for singing was rather large, Standard 5 had to be taken separately on Tuesday mornings and Thursday afternoons. The Students Class took their practical work on Wednesdays instead of Fridays.

A truly war entry on May 14, 'Miss Morley absent today to take leave of a friend who is going to the Front'. June 11 was kept as Empire Day; two boys gained free places to the County Boys'. The Wesleyan Sunday School treat was on July 1, St. Mary's and Congregational on the 15th and St. Luke's, Baptist and Drill Hall on the 22nd leaving only 148 present in the afternoon. The Headmaster was invited to prize giving at the County Boys' on the 27th and the elder children received special lessons on filling up National Register forms on the 29th. School closed on the 30th.

With summer holidays over on August 31, September 1 saw the school opening at 1.45pm and closing at 3.55 p.m. to enable teachers to help in National Registration work. Medical inspections began. The Headmaster gave an address on 'The Navy' for Trafalgar Day, October 21 and had to leave after 11am on December 10 to assist in the work of Lord Derby's recruiting scheme. Christmas holidays commenced December 23.

1916

When school re-opened every boy was inspected by the School Doctor and Nurse. A Board of Education Inspectress of Physical Exercises together with an H.M.I. visited on March 30.

On April 1 the commencement of the school year, 26 boys were admitted from the King Street Infants. Mr. Hammond had been transferred to the Maidenhead C. of E. Boys' School for the duration of the war. The staff was therefore reduced by one and had to be reorganised as follows:-

Class 1 Mr. Murray
Class 2 Mr. Cluff
Class 3 Mr. Bell (Headmaster)

Class 4 Miss Morley
Class 5 Miss Fielder

The order of the lessons in Class 3 sometimes had to be transposed in order to enable the Headmaster to give more supervision to the other classes. Class 3 occasionally had to be grouped with Class 2 or Class 4. As the top division for singing was still large that sometimes had to be divided on Thursday afternoon – Class 1, 2.35–3.5pm and Class 2, 3.45–4.15pm.

Special lessons were given on May 3 to commemorate the 300th anniversary of William Shakespeare's death.

On May 22 children visited Grenfell Park for a special Empire Day rehearsal. All school children in the Borough were invited to assemble in the Park when the Mayor, the High Steward, Col. Foley commanding the troops quartered in the district, and Col. Gorrell, Commandant of the Canadian Hospital at Cliveden, agreed to give an address on 'this most important subject of Empire'. The Town Band provided the music, and oranges and a bun was presented to each child by Miss Coleman. A holiday in honour of Empire Day took place on the 25th.

July 13 saw Cecil Snow being awarded a Spoore Scholarship to the County Boys' School. J. Wesley Walker in his 'A History of Maidenhead' states that by an indenture dated 16th November, 1697, Abraham Spoore provided for the payment of £15 a year for the schooling and teaching of four boys in Maidenhead, to be chosen two out of the Cookham side and two out of the Bray side. In later years the Charity applied to scholarships tenable at the County Boys' (now Desborough), the scholarships being open to boys attending any public elementary school in the Borough of Maidenhead, and awarded in connection with the examination for the Berkshire County Scholarships.

Mr. Cluff attended Reading Barracks for a medical inspection on July 27, the School Shooting Team won the Mason-Macfarlane Cup on the 29th and Mr. Murray was absent on the 31st 'to see a friend going to the Front'. Summer holidays began August 4.

Mr. Cluff was called up for active service in the Army on September 25. On Mr. Cluff's enlistment, Mr. Hammond who had been transferred to the Church of England Boys' asked to return to Gordon Road to fill the vacancy, his request being acceded to. He now took Class 3 (St. IV) plus Class 2 (St. V) in Drill with the Headmaster taking Class 2 and Singing in Classes 1 and 3.

Mr. A.E. Neeve the schools' first caretaker, resigned after nine years. He was succeeded by Mr. Charles Speller. It was about this time that the doorway was made from the garden of the caretaker's house, 35 College Rise, through the school wall.

Medical inspections were on October 16, 19 and 20 and a holiday in lieu of Whitsun Week, October 23–27.

The Managers confirmed the action of the Mayor in granting the use of a room for an inquest on November 7. Five shillings (25p) was paid for such use, 2s. 6d. (12p) to the caretaker for the extra work.

A War Savings Association commenced operation in the school on November 28, teachers carrying out the necessary work. Inefficiency of heating arrangements on December 15 resulted in Room 1 at 11.30 a.m. only 42°F. Although the furnace had been continuously burning for five days and nights all windows had been kept closed since the previous afternoon. Other rooms were not much better. Christmas holidays began on December 21.

1917

The new term on January 9 meant a transposition of lessons for Class 2. Science, Monday 3.15 to 3.45 and Geography, Tuesday 2.5 to 2.35. In accordance with the Circular of the Board of Education, lessons on the 19th were given to the boys on the importance of guarding their tongues and pens so as to avoid leaking information to the enemy.

On February 7 it was announced that Percy Selwood and Harold Hayes, old scholars of the school had been awarded the Military Medal for gallant conduct in action in France. There was poor attendance on the 9th 'owing to bad weather, colds and broken chilblains'. Medical inspections were on the 26th.

Class I were taking a course of lessons on the history of Maidenhead and on March 12 visited the Guildhall where Councillor J.W. Walker showed them the original Charters, Regalia etc. The H.M.I. signified assent to the visit being paid.

The commencement of the school year on April 2 resulted in bad attendance due to snow. 6 boys were admitted from Boyne Hill Infants and 1 from Albert Street but none from the King Street Infants by order of the School Medical Officer owing to the prevalence of mumps and chicken-pox. These boys (31) did not arrive until the 17th making the N.G.R. 241.

Empire Day on May 24 with a visit from the Mayor, Deputy Mayor, High Steward (Lord Desborough), Councillor Chamberlain and the Town Clerk.

On June 5 Standard 5 had to be divided into two sections (Science – A Section to be grouped with Standard 6 and 7, B Section with Standard 4). Geography had to be taken on Monday afternoon in Standard 5 instead of Tuesday afternoon. History, Monday afternoon in Standard 4 instead of Tuesday afternoon. On June 28 Harold Harbut was awarded a Spoore Scholarship and in July four boys free places to the County Boys. School closed on August 2.

Mr. Speller the caretaker died after a very short illness and his widow was appointed to carry on until September 1. In the meantime the post was advertised and Mr. Charles William Richardson was ready to commence duties for the first day of term, September 4. On that day ten boys all from London were admitted and a further eight the following week.

Mr. J.W. Walker visited the school during the afternoon of November 26 to give Standard 6 and 7 a lecture on the manufacture of gas. Twenty of the older boys paid a visit to the gas works on the 28th, Mr. Walker promising to explain the various processes to them.

With 231 on the roll for December 21 it was recorded 'Very poor attendance lately due chiefly to:-

(a) Newspapers arriving late in the morning
(b) Shopping
(c) Fetching coal'.

1918

Re-open January 8. Attendance was adversely affected by snowy weather on the 18th. February 13 saw the cultivation of allotment ground for the growing of potatoes. From twelve to twenty of the bigger boys dug this on a suitable afternoon from 3.15 to 4.15 Mr. Murray being in charge. On these occasions the Headmaster took charge of Standard 6 and 7 as well as his own class (Standard 5). It was necessary to vary the time-table in order that the more essential subjects would not be missed and also because there would be too many boys left in charge of the Headmaster to be put in one room for writing. Medical inspections were on February 21 and Miss Morley left on the 28th.

Mrs. West came on supply from March 1 until June 11. Although a good deal of sickness had been recorded during March the number of casual absences began to diminish owing to the introduction of a partial rationing scheme.

With the re-opening after Easter forty-two new admissions was noted bringing the total N.O.R. to 264. Mrs. E.M. Farmer commenced duties on April 15 with poor attendance the following day due to snow. One pupil was awarded a Spoore Scholarship, Empire Day was held on May 29 due to the Whitsun holiday.

Miss Hilda M. Cook joined the staff on July 1. Poor attendance occurred during the early part of the month due to influenza. There were two Free Places to the County Boys'. Summer holidays August 1 to September 3.

A blackberrying month. The elder children were taken by the teacher to collect blackberries to make jam for the troops on September 6, 13, 16, 18, 23 and 27.

A change of time for the afternoon session commencing October 1. Each lesson was brought forward 30 minutes school commencing 1.30 and finishing at 3.45. Medicals on October 15 and 16 with the school closing after the morning session on the 22nd due to the prevalence of influenza. Christmas holidays began on December 18.

The school was involved in the war effort. The War Savings Association which encouraged war savings in schools had 230 members on its books including 17 former scholars who continued payments after leaving school. In just over two years £1,245 was raised. Miss Goody was the Honorary Secretary. The boys also played their part and during the year made a profit of £4. 18s. 9d. (£4.94) on their allotments.

1919

Re-open January 7. Mrs. Farmer ceased duties on the 31st. Mr. Cluff who had been absent on military service since September 25, 1916 returned on February 3. A new boiler for heating apparatus had to be fitted on the 14th. The afternoon session reverted to the normal time of 2–4.15 on March 3.

The new school year on April 1 saw eighteen admissions from King Street Infants, six from Boyn Hill Infants and two from St. Paul's Infants. N.O.R. 226. May 23 was kept as Empire Day. The Headmaster was away for part of the day on May 26 to attend as a witness at the police court and again on June 29 as a witness at the Quarter Sessions at Reading. A half-day holiday was granted on June 6 for good attendance. Holidays were also granted on July 4 for the Proclamation of Peace and on the 21st in connection with the Peace Festivities.

The Headmaster proposed that a War Memorial should be placed in the Boys' School to commemorate the thirty-two old scholars who died in the war. Mr. Bell submitted a design in oak and bronze and this was officially unveiled by the Mayoress (Miss Cox) on July 23. The Mayor (Alderman Cox), Councillors Norkett and Chamberlain, the Rev. T.F. Lewis, Mr. T.G. Wyatt and the Town Clerk were also present. The following names and inscription appears on the board:-

R. Bates
S. Belcher
G. Bloomfield
M. Bloomfield
C. Bolton
F. Bond
F. Britten
H. Bushell
A. Edwards
W. Folley
L. Gaines
B. Gibbons
A. Goodall
N. Gray
R. Harris

TO THE MEMORY
OF
THE BRAVE SONS OF THE EMPIRE
WHO FELL ON THE BATTLEFIELDS
OF
EUROPE
'THEY HAVE FOUGHT THE GOOD FIGHT'
DYING
IN THE CASE OF
HUMANITY THAT
HONOUR
MIGHT LIVE

T. Leslie
C. Hughes
L. Hughes
F. Marshall
F. Meads
F. Muggridge
H. Poole
F. Pym
H. Rockwell
J. Salmon
F. Smith
F. Stevens
A. White
G. Whitmill
R. Willis

S. Harris G. Wood

This board is in the custody of the Royal Borough of Windsor and Maidenhead Collection and can be seen by contacting the Honorary Curator on 01753 525547.

There were three Free Places to the County Boys' and one Free Place to Borlase School, Marlow. The Headmaster attended a Holiday Course in Geography at Cambridge during the last week of term.

During the summer holidays, August 1–September 9, the outside of the school had been repainted. Handicraft classes re-commenced on September 15. The Mayor, Mayoress and Town Clerk visited on November 4 to distribute 'Peace' medals. November 11 was kept as League of Nations Day although the first meeting of the assembly held in Geneva and attended by delegates from forty-two states did not open until November 15, 1920. Eighty-five elder children attended a lecture at the Picture Palace given by the Rev. F. H. Somerville of the South American Missionary Society on the morning of December 3. Christmas holidays began on December 19.

1920

The new term commenced on January 6, N.O.R. 215. Conferences with the H.M.I took place at the Guildhall on February 10 and March 9. Medical inspections March 8.

Numbers increased to 260 in April when the following pupils were admitted:-

28 from the King Street Infants
7 from the Boyn Hill Infants
9 from the St. Paul's Infants
3 from the Church of England Infants
3 from the Roman Catholic Infants
2 from the North Town Infants.

A half-holiday on May 7 for good attendance. May 21 Empire Day. Another Perambulation of the Borough Boundaries on May 27 this time the boys being Sidney Southgate (13), Frederick G. Blundell (13) and Arthur Wheeler (14). A good attendance half-holiday on June 10. At the suggestion of the H.M.I. the order of lessons could be varied when boys have to attend the Handicraft Centre. Poor attendance on July 30 as many of the Scouts had been in camp. The remainder enjoyed a half-day holiday. There were three Free Places to the County Boys'.

Re-open after the summer holidays on August 31. Handicraft classes were discontinued from September 28 until December 6 pending the appointment of a new Instructor.

The Educational Conference was held in Reading on October 1 and became an annual event. Medical inspections on the 25th and the following day some of the elder boys would, in future, be taken to the park (weather permitting) by one of the assistant masters to play football during the last hour on not more than one afternoon each week. The deposits of the boys in the school National Savings Association had now reached £1,000.

With a N.O.R. of 231, November 5 saw the average attendance of 226.1 (97.8%) as the highest in the history of the school. Although Armistice Day on the 11th was a special celebration attendance was very poor owing to the absence of all the Scouts both morning and afternoon. The Headmaster usually received an invitation to the prize giving at the County Boys' School during the month. Christmas holidays began December 19.

1920–21 saw the use of the school in the evenings. On alternate Wednesdays, the hall was used for recreational purposes, on another night a room for the use of the Allotment Holders' Association and the 1st Maidenhead Company of Girl Guides used the central hall, and in the summer months, the playground on Thursday evenings.

The Chairman of the Managers (Councillor Hope) presented goal posts and netball apparatus for the use of the older children which was erected on the land in front of the school adjoining Gordon Road.

1921

Re-open January 11. N.O.R. 214. Medical inspections February 16.

Winners of the Grenfell Shield 1921.

With forty-six new admissions on April 5 numbers increased to 251. Empire Day was held on May 27. Eighty-one boys were absent on the afternoon of June 30 owing to the Scouts' Sports being held in Kidwells Park.

The school won the relay race at Burnham School Sports against ten other entries on July 8. There were five Free Places to the County Boys'.

F.W. Gilroy, a cadet on H.M.S. Worcester and formerly a scholar of the school, was presented with the King's Gold Medal by H.R.H. the Prince of Wales on July 28. Summer holidays July 29–August 30.

The school won the Pitcher Shield (for running) at Kidwells Park on August 1. Classrooms had been whitewashed and distempered during the holiday period. Medical inspections September 20 and 21, Education Conference on the 30th. Standard II boys went to the Thicket for a nature walk and lesson on 'Berries' on October 25. There were fifty-one absent on November 11 owing to the Scouts Armistice Service at the War Memorial, designed by the Borough Surveyor Lt. Col. Percy Johns, and which stood adjoining the Public Library in St. Ives Road. Christmas holidays started December 23.

The School Football Team had been very successful during the term. In the Grenfell Shield Competition results show:-

Matches won	9	Lost	0
Goals for	56	Against	0

1922

The new term commenced on January 10. N.O.R. 228. Poor attendance due chiefly to mumps and influenza. School closed on February 28 for the wedding of Princess Mary. A busy March. Medical inspections on the 16th; Standards 6, 7 and the Students' Classes visited the Guildhall and were shown the Charters and

Winners of the Grenfell Shield 1922–23.

Regalia by Mr. J.W. Walker (Manager) on the 21st; on the following day Mrs. Morgan gave an address on the League of Nations, and on the 23rd the Mayor (Councillor Stuchbery) visited to present the football provided by members of the Education Committee. He was accompanied by Councillor Hope (Chairman of the Managers) and Councillor Chamberlain.

In all the football team had played ten matches in the Grenfell Shield Competition during the season 1921–22 of which none had been lost. They had scored sixty-five goals without having one goal scored against them. This was a record for the school and considered to be a remarkable achievement. The Managers directed their congratulations to be forwarded to the Headmaster, the trainer, Mr R.W. Murray, and the team, thus the presentation of the new ball. The team also won the final match in the competition by four goals to one. This was the first time the Grenfell Shield had been won by a Maidenhead team since the British School won it in 1906.

At the commencement of the school year on April 1, twenty-two were admitted from the King Street Infants', six from Boyn Hill and three from St. Paul's. N.O.R. 259. Empire Day May 24.

Mr. Murray was absent on the afternoon of June 22 to attend a conference with the H.M.I. at the Technical Institute. With Robert Woods gaining a Junior County Scholarship this meant that one Senior, one Intermediate and two Junior Scholarships had been awarded to boys who were formerly pupils of the school. On June 30 the percentage of attendance during the past quarter was 96.7 the highest in the school's history. Seventy-four boys had completed the quarter without being either absent or late.

The hall, corridors and cloakrooms had been whitewashed and distempered during the holiday period August 4–September 5. A considerable number of boys were still on holiday when term commenced. Mr. Maurice William Charles Lukeman commenced as Student Teacher. The Educational Conference was on September 29, twelve boys were excluded in October for Impetigo, medicals October 10 and 12, Standard 2 entertained the rest of the school for the last hour on December 20, Christmas break began on the 22nd.

1923

Re-open January 9. On February 10 the school was used for sleeping accommodation for a party of about two hundred hunger-marchers. The rooms were disinfected and cleaned immediately after the men left on the Sunday and were ready for use on Monday morning as usual.

Medical inspections on March 19 and on the 28th the percentage of attendance for the WHOLE year was 94.9 again the highest in the history of the school.

With thirty-four new admissions from the King Street Infants', six from Boyn Hill and five from St. Paul's the N.O.R. stood at 267. School closed on April 26 for the wedding of H.R.H. the Duke of York to Lady Elizabeth Bowes-Lyon (now the Queen Mother).

Again the football team won the Grenfell Shield on May 7 by beating Eton National 1 goal to nil in the Final. The Headmaster was absent for most of the morning of the 18th to make arrangements for the performance of 'Julius Caesar'. A half-holiday was given to enable boys to attend the play by the Ben Greet Players. Empire Day was celebrated on the 31st.

There was one County Junior Scholarship, two Spoore Scholarships and one Free Place to the County Boys'. Dr. Paterson (M.O.H.) gave the elder boys a lecture on his visit to Austria and showed pictures and specimens. Mr. Lukeman the Student Teacher's engagement terminated on July 31.

The interior woodwork was re-varnished and teachers rooms whitewashed and distempered during the summer closure (August 3–September 4).

The new Student Teacher was Mr. C.N. Pearson. Educational Conference September 28. The Headmaster attended the Regional Conference of National Savings Associations on October 19. Medicals 24th and 25th.

The Committee learned with great pleasure and satisfaction of the success of Ronald P. Bell, son of the Headmaster, in gaining with distinction an open scholarship at Balliol College, Oxford, at the age of sixteen. For three and a half years he was a pupil at Gordon Road from which he gained a free place to the Maidenhead County Boys' (now Desborough School) where he had been for the past six years. Four members of the Education Committee, the Rev. T.F. Lewis, and Councillors Chamberlain, Oldershaw and Norris were present at a ceremony held in the hall on December 20. An extra half-day holiday was granted to mark his success.

1924

The new term commenced on January 8. N.O.R. 229. Average attendance 209. (89%). Figures dropped for the first week of February – 197.4, 86.5% – due to the prevalence of colds. The Headmaster was absent for part of the afternoon of February 7 to attend the funeral of a scholar who was accidentally drowned.

The new school year saw thirty admissions from the King Street Infants' and six from Boyn Hill Infants'. A further eight from the Scattered Home in Courthouse Lane arrived on April 29. Empire Day was May 23.

Standards 6, 7 and Ex 7 visited the British Empire Exhibition at Wembley on July 21, there were three Spoore Scholarships and one Free Place to the County Boys' and Mr. Pearson the student teacher completed his duties on July 28. Summer holidays August 1 to September 2. The Educational Conference was on September 26, medical inspections on the 29th, Christmas holidays beginning on December 19.

1925

School resumed January 7. Alderman J.W. Walker gave a lecture to the elder boys on February 3 entitled 'The Poor Law' and showed documents in connection with lessons on 'Citizenship'. Medical inspections took place on the 24th.

With twenty-four admissions from King Street and six from Boyn Hill the N.O.R. on April 1 topped 262. The school again won the Grenfell Shield for football at the end of the month.

Empire Day this year was May 25 with a very special visitor – Dr. Popovic the Medical Officer of Health, Novi-Sad, Yugoslavia.

Two former scholars were awarded Intermediate Scholarships

and two pupils and a former pupil Junior Scholarships by Berkshire County Council. There was one Spoore Scholarship. Thirty-four boys from Standard 6 visited the British Empire Exhibition at Wembley on July 3. The school won the Oppenheimer Challenge Cup (Relay Race) at Waltham on the 18th but by term end on the 31st attendance was adversely affected by:-

(a) chicken pox and German measles
(b) Sunday School treats and choir outings
(c) boys away on holiday.

The school won the Pitcher Challenge Shield (Relay Race) on August 3 when on the following day it was announced there was one Cherry Scholarship at the County Boys'.

By the time the new term began on September 1 the whole of the exterior of the building had been re-painted. The report of H.M. Inspector's was also to hand. It contained:-

(1) The general condition of the school is very satisfactory. Buildings are good and kept in excellent repair. The department has a central hall, six good classrooms each accommodating 50 children and two teachers rooms each with offices of their own. The chief disadvantage (boys and girls departments) is the Infants' Department is in temporary premises about a mile away although space has been left on site for an Infants' School. This probably accounts to some extent for the fact that the boys' department has about 60–70 spare places although it is in such excellent buildings and is as regards work one of the best boys schools in the county.
(2) The staff is a good one, the two lowest classes taken by women assistants the four upper classes by three male assistants and the Headmaster. This proportion of four male teachers and two women teachers is a fairly satisfactory one for a boys school of this size.
(3) A good proportion of the boys pass through Standard VII and there is a Standard Ex VII of 27 boys taken by the Head Teacher and doing very good work meaning promotion is on sound lines and the brighter boys are looked after and given work suited to their special ability. In Standard V for instance out of 48 boys, two were nine years of age and nine were ten.
(4) All staff work hard and prepare their lessons carefully. Lessons given clearly, teaching thorough.

(5) Boys are taught to think for themselves and one of the chief impressions retained is the quickness and intelligence of the answers given by the boys in every class.
(6) Another point noted is the excellent general knowledge of the boys due to good lessons in History, Geography and Elementary Science and to copious reading.

Medical inspections were on October 14 and 15. Christmas holidays commenced December 23.

1926

Resume January 12. Poor attendance on the 15th due to snow. A member of the R.S.P.C.A. gave an address on February 15. There were twenty-nine admissions for the new school year in April. Empire Day was May 21.

There was one Intermediate County Scholarship, one Junior County Scholarship, three Free Places, two Spoore Scholarships and one to Cheltenham Grammar. Again the school won the Pitcher Shield for the Relay Race.

Autumn Term commenced on August 31 with a poor attendance, many boys still away on holiday. The Educational Conference was on September 24. Standards 6 and 7 visited Maidenhead Waterworks and was shown around by the works Manager on October 19. Poor attendance on Armistice Day, November 11 with Scouts, Cubs, Choirboys and War Orphans attending the Cenotaph. Christmas holidays commenced December 23.

The deposit in the Boys' School National Savings Association had now reached the £2,000 mark.

1927

Re-open January 11. The 18th unfortunately saw the death of Mrs. Bell, wife of the Headmaster. Dental inspections took place on the 24th.

Twenty-four admissions from King Street Infants' and five from

Boyn Hill brought the N.O.R. to 235 on April 1. Medicals on the 6th. The football team were again successful in winning the Grenfell Shield by beating Langley 4 goals to 3 in the final. Empire Day fell on the correct date, May 24.

During the months of June and July about 90 boys (in classes of 30) attended at stated time at the Corporation Baths for swimming instruction. A teacher was in charge of each class. When this ceased on July 29 special mention was recorded of the voluntary help that had been given by Mr. Richardson, the caretaker, for his assistance in this matter. The school won the Curtis Shield for swimming – a great achievement being the first time since the contest began in 1907.

There was one Spoore Scholarship and one Free Place to the County Boys'. Summer holidays July 29 to August 30.

Two boys were awarded Art Scholarships to attend the Technical Institute each Wednesday afternoon and Thursday morning as from November 4. Medical inspections were held on November 7 and 8 and from the 11th the prevalence of measles and mumps affected the attendance for the rest of the term. The Town Clerk and Capt. Dibb visited the school on November 23 in connection with a treat that was to be given to poor children by the Rugby Football Club. Christmas holidays began on December 22.

Berkshire Education Committee applied to use the school for lectures in music to teachers in Maidenhead and district on four Saturdays during October, November and December.

1928

Re-open January 10. N.O.R. 221. Average attendance 203.1 (91.9%). Medical inspections March 20. The Headmaster attended the Prize giving at the County Boys' School on the 22nd. April 2 began the new School Year. With forty-two admissions number rose to 258. The School 'came of age' on the 4th.

Dental inspections on May 23, Empire Day on the 24th when registers closed at 9.05 a.m. After one hour's secular instruction, boys marched through the town to the newly opened Rialto Picture House where they were addressed by the Mayor

(Alderman Cox) and Empire films were shown. The afternoon was declared a holiday.

Swimming classes commenced on June 5 and finished on August 1. A good number of boys learned to swim during this period, the school again winning the Curtis Shield for swimming. Mr. Richardson the caretaker was thanked for his invaluable assistance. Summer holidays August 3 to September 4 the playground being re-tarred during this period.

Regular register checks were made by various educational officials, council members or managers. Names were called, heads counted and an entry to that effect made in the School Log Book. The annual Education Conference was on September 28. Medicals were on November 6 and 8 and on the 9th the Headmaster took the Students' Class to the Guildhall to witness the election of the Mayor (Councillor Archer, Chairman of the School Managers). Christmas holidays commenced on December 21. This year saw one Junior County Scholarship and two Free Places to the County Boys'.

1929

The new term began on January 8. Three boys were awarded Art Scholarships at the Technical Institute. February saw low attendance mainly through influenza and chills.

With only thirty-eight admissions in April numbers were slightly down at 252. Medical inspections on May 1 and 2. The Boys' School football team were successful once again in winning the Grenfell Shield and the North East Berkshire Elementary Schools Shield and a half-day's holiday was granted on Friday May 10 in recognition of these successes. May 17 was kept as Empire Day.

Swimming instruction began on June 4, dental inspections on July 17, and the Running Team won the Oppenheimer Cup for the Relay Race on July 27. There were three Spoore Scholarships and two Free Places to the County Boys'. Summer holidays August 2 to September 3.

The Headmaster with some of the elder boys visited the Health Exhibition at the Town Hall on the morning of September 20. School closed for the Educational Conference on the 27th.

Standards 6, 7 and Ex 7 went to the Town Hall at 3.15 p.m. on October 17 to hear a gramophone lecture on 'The instruments of the orchestra'. Scouts and Cubs attended the service at the War Memorial on November 11, the two minutes silence being observed in school. Medicals were on the 7th and 12th, Christmas holidays beginning on December 20. A new flag pole had to be erected as the old one had become unsafe.

1930

The term 'primary school' was adopted by the Hadow Report on The Education of the Adolescent (1926). Under this Report the question of the re-organisation of the schools in the Borough necessitated the provision of Junior Schools for children under eleven years of age and Senior Schools for children eleven years and over. In Maidenhead at this time the Board of Education no longer recognised the King Street Infants' School which was behind the Wesleyan Church (now the Methodist). There were two methods in which the re-organisation could be carried out:-

1. Making the school at Gordon Road a senior school and the remaining non-provided schools in the town (except the Roman Catholic School) junior schools.
2. The Council to make Gordon Road a senior school and provide a junior council school upon another site leaving the non-provided school managers to re-organise their own schools.

The Sub-Committee recommended that Gordon Road be re-organised as a senior council school and a new school for junior and infants be built 'at the rear of houses on the east side of Cookham Road and of houses on the west side of Lower North Town Road'. Additional accommodation would be needed at Gordon Road to make buildings available for 640 senior scholars. Later in the year the Headmaster paid a visit to see the new 'Modern' school in Windsor.

School re-opened January 7, N.O.R. 230, average attendance 216.7 (94.2%). At the end of the month the Chairman of Managers and the Borough Surveyor visited to see what repairs would be needed during the ensuing year. One of the items was the renewal of the whole of the blinds to the windows of some of the classrooms on one side of the central hall. A tender of £18 from Mr. E.V. Morris was accepted. Medical inspections were held on March 20.

For the new school year on April 1, twenty-four were admitted from King Street and five from Boyn Hill. N.O.R. 244. The afternoon session commenced at 1.45 p.m. on April 9 to enable boys to attend the final match in the Grenfell Shield Competition at Slough. On Tuesday evening April 15 the football team beat Twyford School team in the final of the North East Berkshire League, thus retaining the Championship Shield won last year. A Sub-Committee of Managers called to enquire regarding the staffing position on May 7. Empire Day was the 23rd.

Swimming commenced for elder boys on June 2. Prize giving at the County Boys' July 25. Summer holidays August 1 to September 2. There were four Free Places. There was poor attendance, twenty boys made no attendance on the 2nd and still nineteen no attendances on the 12th. The Mayor and Mayoress (Councillor and Mrs. Norris) distributed prizes given by the Chamber of Commerce for essays on the British Empire on October 2, school closing on the 3rd for the Educational Conference. The Headmaster took ten of the elder boys to witness the election of the Mayor (Councillor Norris) at the Guildhall on November 10. Medicals were on the following day, the girls entertaining the boys on the last day of term – December 18.

In 1930 it became a requirement of the Board of Education that playing fields should be provided for all new senior schools. Two sites were suggested and the Town Clerk directed to make enquiries as to the terms upon which one of these could be acquired for the purpose proposed. Negotiations with a Mrs. Simpson about land adjoining the eastern boundary was made.

1931

Resume January 6. N.O.R. 231, Average attendance 217.5 (94.1%). On the 28th every child present was inspected by the School Dentist. On April 1 thirty-five were admitted from King Street, six from Boyn Hill and one from St. Mary's Roman Catholic. N.O.R. 265. Miss Fielder tendered her resignation through ill-health after twenty-four years service and was granted a testimonial under the seal of the council. Mr. L.E.J. Adderson was appointed as an assistant teacher.

'Special' medicals were held on May 7, Empire Day on the 22nd. Miss I.K. Warburton should have commenced duties on June 2 but owing to illness could not start until the 8th. There were three Spoore Scholarships and four Free Places. A holiday on the afternoon of July 23 for the Elementary Schools Swimming Gala. The school won the Curtis Shield and in conjunction with the Girls' Department the Norris and Richardson Cups. The Headmaster attended the County Boys' Speech Day on the 24th. Attendance was poor with boys being away on holiday, Sunday School treats and Choir outings. Summer holidays July 31–August 31.

Mr. Donald R.A. Mott commenced as a Student Teacher on September 7. Closed for Educational Conference September 25. There was one Art Scholarship to the Technical Institute. Boys attended the Guildhall for the election of the Mayor on November 9, medical inspections on the 10th and 11th and head inspections on the 26th. There were cases of chickenpox during November and December. Standards 2 and 3 entertained the rest of the school on December 22, Christmas holidays commencing the following day. Folk dancing classes were held in the hall on Wednesday evenings from September 30 until December 2. The amount which had been deposited in the School's Savings Association now exceeded £3,000. The Education Committee was able to purchase the caretaker's cottage when the owner decided to sell.

1932

School re-opened January 11. N.O.R. 230, average attendance 214 (93%). There were two further Art Scholarships at the Technical Institute. J. Wesley Walker had just had his book 'A History of Maidenhead' published and Standard 6 who had been having a course of lessons on this visited the Guildhall and were shown the Charters, Maces, etc. by the Town Clerk on February 24. Medical inspections were on March 10 and the school closed for Easter holidays on the 23rd.

As from April 1 the school will be re-organised as one mixed department with senior and junior divisions.

7
Girls' Department

1907

The Head Teacher was present at school on Friday April 5 to admit scholars and when school officially opened on the 8th 217 girls were on the roll.

Staff:-

Miss Bertha Partlo	Head Teacher
Miss Gwladys Evans	
Miss Laura Brett	
Miss Beatrice Freeman	
Miss Alice B. Goody.	

Arranged:-

Standard II	Miss Freeman
Standard III	Pupil Teachers
Standard IV	Miss Goody
Standard V	Miss Brett
Standard VI & VII	Miss Evans

The pupil teachers arrived on April 12 and were Nana Gemmel and Linda James assisted by a monitor, Violet Tilbury.

April 23 being Shakespeare Day the Head Teacher took Standards IV–VII in the Hall and talked to the girls about the poet's life and work.

Standard 6 Girls School 1907–8 From a Postcard owned by Luke Over.

PROPOSED SCHEME OF WORK IN OUTLINE

Arithmetic

Standard II	Notation to 999, exercises in four simple rules in problematic form, tables to 12 x 12, simple addition, subtraction, multiplication, division and reduction of money, measuring and weighing common objects.
Standard III	Notation to 999, 999, simple multiplication and division by factors, compound (as above), measuring, weighing, etc.
Standard IV	Weights and measures, factors and multiples, the metric system (simply).
Standard V	Vulgar fractions, square measure, mensuration, bills of parcels, aliquot parts, metric system.
Standard VI	Decimal fractions, simple proportion, mensuration – solids, simple interest, averages.
Standard VII	Averages, percentages, profit and loss, compound proportion.

In all classes, exercises would be given in problematic form, revision of work of previous standards in all cases.

Reading Books

Standard II	'The Golden Staircase' Part I; 'My Book of True Stories'; 'Round the World'; 'The Snow Queen'; 'Bunny and Furry'.
Standard III	'The Golden Staircase' Part II; 'Eyes & No Eyes' Parts I and II; 'The Young Briton History Reader' (Junior); 'Wide-World Reader' Book I; 'Sasha the Serf'; 'Andersen Reader'.
Standard IV	Selected Poems from Tennyson; 'Eyes & No Eyes' Parts III & IV; 'Young Briton' (as above); 'Wide-World Reader' Book II; 'Swiss Family Robinson'.
Standard V	Tennyson (as above); 'Eyes & No Eyes' Parts V & VI; 'MacMillan's New History Reader' (Intermediate); 'Wide-World Readers – Europe'; 'The Story of King Arthur'; 'Little Nell'.
Standard VI & VII	'The Laureate Poetry Book' (Tennyson); 'The Merchant of Venice'; 'Nature Reader Monthly'; 'Mac. New History' (above); 'Wide-World Reader – British Empire'; 'The Children of the New Forest'; 'A Christmas Carol'; 'The Mill on the Floss'.
Standard VII	'Kenilworth'; 'Alice's Adventure in Wonderland'.

Needlework

Standard II	Hemming, sewing, fixing, sew and fell seam; darning on canvas; knitting; simple cutting out and garments.
Standard III	Herringboning on canvas: fixing and working hem on square; wide hem; band; stitching; running; sewing selvedges, knitting 4 pins; cutting out from lines and patterns; simple garment.
Standard IV	Sewing on hooks and eyes, run and fell seam; herringboning on flannel; darning, pleating, flannel seam gathering, knitting toe and heel.
Standard V	Darning; patch – calico and flower; feather stitching (simple); false hem; button and buttonhole; knitting-increasing; cutting out – more advanced; simple garment.
Standard VI	Tucks; eyelet-hole; darn in linen; front opening; tapes; print patch; cutting out paper patterns of all garments made in school; mending garment; sewing machine.
Standard VII	Gusset; whipping; flannel binding; cutting out and adapting patches; mending, machining garment.

English	
Standard IV–VII	Lessons on correct speaking and writing; simple analysis, parts of speech.
Standard II–VII	Selections from Tennyson's works; stories of 'Idylls of the King' and other stories; stories from Shakespeare and other poets.
Health	Simple talks on this subject in all classes.
History	
Standard II	Simple stories from English History.
Standard III	Stories from famous Englishmen.
Standard IV	Outline of English History from early times till 1485.
Standard V	Outline of English History from early times till present time. Special attention to social life.
Standard VI & VII	Outline of English History. Special attention to growth of British Empire.
Geography	
Standard II	Definitions, plans, etc. 'Boys and Girls of Other Lands'; Local geography.
Standard III	England and Wales descriptive lessons; local geography – our town, neighbourhood and river.
Standard IV	British Isles; our County and its neighbourhood.
Standard V	Europe – descriptive lessons; towns of the Thames Valley.
Standard VI & VII	British Empire; London.

In all classes, visits and walks would be arranged to illustrate the lessons.

Singing	
Standard II–VII	Solfa. In all classes, voice production etc. for few minutes every day. Simple time and tune exercises, also ear tests. In upper classes simple staff also.
Composition	Oral and written in all standards, lower chiefly oral, upper chiefly written.
Standard II & III	Reproduction of lesson, description of picture, object or flower. Reproduction of simple story, description of action performed. Imaginative subjects.
Standard IV	As above. Also friendly letters.
Standard V	As above plus simple essays.
Standard VI & VII	As above plus autobiographies, essays, business letters.

Nature Study	In all standards lessons suitable to the time of year to be arranged. Observations of plants grown in rooms. Nature walks at least once each season.
Drawing	All standards. Free-arm – simple forms on boards or brown paper. Brush and pencil drawing from nature to follow nature lessons where possible.
Drill	According to model course. Games in each class.

From May 3 each teacher in turn stayed in charge of dinner children from 12–2 p.m. when weather was not suitable to be outside. On the 6th the school became affiliated with the 'League of Empire'. Through this association the girls will correspond with school children in the Colonies. Miss Gwen Lobb joined the staff on the 14th and as Empire Day this year was celebrated on Friday 17th the girls had been preparing a suitable song. Whitsun holidays began, re-opening on the 27th.

Standard V started the nature walks on May 28. The Agricultural Show on the 30th resulted in poor attendance. 38 girls went from the school leaving only 52 behind. Miss Evans left on the 31st after only two months.

Miss Catherine Granville became the teacher of Standard II on June 3, Miss Freeman moving to Standard VI. Standards VI and VII began their nature walks, and the school commenced to send flowers to Popham Road Girls' School, Islington, a school situated in a very poor part of London. It was hoped to send a box every week consisting chiefly of wild flowers.

Special lessons on June 15 as a reminder of the signing of Magna Carta (June 15, 1215). The same on the 18th, the anniversary of the Battle of Waterloo (1815), when each teacher spoke to their class on this great event during the optional lesson.

On the previous Saturday, 34 girls from Standards VI and VII accompanied by three staff paid a visit to London. Assembling at Maidenhead Station, they caught the 8.59 train to Paddington, thence by the Metropolitan Railway to Mark Lane. They visited the Tower of London being shown round by a special warder, from there on to Tower Bridge, walking past The Monument to St. Paul's noting the chief monuments and then going into the crypt. They then caught a bus to Charing Cross and Trafalgar Square, walking along Whitehall to Westminster, through the Houses of

Parliament into Westminster Hall, visiting the Abbey, Chapter House and Cloisters. After tea at Westminster, they walked through St. James's Park to Buckingham Palace, along Constitution Hill to Hyde Park Corner through the Park to Marble Arch. Catching buses to Paddington they returned to Maidenhead 8.28·p.m. Although somewhat marred by heavy rain during the early part of the day, a very enjoyable and instructive time was had by all. The total cost including tea was two shillings each (10p).

Lessons had been given during the previous week on the buildings to be visited but the girls had to write an account of their outing, each girl drawing up a plan showing the route taken and places visited.

The school closed on July 8 owing to a Fete at Taplow Court (The High Steward of Maidenhead, Lord Desborough's residence).

Lord Tennyson having been chosen by the school as the poet for the year featured in lessons for Standards IV–VII on July 9. Several girls read poems which they had prepared, others recited poems which had been studied during the term and the two songs 'Home they brought the warrior dead' and 'Crossing the Bar' were sung by the older girls. In conclusion all sang 'Strong Son of God'. The event was so successful it was hoped a similar lesson could be arranged each term.

Summer holidays – August 2–September 2.

When school re-opened Miss Madge Bloomfield commenced as a first year pupil teacher making four in the school. Cookery classes started at the Technical Institute in Marlow Road, 9 girls in Course III, 44 in Course II. On the 18th Standard V visited Windsor Castle. Walking to the railway station to catch the 9.25 they first went to Eton to see the College, then the State Apartments and Round Tower, went up the Long Walk where they had lunch, returning to see the Royal Stables, St. George's and the Albert Memorial Chapels concluding with a walk in Alexandra Gardens. They returned via the 4.33 from Windsor. Nature walks for Standards VI and VII on the 23rd. Divided into four divisions the object was to gather as many different kinds of berries as possible. It was Standard IV's turn the following day.

Mr. Ellicock, an H.M. Inspector of Leicester Schools and

formerly Headmaster of the Maidenhead British School visited during the afternoon of the 24th. Miss Granville left on the 30th.

The Education Secretary gave a lecture on chalk formation to Standards VI and VII on October 11 when specimens were shown under microscope. Miss Hilda Maddison was appointed to teach Standard III, Miss Lobb having moved to Standard II, as from the 14th.

Children 'marched' everywhere in those days and November 1 was no exception when the annual visit to the Chrysanthemum Show was made. The four pupil teachers completed their period of ten week's practice returning to the High School for the remainder of the school year. They would only return for short periods when that school closed for the holidays.

To celebrate their first Christmas, classrooms were decorated and girls painted cards on December 17. Singing, recitations and dialogues in the Hall closed the term on the 20th.

1908

Poor attendance on the first day of term, January 6, with only 172 present. On the 14th a new girl was admitted but left because there was no Infant School attached to which her younger brothers and sisters could come.

February 10 saw a scholar suspended for stealing 1s. 0½d. the property of another girl. Many things appeared to have been stolen during the past few months. Miss Maddison's class visited North Town Moor as part of a geography lesson on the 14th.

The H.M. Inspector's Report was received on March 10 and stated 'The Head Mistress fulfils her duties with thoughtful earnestness and the class teachers prepare their lessons with much care. The instruction is in most respects praiseworthy both in aim and results, but there is a tendency to help the girls too much instead of making them think and observe for themselves. Although dull and unintelligent in oral arithmetic they work their written sums with neatness and satisfactory accuracy. Discipline excellent'.

An exhibition and sale of the needlework garments made during the year was held in the Hall on March 11. Parents and friends were invited to attend.

April 1 and the start of the second school year. 18 pupils were admitted from the Council Infants' making 222 on the nominal roll.

Organisation:-

Standard II	Miss Goody
Standard III	Miss Brett
Standard IV	Miss Maddison
Standard V	Miss Lobb
Standard VI & VII	Miss Freeman
Ex VII (Students' Class)	Miss Partlo.

April 13 saw the commencement of Cookery Classes at the Technical Institute in Marlow Road. There were 5 more new admissions when school re-opened after the Easter holidays on April 27. The following day extra drill lessons began in preparation for the Empire Day celebrations.

Standards IV and upwards marched to Kidwells Park on May 4 for the first united drill practice. Three further rehearsals took place when on the 21st the whole school assembled in Grenfell Park at 1.30 p.m. marched in procession through the town to Kidwells Park where older scholars took part in the Drill Display finishing with inter-school races. On May 22 Standard VII reached 100 per cent in attendance during the week, the second time this year the class had done so. They went on a nature walk to the Thicket on the 27th.

Four teachers were in charge of a party of 15 older children who visited Stoke Poges. The majority went by train to Slough but a few ventured the journey on bicycle. On June 18 only 157 girls were in school due to the Wesleyan Sunday School treat.

The school closed on July 3 because of Taplow Court Fete, now an annual event. Over 100 absent on the 23rd due to four 'treats', school closing on the 31st for the summer break.

Nature walks during September, on the 9th Standards VI and VII, the 10th Standard V and 16th Standard IV. On the 21st seven older scholars visited the White City, the name given to the buildings erected at Shepherds Bush for the Franco-British Exhibition of 1908. At the Harvest Thanksgiving Service at the close of school on the 24th, the gifts of fruit, flowers and vegetables were sent to a poor London School and the local

Workhouse Infirmary. On the 30th, 32 girls (Standard V) marched to the station, proceeded to Windsor by the 9.27 train, visited Eton College and the State Apartments, returning on the 4.33 from Windsor.

On October 9 Standard II gave a short concert, the Chrysanthemum Show in the Drill Hall, Marlow Road (a gift to the town by Mr. J.D. M. Pearce, publicly opened in 1903) on the 30th; Standard III's short concert on November 13; and on the 26th a letter received from a parent asking that a pupil be withdrawn from religious instruction as they were Roman Catholics. This was the first case ever known.

Special lessons on the work of John Milton were given on December 9 to mark the tercentenary of his birth. School closed on the 23rd with an end of term concert.

1909

Back on January 11. Several mothers were present on the 12th when medical inspections began. When these finished on the 18th thirteen girls were found to be suffering from defective eyesight.

Standard IV gave the half-hourly monthly concert in the Hall on February 5 and on the 10th nearly one hundred people availed themselves of the opportunity to see the girls at work.

The H.M.I. Inspection was on March 4; the exhibition and sale of needlework on the 16th and the monthly half-hour concerts given by Standards VI and VII on the 31st. Miss Maddison left the school.

Seventeen new girls were admitted for the start of the new school year on April 1. Miss L.E. Hambly who had been engaged as a supply teacher for the past four months replaced Miss Maddison taking over Standard IV. Nature study walks for Standards VI and VII began on the 21st, the Students Class the following day.

Standards IV–VII marched to the Park for the first rehearsal for Empire Day on May 19, the final rehearsal on the 26th with Empire Day the 27th.

Five pupils attended for oral examinations for free places at the

Secondary School on June 18; medical inspections June 25–28; Sunday School treats June 24, July 1 and 15; Taplow Court Fete July 19, school closing on the 30th.

School re-opened on August 30 with Miss Violet Tilbury a former pupil teacher commencing as an uncertified assistant teacher in place of Miss Hambly who was only temporary until July 30.

It was announced on September 2 that one pupil had passed the Oxford Junior Local Examination. Standard V visited Windsor Castle on the 15th, a lesson had been given in preparation for the visit but essays had to be written by the girls after their return. The Harvest Festival arrangements on the 22nd were similar to last year.

A nature walk for Standard V on October 12; the Chrysanthemum Show on November 12; school closed for the Christmas holidays on December 23.

1910

When the new term began on January 10 only 164 were present owing to bad weather. No school on the 25th due to the General Election. The annual Exhibition and Sale of Needlework garments raised £17. 7s. 1d. on March 10.

Medical inspections were held on three afternoons from April 21 and although 62 pupils were examined parents of 6 scholars objected and withdrew their children. 6 girls entered the Labour Examination, 2 passed.

Empire Day drill commenced on May 4 and again 20 girls were withdrawn by their parents from taking part in the proceedings. The girls marched to Grenfell Park on May 9 to be present at the Proclamation of King George V. Lessons were given throughout the school on the 24th 'On the Empire and our duty as citizens of the Empire'.

Special lessons were given on June 14 to Standards VI and VII on famous buildings in London in preparation for a visit the following Saturday. 44 girls accompanied by 3 staff visited the Tower of London in the morning, after lunch the Houses of Parliament and Westminster Abbey and after tea, through the parks to Marble Arch. The total cost (including tea) for each girl was 2s. 1½d.

Summer holidays began on July 29 until August 29, Standard V's trip to Windsor was on September 7; it was announced on the 14th that 4 girls had been awarded free places to the secondary school; the annual Harvest Thanksgiving was on the 21st; nature walks for various classes took place on September 22, 27, October 4 and 6 and six cases of mumps in Standard II was reported to the Medical Officer of Health on the 10th. The second fire drill took place on October 29 all the girls having evacuated the building within half a minute.

The usual break-up concert and lessons of a Christmas theme was held on December 20.

1911

School re-opened on January 9. Three very backward girls aged respectively 10, 11 and 12 were admitted on January 16. None could read. Needlework was on view and purchases to the value of £17. 11s. 6d. were made on February 16. The previous day the Mayor and Deputy Mayor called to enquire about girls in need of boots.

On March 10, by permission of the Chairman of the Education Committee, the Rev. Shepheard Welwyn addressed the girls on behalf of the Imperial Sunday Alliance. Two girls who had reached the age of 15 were dismissed from school on March 31.

The new school year commencing on April 3 saw twenty new admissions. During this coming year Hygiene would be taught instead of Nature Study as a class subject in Standards VI, VII and Ex VII. In Standard V one hygiene lesson would be substituted for one nature study. Geography would be taught on Monday afternoons instead of mornings in VI and VII. One girl passed the Labour Examination on April 8.

On Empire Day (May 24) the Mayor, Deputy Mayor, Town Clerk and the Education Secretary addressed children of both departments, a half-day holiday being granted for the afternoon. A nature walk for Standard II was the following day.

An extra needlework lesson was given on June 13 in order to

finish scarves in readiness for Coronation Day. In accordance with the King's wish all schools closed on the 16th for one week for the Coronation celebrations.

Summer holidays August 4 to September 4. Two girls had passed the examinations for free places at the Girls' Secondary School. Nature walks for Standard II on September 26 and Standard IV on October 3. Standard V annual visit to Windsor, September 13.

A Drawing Inspector visited the school on November 21 to examine drawings. Each class did an exercise in pencil and brush drawing. Another H.M.I. Inspection on November 30 and December 1, girls in the top classes were given a demonstration in First Aid and bandaging also on the 1st. The usual break-up arrangements took place on the 21st.

1912

The new term began on January 8. The H.M.I. Report issued on January 19 related to both boys and girls departments (see also boys' section). In the case of the Girls' School it read:-

'The first class sing folk songs sweetly and their free physical exercises are most praiseworthy. Needlework is excellent being thoroughly practical and sensible. It is as pleasing as it is rare to find three sewing machines in constant use. Much of the drawing is of a promising character, the pencil drawing in the first class showing the most successful effort. The exercises for a considerable time have been drawn from nature and the water-colour drawings have been the least successful, particularly in the lower parts of the school, conventional renderings being numerous. It is good to see a bird-table well supplied with food by the girls'.

Owing to low temperatures in the class rooms on February 5 the Chairman of the Managers authorised fires to be used to augment the heat from the pipes. On the 20th school commenced 1.30pm and was dismissed at 3.30pm. At the Exhibition and Sale of Needlework held in the hall afterwards, several parents and friends inspected the work and made purchases, the sum of £21. 2s. 8d. being handed over to the Town Clerk.

The new School Year commenced on April 2 with an additional 35 scholars.

Organisation:-

Standard II	Miss Lobb
Standard III	Miss Tilbury
Standard IV	Miss Goody
Standard V & Ex VII	Miss Brett
Standard VI & VII	Miss Freeman

The Head Teacher in addition to the supervision of the whole school was responsible for the teaching of Arithmetic, Algebra and Needlework to Standards VII and Ex VII and for Hygiene in Standards VI, VII and Ex VII.

At a fire drill on April 25 the total evacuation of the building took 30 seconds. The Mayor and Deputy Mayor addressed boys and girls for the Empire Day celebrations on May 22. Annual medical inspections took place on June 17 and 18. The annual visit to London by Standard VII and Ex VII was on June 24. Girls in the Relay Race Team were absent on the afternoon of July 10 owing to the Cup Race at Cranbourne. Cookery exams for Standard V and VI began on July 12 ending on the 25th. Sunday School treats, July 18 and 25th. Summer holidays August 2 to September 2.

The annual visit of Standard V to Windsor was on September 18, leaving Maidenhead 9.30 a.m. returning 5.00 p.m. Visiting Eton College, the State Apartments, Royal Stables and the Chapels, every girl in the class went on the excursion each paying their own expenses of 7d.

All girls assembled in the Hall for the usual Christmas concert on December 19, term ending on the 20th. For the first time the names of the top girls in the examination in each class was recorded in the Log Book.

Standard II	Marjorie Taylor
Standard III	Doris Taylor
Standard IV	Florrie Hoiles
Standard V	Gwennie Muggridge
Standard VI	Mary Fraser
Standard VII	Hilda Whitlock.

1913

Re-open January 6 with four new scholars. School commenced at 1.45 p.m. and closed at 4.00 p.m. on the 7th to allow the upper standards to leave early for the tea and entertainment at the Town Hall being given by the Mayor.

Medical inspections on February 6 with the annual sale of needlework on the 20th. Miss Freeman, one of the original teachers, resigned after six years on March 19 owing to her forthcoming marriage. Miss Hilda Muriel Adams commenced in charge of Standard II on April 1. Miss Lobb transferred to Standard V with Standards VI, VII and Ex VII the responsibility of Miss Brett and the Head Teacher. Forty one girls commenced Course III in the Cookery Class and an alteration in the time-table meant the hygiene lesson being given instead of nature study in Standards II to V.

Empire Day was observed on May 23 when the Mayor (Councillor Chamberlain) accompanied by the Mayoress, Councillor Stuchbery, the Town Clerk and two School Managers addressed the whole school (boys and girls).

The annual visit to London by Standard VII and Ex VII was made on June 10. The morning was spent at the Zoo and the afternoon at St Paul's, the Guildhall and Westminster Abbey. Total expenses for each girl (including tea) 2s. 3d.

Playtime was omitted on the afternoon of July 10. School was dismissed at 4.10 p.m. because so many girls were wet through due to a heavy storm just before 2.00 p.m. Summer holidays began on July 31 but in the afternoon Standards VI and VII attended a treat at Cliveden by invitation of Mrs. Astor. Four pupils obtained scholarships to Secondary Schools.

The new term began on September 1, Standard V annual visit to Windsor on the 29th.

More violent storms in October. Sixty-three girls were absent on the 2nd when torrential rain fell between 1 and 2 p.m., and again on the 7th when fifty were away. Alterations were made to the time-table on December 16 to allow Christmas items – painting cards, Christmas songs, etc. to take place. All classes assembled together for the break-up concert on the 18th, school closing the following day.

1914

School re-commenced on January 5. The sale of needlework was on February 26; twenty-five scholars were admitted for the new school year on April 1; Empire Day, May 22 and the Relay Race Team were absent on July 8 owing to the Cup Race taking place at Cranbourne. Sunday school treats accounted for poor attendances on July 16 and 23rd. Two His Majesty's Inspectors' visited the school on July 22 and were present during the morning and afternoon sessions. Summer holidays July 31–August 31.

The H.M.I. Report was received on September 11 and read: (GIRLS SCHOOL),

'The girls generally are in excellent order and the tone is very pleasing except that there are a few girls in Standard V who are not working on nice terms with their teacher. The ordinary subjects of instruction show good results. Reading deserves praise for its ease and pleasing expression, Arithmetic is sensible and practical, Writing is good and Composition very good, except in Standard V where writing, spelling and expression show carelessness.

Very good teaching is noticcable in History, Hygiene and in the Geography of Standards VI and VII. In the other classes, geography is not taught on modern lines nor are there any modern books either for teachers or children. The girls are readily responsive to questions, they make statements in good form and frequently ask questions. The older girls, some of Standard VI and all VII are very thoughtful and intelligent and are doing excellent work in many directions'. (Refer also to BOYS SECTION).

Two girls were awarded Free Places at the County Girls' School.

Various specimens of work done at home by the girls of Standards VI and VII were on view during the afternoon of November 17. The arrangement and preparation of these articles caused a slight alteration to the time-table in those classes – singing and recitation being omitted. Medical inspections were on the 23rd.

The painting of cards and this year, preparations of Christmas puddings took place on December 21. The breaking-up concert was on the 23rd.

1915

The new term began on January 12. The highest temperature recorded in any room was 50°F. Standard VI moved from Room XI to Room XII as the Cookery Class was to be held in the school temporarily. Standard VII would work in the Hall for the lessons which they took separately from Standard VI. This necessitated changing Drill and Recitation in Standard II on Tuesday afternoons. The Cookery Class commenced in Room XI on February 1.

During the week of February 19 the attendance of 78.8% was the lowest recorded during the eight years the school had been open. This was due largely to influenza which was very prevalent among the girls. The sale of needlework was on February 25.

Thirty-three new pupils were admitted after the Easter holidays. With thirty girls in VII and Ex VII this class was obliged to work in the Hall.

Organisation:-

Standard II	Miss Adams
Standard III	Miss Lobb
Standard IV	Miss Tilbury
Standard V	Miss Goody
Standard VI	Miss Brett
Standard VII and Ex VII	Miss Partlo (Headmistress).

For some oral lessons VI, VII and Ex VII would be taken together by Miss Brett.

June 11 was kept as Empire Day. The Mayor (Councillor E. Norkett) accompanied by Alderman Cox, Councillor Chamberlain and the Town Clerk visited the school, girls assembling with the boys and infants. A suitable song and hymn was sung, the Mayor gave an address, the remainder of the day being declared a holiday.

A girl who was impertinent and defiant to a teacher and then defied the authority of the Headmistress had not attended school since July 14. The mother was sent for and found to be upholding her. After a week's interval her father brought her to the school but refused to allow her to receive punishment and took her home again. This matter was reported to the Town Clerk. (See also H.M.I. Report September 1914).

Summer holidays July 30–August 31. Teachers were asked to give assistance with clerical work in connection with National Registration papers. On September 1 school commenced 1.45 closing 3.55 to allow for this. Cookery School moved back again to the Technical Institute with Course II commencing in the morning. A demonstration in First Aid was given to Standard VII and Ex VII on the 22nd. Nature walks on the Thicket for Standard III on the 23rd and Standard II on the 30th.

Medical inspections on October 6, 7 and 8 and to mark Trafalgar Day special lessons on The British Navy and its work took place on the 21st.

Another H.M.I. inspection on November 3; Miss Brett was absent on the 15th as her brother was home on leave from the Front, and all assembled for the Christmas break-up concert on December 23.

1916

Back to school January 11. The classroom was required again for the Cookery School as from the 13th, Standard VII girls returning to be taught in the Hall. Average attendance for the first week, 220, N.O.R. 231. The Drawing Inspector saw work in that subject in every class on January 28.

Colds resulted in much lower attendance figures all through February. Takings at the Sale of Work on February 24 amounted to £32. 15s. 5d. Miss Tilbury spent the morning of the 28th at the Council Infants' School to observe methods used in teaching various subjects in readiness for her work with Standard II next year (April). Miss Adams resigned on the 29th to take an appointment in the clerical department of London County Council, resulting that for the next month the Headmistress taught Standard II. Standard VII would work with the Headmistress for some lessons only taking the rest with Standard VI.

Mrs. Roadnight commenced work on the afternoon of March 8 on supply for two days as the Infants' School was closed due to measles. Miss Gandy commenced on the 13th for the same reason. On the 12th a scholar of Standard II died in hospital after an operation for appendicitis. She had been taken ill in school the previous Wednesday. On the 27th Miss Brett was granted a week's leave of absence owing to the return of her fiancé from the Front. She married and became Mrs. White.

On March 30 an H.M.I. together with the Inspectress of Physical Exercises saw a drill lesson given by Miss Goody to Standard V.

Mrs. White returned on April 3 ready for the commencement of the tenth school year. Thirty-three girls were admitted making a total of 254, the highest in the history of the school.

New organisation:-

Standard II	Miss Tilbury
Standard III	Miss Partlo (Headmistress)
Standard IV	Miss Lobb
Standard V & Ex VII	Mrs. White
Standard VI & VII	Miss Goody.

In needlework Standard VII & Ex VII in addition to Standard III would be taught by the Headteacher who would also teach History in Standards VI, VII and Ex VII. The time-table in Standard III would sometimes have to be altered to allow the Headteacher to inspect the work of other classes. On April 13 a scholar in Standard VI was awarded a scholarship tenable at the County Girls' School from September, this being given by the Trustees of the Maidenhead Charities.

A rehearsal for Empire Day taken in Grenfell Park was on May 22. (see Boys' Section).

Notice was received that there would be no Whitsuntide holiday this year. A pupil of the school for the past five and a half years died on the previous Saturday morning, the funeral taking place on the afternoon of June 21. The Headmistress took nine of the senior pupils to the cemetery for the service from 3–3.30 p.m.

Four girls were successful in securing a Free Place to the County School.

Summer holidays were from August 4–September 4. Nature Walks, September 28 and October 5. Medical inspections,

October 18. Songs, games, etc. instead of the usual lessons for the last school day on December 21.

1917

Re-assemble January 9. Cookery Classes were suspended for a short time from the 15th owing to the unavailability of the tutor.

Only 145 attended school on February 5 owing to snow. The sale of needlework amounted to £41. 17s. 10d. on February 22. Further medical inspections on the 28th.

Owing to an epidemic of chickenpox and mumps in the Infants' School no new scholars were to be admitted from this school until after the Easter holiday. Low attendance again on April 2 due to heavy snow.

The Headteacher was at a meeting of the Food Economy Campaign on May 1 and with the Executive Committee on the 2nd and 4th. Two pupils had passed the Labour Examinations. Special cookery demonstration lessons were being given to older scholars. Standard VI and VII attended in the mornings, Standard V in the afternoons. They dealt chiefly with substitutes for wheaten flour. Boys and Girls rehearsed the song and hymn for Empire Day on the 21st and 23rd in readiness to welcome the Mayor, Lord Desborough and members of the Corporation on the 24th.

The Headteacher attended a meeting for women in the Town Hall addressed by Dr. Mary Scharleib on June 21.

In connection with the National Baby Week, the Matron Superintendent of the V.A.D. (Voluntary Aid Detachment) hospital visited and addressed older pupils on 'How to mind Baby'. Three Free Places were awarded to the County School. Holidays August 3 to September 4.

By October 8 the number on the roll had risen to 255. Admissions had been stopped pending the decision of the Managers on the matter. Five new pupils were admitted to Standard VII on the 16th as there was room in that class. Medical inspections again on the 25th.

Mr. J. Wesley Walker gave a lesson to Standard VII on 'Gas' in preparation for their visit to the Gas Works on December 7. Christmas holidays commenced on the 21st.

1918

The new term began on January 8, an H.M. Inspector visited on the 9th and a special cookery demonstration to Standard VII was on the 11th. A half-day holiday and sale of needlework was on February 21 raising £34. 13s. 11d.

For the new school year classes changed to:-

Standard II	Miss Lobb
Standard III	Miss Tilbury
Standard IV	Miss Partlo (Headmistress)
Standard V & Students	Miss Goody
Standard VI & VII	Mrs. White.

N.O.R. 263. Five girls out of six passed the Labour Examinations on April 20.

Mrs. White left on the afternoon of May 1 as she had been granted leave of absence for an indefinite period to be with her husband who was ill. This resulted in three classes without teachers on the 6th. Mrs. Hill, Mrs. Bell, Mrs. Nicholls and Miss Dover were called in to help.

Empire Day was to be kept on May 17. Extra singing and recitation lessons were given in order to teach the hymn and song but notice was received on the 16th that the Mayor would be unable to visit owing to illness. This finally took place on the 29th.

Miss Tilbury returned on June 24 after a period of eight weeks absence. Miss Eleanor Freeman commenced on supply in Mrs. White's place. Summer holidays August 1–September 3.

Miss E.M. Dover was appointed to the permanent staff for the new term. Registers were not marked on the afternoon of the 6th as most of the older girls had gone blackberrying. The Headteacher visited the Girls' Elementary and Girls' Intermediate School at Clewer St. Stephen on the 12th. Blackberrying again for the upper standards on the 13th, 20th, 24th and 27th. The girls received payment for their blackberries on October 2. The total amount gathered was 226 lb., the pay, three pence (old money) per pound. Medical inspections were on October 8 and 9.

The influenza epidemic began taking its toll on pupils and staff.

On October 18 only 174 scholars were present, on the 21st the Sanitary Authority acting on the advice of the Medical Officer of Health closed the school until November 4, it opened only to be closed for another week, opened on the 11th with 161 in the morning and 120 in the afternoon, closed on the 12th, re-open with 189 on the 18th, 171 on the 22nd reaching a high of 208 on December 10, the largest number since October 10. The last day of term ended with singing, recitation and games on December 18.

With the Education Act of 1918 the minimum leaving age became 14.

1919

Still poor attendance for the first day of term – January 7. The sale of needlework on February 27 realized £57. 7s. 0d. The N.O.R. on April 1 was 241. The average attendance for the first week of the new school year was 225.6. Percentage of attendance 93.6. Empire Day was celebrated on May 23.

As the required 90 per cent of attendances was obtained for the month ending May 30, the school closed after the morning instead of the afternoon session for the Whitsun holiday. By order of the Mayor, the school closed on the first Friday afternoon in July to celebrate the Peace. Another half-holiday given in the afternoon of July 11 for the 90 per cent attendance figures during the month of June. Tea was given in the school on Saturday afternoon (19th) to all children in connection with the peace celebrations, and although the school assembled on the morning of the 21st the girls were dismissed for another day's holiday.

Girls assembled with boys at 3.30 p.m. on the afternoon of July 23 for the unveiling ceremony of the memorial board recording the names of former pupils killed in the war.

For the first time, five weeks was granted for the summer holiday (August 1 to September 9). Arrangements had been made for Miss A.C. Martin to commence on October 1. She visited the school on September 17 to observe lessons in various classes in order to obtain a general idea of the working of the school. She had been given specimen lessons in different subjects for her benefit, but, in the absence of Miss Tilbury, began duties on supply as from September 19. Unfortunately her resignation was received on October 31. Miss Dover completed work on the permanent staff on September 30 but did assist from time to time on supply.

Medical inspections October 8 and 9 and nature walk for Standard V on the 14th. The Mayor accompanied by the Mayoress and Town Clerk addressed girls and boys assembled in the hall on November 4 in connection with the distribution of Peace Medals. On November 11, the first anniversary of Armistice (or Remembrance) Day, the occasion was marked by singing a special hymn and National Anthem, reading the King's Message and observing the two minute silence. Instead of the usual history lesson in each class, each teacher gave a short address on the 'League of Nations'. (The first meeting of the League of Nations was held at Geneva, Switzerland on November 15, 1920. It was an international association of countries created to maintain peace among the nations of the world. The League was dissolved in April 1946, its successor, the United Nations).

Miss D.A. Tarrant commenced as a temporary assistant on November 20 and Miss A.L. Lillystone as an assistant on the permanent staff on December 2. Eighty five girls attended a lecture in the Maidenhead Picture Theatre given by the Rev. F.H. Somerville on 'Missionary Work among the Indians of South America' on December 3. This was illustrated with cinematograph films. Each class contributed an item towards the end of term concert on the 19th.

1920

The new term commenced January 6, N.O.R. 226. The sale of needlework raised £82. 7s. 5d. on February 26. Medical inspections for girls aged 8 and 12 on March 11. Miss Tarrant resigned on March 31.

Miss Partlo the Headmistress who had been on long term sick leave, returned to school on April 13. Miss Goody had taken charge during her absence assisted by Miss Lobb. Numbers had increased to 264. Classes were now arranged as follows:-

Standard II	Miss E.F. Freeman
Standard III	Miss V.A. Tilbury
Standard IV	Miss A.L. Lillystone
Standard V	Miss A.B. Goody
Standard VI & VII	Miss G. Lobb.

The Headmistress was still responsible for some subjects with Standard VII and for this term one division of Standard II in needlework. An alteration in the time-table of Standards VI and VII resulted in one oral subject omitted, handwork taking its place. On April 29 Miss Partlo supervised the cutting out of garments by the older girls. It was impossible to get all the large garments cut in the needlework lessons – the girls came for cutting-out as they could be spared from other lessons. All Standard VI girls had cut out a woman's pinafore.

A half-day holiday was given on the afternoon of May 7 for good attendance during April, all departments having reached the required percentage. A rehearsal for Empire Day on May 20 in readiness for the Mayor's visit the following day. Many parents and friends were present on this occasion.

The mid-term arithmetic test was given in all classes on June 7. The following day Standards IV and V were given an oral arithmetic test. Another half-holiday on the 10th for good attendance during the month of May. As the new drill books had arrived during the week of the 18th, the Headmistress took drill examination in all classes on the old course so that teachers could at once start the new course.

July 2 was the first week of this school year that the percentage of attendance had fallen below 90. This was, of course, due to two Sunday School treats. Poor attendance again on the 9th due to wet weather and the 16th owing to three Sunday School treats. The school closed on the morning of the 30th for the summer holiday the afternoon being given for good attendance during June.

Re-open August 31. Miss Tilbury was married during the holiday and became Mrs Robinson. She continued teaching until the end of September. No further pupils were being admitted to Standard II as the number in that class had reached 60. A nature walk to the Thicket for Standard III on September 9 while

Standard V were given a special lesson on the 'Mayflower' to mark the tercentenary of the little sailing vessel of 180 tons which carried the Pilgrim Fathers to America in 1620.

Three scholars had gained Free Places to the County Girls' School this year. The school closed on September 30 as all teachers attended the conference on 'Educational Subjects' at Reading.

Miss Eliza Jane Tiller replaced Mrs. Robinson on October 4. By the 15th the N.O.R. had risen to 254, 26 higher than the corresponding week last year. The mid-term test in arithmetic was given throughout the school on the 20th, the oral arithmetic on the 21st. (Now a termly procedure).

The Armistice short service and two minute silence was adhered to on November 11. This was a memorable occasion as the body of the Unknown Warrior was brought from one of the war cemeteries in France to be buried in Westminster Abbey. Attendance had improved and a half-day holiday was granted on the 19th for October's figures.

A North American Negro gave an address to the children on the negro people in America on December 10. After the address he sang negro songs and hymns. During the afternoons of the last week of term painting Christmas cards, calendars and singing carols took precedence. The first hour of the afternoon on the 23rd was devoted to the Christmas concert, the last hour in classrooms having music and games.

1921

The new term began January 11. Medical inspections, February 14. The annual sale of needlework, February 17, a high of £77. 8s. 4d. being recorded. A new monitress, Miss Ethel Annie Brooks commenced work on April 5. All girls spent some time in the playground on the morning of the 8th watching the eclipse of the sun. Arrangements for Empire Day on May 27 followed similar lines to last year.

The highest number on the roll to date, 279, was on June 3. On June 30, Dr. Paterson the Medical Officer of Health made a special intelligence examination according to the Binet-Simon system for the measurement of intelligence. Two girls were tested, a girl distinctly above the average and a very backward girl. These tests continued on July 4. (Alfred Binet and Theophile Simon, two French psychologists, had been commissioned during the early part of the century to find out why certain children in the schools of Paris lagged behind their classmates in school work).

Two pupils gained Free Places to the County School, one of them being the girl who had the intelligence examination back in June. Summer closure July 29–August 30.

Miss Kathleen E.F. Phillips commenced as a Student Teacher on August 30. Through the kindness of the Chairman of Managers, Councillor Hope, who supplied the apparatus, older pupils were now able to enjoy a game of netball.

A nature study walk to the Thicket for Standard III on September 6; medical inspections on the 27th and 28th; school closed for the teachers annual conference in Reading on the 29th.

Standard IV gave a short selection play taken from 'As You Like It' on October 21. It was prepared in Literature lessons during the term and was enjoyed by all classes. Many colds and five cases of mumps was reported on November 4.

A play entitled 'The Crowning of Peace' was performed by the upper girls on December 1. Boys and their teachers were invited. Special Christmas lessons took place on the 19th, the Christmas concert, each class contributing one item to the programme was on the 22nd, school closing on the 23rd.

1922

Re-open January 10. Miss Lobb was absent owing to serious illness in her home. A short address was given by the Headmistress to mark the second birthday of the League of Nations. The lowest attendance since week ending November 15, 1918 was recorded on January 20 owing to bad influenza colds.

Miss Ethel Brooks the monitress left on February 13 to commence at the County Girls' School. She would continue to help but only when that school was closed for holidays. All girls assembled in the hall on the 17th to see 'The Wild Swans' composed and acted by Standard IV. The annual exhibition and sale of needlework was on the 23rd.

It was the wish of King George V that all schools should close on February 28 for the wedding of his only daughter, Princess Mary, to Viscount Lascelles, later to become the Earl of Harewood.

March 10 showed the best attendance since week ending June 24, 1921. Medical inspections on the 13th and 14th. Miss Tiller who would be responsible for the lowest class in April spent the morning of the 15th observing teaching methods used in the Infants' School. Mrs. G. Morgan addressed boys and girls on the League of Nations on the 22nd and the girls of the netball team played their first school match with Boyne Hill Girls and won by 5 goals to 2 on the 29th.

With thirty two admissions from Alwyn Road, St. Paul's, East Street and the Infants' School organisation was:-

Standards	*No.*	*Teacher*
VII & Ex VII	36	Miss Partlo (Headmistress)
VI	42	Miss Goody
V	45	Miss Lobb
IV	48	Miss Lillystone
III	49	Miss Freeman
II A & B	53	Miss Tiller
	273	

Handwork lesson for upper standards on Tuesday afternoons was replaced by a reading and an optional lesson. Fancy needlework would be included with the plain needlework. Several changes to the position of lessons in the upper standards were made in order to arrange for Miss Lobb to teach singing to Standards VI, VII and Ex VII as well as to Standard V.

Half of Standard IV visited the Museum to inspect the historical collection on May 1, the remainder on May 3. The same arrangements for Standard V on the 11th and 12th. Mrs. Harding-Andrews gave an address to upper classes on people of Austria and Czechoslovakia on the 22nd. Empire Day celebrations on the 24th.

On May 29 girls assembled in the hall to witness the performance of 'The Trial Scene' from 'The Merchant of Venice' given by Standards VII and Ex VII who had been studying the play in literature lessons.

The school was presented with a large and interesting collection of shells on June 1. On the 23rd Mr. Thompson, a North American negro, spoke on the history of North America and sang negro folk songs. The percentage for the quarter ending June 30 was 93.4 the highest recorded since June 1914.

On July 17 Standard IV performed a play entitled 'Moonshine' adapted from 'A Midsummer Night's Dream'. It proved impossible for the Headmistress to take the termly examinations in all subjects throughout the school as she was responsible for teaching Standards VII and Ex VII. Drawing and Recitation marks in Standards II–V had been given by the assistant teachers. Singing and Drill had not been examined.

Miss Phillips completed her period of training as a student teacher on August 4. Summer holidays commenced until September 5. One 'Free Place' was awarded to the County Girls'.

Two new student teachers, Miss Louisa Mary Badcock and Miss Dorothy May Snow, commenced on September 5. Mr. E.D. Ford, an American, spoke to upper classes on the League of Nations on the 20th. No school on the 29th due to the annual Educational Conference in Reading.

Saturday October 7 saw Standard IV visiting Reading Museum and the Abbey Ruins and being shown objects of special interest. Medical inspections, 11th and 12th and a series of talks on 'The Care of the Baby' was given by the school nurse to older scholars during October and November.

Girls assembled in the hall on November 30 for a little celebration on 'Home'. Short readings on the subject were given, hymns were sung by the girls, songs rendered by Mrs. Robinson (a supply teacher) and Miss Lobb and a pianoforte solo by Miss Badcock. In an address Mrs. Elwin Nash gave some beautiful thoughts on 'Home' and set before them, a high ideal of womanhood. At the close of the meeting all repeated together the words of a short dedication.

A netball match with Boyne Hill Girls' on December 7 resulted in a win by 11 goals to 5. Each class contributed an item to the Christmas concert programme on the 21st, school closing on the 22nd.

1923

The new term began on January 9. Daphne Franks, a Standard V scholar, won First Prize (£25) in Gamages Essay Competition open to all children under twelve years of age. Lessons on the geography and history of the town of Maidenhead were given in all classes on the 26th in preparation for 'our second celebration' taking place on the 30th. Readings bearing on the subject were given and the two hymns 'The Golden City' and 'The Hymn of the City' were sung. Mrs. Robinson gave a beautiful rendering of 'Jerusalem'. The Mayor (Councillor T. Stuchbery) spoke on Maidenhead, its past, present and future and set before them their duty as the future citizens of the town. At the close, the girls repeated the words of a short dedication in which they pledged themselves to the service of the town.

The sale and exhibition of needlework was on March 1 raising £47. 8s. 4d. and medical inspections on the 21st and 22nd.

A slight change in the organisation for the new school year.

Standard Ex VII	Miss Partlo (Headmistress)
Standard VII	some lessons with Miss Partlo and Miss Goody
Standard VI	Miss Goody
Standard V	Miss Lobb
Standard IV	Miss Lillystone
Standard III	Miss Freeman
Standard II & girls below Std. II	Miss Tiller.

The number on the roll, 280, was the highest since the school opened.

It was the wish of King George V that all schools close on April 26 to mark the occasion of the marriage of the Duke of York to Lady Elizabeth Bowes-Lyon. The girls sent a large box of flowers to a London Infants' School on the 30th.

On the afternoon of May 10 girls of Standards VI, VII and Ex VII each represented one of the countries in the League of Nations. They had collected products etc. of the country and these were exhibited in the hall. Many of the girls were in the national dress, each being provided with the flag. At 3 p.m. other classes came to view the exhibits and to gather information. The proceedings closed with the singing of a suitable song. School closed on the morning of the 18th for the Whitsun holiday in order to allow children to attend the performance of the play 'Julius Caesar' in the afternoon. A belated Empire Day took place on June 1.

Dr. Paterson the Medical Officer of Health spoke to pupils on his recent visit to Austria on July 5. The engagements of Miss Badcock and Miss Snow – student teachers – terminated on the 31st. They were replaced by Miss Winifred Irene Taylor and Miss Ena Kathleen Morris on August 1. Holidays August 3–September 4.

Nature walks to the Thicket for Standard II on September 6 and Standard III on the 13th. Half of Standard IV visited the Museum on October 17, the remainder on the 22nd and Ex VII on November 9. The netball team played Alwyn Road on the 19th and won. The third of the series of celebrations 'Our Country' was on the 23rd. Readings, recitations, hymns and songs were given by girls and teachers. Lady Gardner (wife of Ernest Gardner the local M.P.) was present and spoke to the girls on their duty to England. The short dedication was repeated.

Several cases of measles among the lower classes was reported on November 30 and December 7. The Christmas concert was on the 19th and girls assembled with the boys on the 20th to do honour to R.P. Bell, a former scholar who gained a scholarship to Balliol College, Oxford. (see Boys' section).

1924

School commenced on January 8. Rooms were very cold and the temperature in Standard V at 10 a.m. was only 41°F. The following day at 9.30 a.m. no room was higher than 47°F with all windows closed. Statistics for the first week – N.O.R. 247, average attendance, 216.25, percentage, 87.5. Owing to the rail strike on the 21st, Miss Lillystone did not arrive in school until 11.45 a.m.

£36. 13s. 3d. was raised at the sale of needlework on March 6. Winifred Lowe, a former scholar, passed the Civil Service Examination (made compulsory for entrance into the British Civil

Service during the 19th century) and was third on the list of 1500 candidates.

Thirty two admissions from the Infants' School brought the new school year roll to 270. A change in some classes:-

Standard II	Miss Tiller
Standard III	Miss Lobb
Standard IV	Miss Freeman
Standard V	Miss Lillystone
Standard VI	Miss Goody
VII & Ex VII	Miss Partlo (Headmistress).

Girls assembled with boys for the Empire Day celebrations on May 23. In connection with the centenary of the R.S.P.C.A. special lessons on 'Kindness to Animals' were given during the month of June.

Miss Lobb on Doctor's advice, would be absent until the summer holiday resulting in the Headmistress taking Standard III in addition to VII and Ex VII.

The great British Empire Exhibition was held at Wembley during 1924–25. All classes became involved.

On June 30	an Empire pageant was given by Standard V
On July 4	Standard II gave a play entitled 'Britannia and her Children'
On July 11	an Empire play by Standard IV
On July 18	an Empire play by Standard III
On July 21	Standards VI, VII and Ex VII (72 girls) visited the Exhibition at Wembley. They were conveyed in a char-a-banc from the school gates at 9 a.m. returning 8.30pm.

On Saturday September 13 nineteen girls from Standard V visited Wembley.

Frances Wilson gained a Junior County Scholarship, the first time this had been won by a pupil of the school. On July 31 Miss Morris and Miss Taylor completed their period of training. There was one Free Place to the County Girls' and although four others passed the examination they were not elected to a 'Free'.

When school re-assembled after the summer recess Miss Phillips commenced as a permanent assistant. The annual Educational Conference was on September 25.

A distinctive school hat with a badge became fashionable and many of the girls voluntarily adopted it. The netball match between Boyne Hill was played on home ground on October 23, Gordon winning. It was announced that at the Board of Education Certificate examination for teachers held in July, Miss Phillips passed gaining 'credit' in six subjects.

A short service commemorated Armistice Day on November 11. 'O God Our Help' was sung and the two minutes silence observed. Twenty girls who were in the Girl Guide movement were absent.

A correspondence between girls of the school and the Pershing High School, Tulsa, Oklahoma, U.S.A. began. The first batch of letters from America arrived in early December. A scholar of Standard III died on December 14, the Headmistress attended the funeral on the 17th. The usual Christmas concert closed the term.

1925

Several pupils were absent on January 7 because of floods. A lot of illness was reported during the month owing to influenza and bad colds. At one time, three teachers were absent from the Boys' School and Miss Phillips assisted there.

The girls assembled for a celebration of the League of Nations on February 5. Poems, songs and hymns bearing on the subject were given by all classes. Mrs. Williams recited and Mrs. Robinson and Miss Lobb sang the duet 'O Lovely Peace'. A fair number of parents attended the Needlework Sale on the 26th where garments were on view in the hall. Three staff began attending a course of lectures on 'The Teaching of English' being held at Reading on Saturday mornings.

On one Saturday during March some pupils of Standard V travelled with Miss Lillystone to Reading. They were met by the Misses Freeman, Phillips and Partlo, visited the Museum and picture gallery and then the Abbey Ruins returning on the 3 o'clock bus. A few upper girls visited the Exhibition of Handicraft of the children of various European countries which was shown in St. Luke's Institute on the 12th. Standard V gave selections from 'As You Like It' on the 20th, thirty girls attended a lecture on

Canada at the Drill Hall in the evening, a Drill Inspectress from the Board of Education visited and saw drill lessons given in Standards II, IV and VI and netball played by Standards VII and VIII on the 27th and the school year ended with the girls being promoted to higher classes on the 31st.

With twenty-six new admissions on April 1 it was all change for teachers and classes:-

Standard II	Miss Tiller
Standard III	Miss Goody
Standard IV	Miss Freeman
Standard V	Miss Lillystone
Standard VI	Miss Lobb
VII & VIII	Miss Phillips and Miss Partlo.

The Headteacher would be responsible for Standard VIII in subjects which are not taken with VII, also for some lessons with all the upper girls and certain lessons in Standards III and VI.

Standard VI gained 100 per cent in attendance for two consecutive weeks in May. In the examination for Junior Scholarships held during the month, Inez Cox was successful, being placed seventh on the County list.

Visits to the Museum:-

Standard VIII and part of VII	May 21
Remainder of Standard VII	May 28
Part of Standard VI	June 11
Remainder	June 15

Empire Day was observed on May 25.

June 18 saw four girls from Standard VIII upper division visit the Public Library for a lesson on 'The Uses of a Public Library'. Twenty-nine pupils from Standard VI went to the Wembley Exhibition on July 3. There were two Free Places to the County Girls' and the summer vacation from July 31–September 1.

Miss Kathleen Rose Swaffield, a bursar at the County Girls' School became eligible and was appointed as a student teacher. An H.M.I. inspection was carried out on the 14 and 16 of July and the main points in their report included:-

'Work done in majority of classes good, in some classes very good. The lowest class in which the majority of the children have just left the King Street Infants' School where the teaching is excellent, is particularly good and the two classes above leave a very good impression. The top class is in charge of a capable teacher (formerly a student teacher in the school).

The school is in quite a satisfactory condition in many ways. The majority of the girls come from very good homes and are capable of fairly hard work. As there is no Central School in the town and only two or three girls per year leave for secondary school the higher classes have not lost the best of the children at about the age of eleven. The girls in the upper classes are in many cases almost of central school type, some even of secondary school type. Some statistics obtained go to prove this. More than a third are having private tuition in playing the piano, several in one class had wireless apparatus at home and more than half were accustomed to listen to wireless, nearly all had boxes of water colours and nearly all had access to good reading matters such as copies of Shakespeare and so on.

With such material, obviously a school where in the absence of a Central School locally, there should be a definite "advance course of work" for the older children.

The chief suggestion is that the teaching of Literature (a subject which generally appeals to girls) should be very much extended. History and Geography should also receive a rather freer treatment with a view to increasing the general knowledge of the girls.

Of other subjects, Singing and Music are possible subjects in which improvement is possible – in view of the large number who have private musical instruction. In the Infants' School a teacher of more than average musical ability could, on two or three afternoons a week, interchange on a suitable arrangement basis'.

The older girls in Standards III and IV were put in a special class – Standard VI (b). They would work under Miss Lobb with Standard VI. School closed on September 28 for the annual Educational Conference.

October 5 and a walk in connection with the course of history lessons taken on Saturday afternoon by Standards VII and VIII. By permission of Sir Edward Barry, they visited Ockwells Manor and walked round the grounds to see various buildings. Afterwards they proceeded to Bray and visited the church and Jesus Armshouses (built 1623–28 and celebrating their tercentenary). A nature walk to the Thicket for Standard II on the same day.

Standard V visited the Museum, half the class on the 6th the remainder on the 7th. Harvest Festival was on October 8. Girls brought flowers, fruit, vegetables, eggs, etc. which was displayed in the hall. A short service followed, the produce being distributed to the Infirmary of the Poor Law Institution, the Isolation Hospital and Maidenhead Cottage Hospital. VII and VIII girls accompanied by teachers took grapes, eggs and flowers to the Infirmary and sang school songs and hymns to old people in the wards.

Miss Goody attended a Conference of the National Savings Association at Salisbury on October 15. Medicals 20th and 21st.

Miss Lillystone presented six large posters depicting British Empire scenes to the school on November 3. The usual Armistice Service on the 11th and the twelve oldest scholars visited the Public Library on the 18th and 25th to be instructed in the use of encyclopedias and books of reference. The Christmas concert was on December 23.

1926

Re-open January 12. Attendance only 88.6 on the 15th owing to a heavy snow storm. A scholar of Standard III who had been suffering from rheumatic fever for some weeks died on the Saturday. Standard IV to the Museum on the 27th and 28th.

An address on the 'Kindness to Animals' by a member of the R.S.P.C.A. was given on February 15. A Band of Mercy in connection was formed with fifty girls joining on the 22nd. Sale of needlework on the 25th.

A teacher from the East Street Infants' School gave a talk on Irish poetry on March 4. It was illustrated by readings of poems and by Irish songs on the gramophone. Girls were very interested and willingly stayed after school hours. Miss Lobb visited the Infants' School to observe musical work on that day and returned again on the 9th to see the work of the girls who would be promoted on April 1. A First Aid demonstration was given to Standard VII on the 25th. There were twenty-seven new admissions after the Easter holidays. Empire Day celebrations took place on May 21.

Vera Madge Green was successful in the recent examination for

Junior Scholarships open to all schools in the County. She was the top girl on the list. Three other pupils won Free Places. Miss Swaffield completed her period of training on July 30. Summer holidays until August 31.

Miss Tiller who was granted a year's leave of absence on Doctor's advice back in January, never returned and resigned on August 27.

A nature walk for Standard III on September 14 and Standard II on the 23rd. Harvest Festival (as last year) was on the 22nd. Educational Conference the 27th.

A former pupil gave a selection of pianoforte solos from some of the great composers to upper girls in the singing lesson on October 5. A lesson on Ockwells Manor had been given on the 14th to prepare the top class for their visit the following day. The usual Armistice Service took place on November 11. All classes observed Shakespeare Day on the 18th with a varied programme:-

Fairy Scene from 'Midsummer Night's Dream'	Standard II
Song 'When Daisies Pied'	Standard III
Shakespeare character recitations	Standard VI
'As You Like It' (two scenes)	Standard V
Song 'Who Is Sylvia'	Standard VI & VII
'Hubert and Arthur' from 'King John'	Standard IV
Song 'Where The Bee Sucks'	Standard V
'Julius Caesar' (four scenes)	Standard VII
'The Princes in the Tower' from 'Richard III'	Standard III

Mrs. Janie Urquhart Bailey was engaged on November 17 to cover Miss Lobb's absence through illness. With the dentist's visit to Standards II and III on the 26th all heads were inspected on December 2. Ten of the older scholars were taken to see a film on India at the Drill Hall after school on the 3rd and the Christmas concert closed the term on the 23rd.

1927

The new term commenced on January 11. Miss Lobb was still absent and Mrs. Alice E. Carter came in on supply. She did not return until February 21. The sale of needlework was on March 10.

Miss Freeman retired from teaching on March 25 pending her forthcoming marriage. Miss Louisa M. Badcock, a student teacher in 1922–3, was appointed as her replacement from May 1.

April 1 saw thirty-two admissions with staff arrangements:-

Standard II	Miss Phillips
Standard III	Miss Badcock (from May 1)
Standard IV	Miss Lillystone
Standard V	Miss Goody
Standard VI	Miss Lobb
Standard VII & VIII	Miss Partlo (Headmistress).

Girls brought in wild flowers to send to three schools in London on May 2; Sixty scholars attended the Picture Theatre on Saturday morning (14th) to see R.S.P.C.A. films; seven sat for examinations with only one 'Free' Place; Empire Day celebrations (24th).

Swimming instruction (first time ever mentioned) began at the Public Baths on June 2. Standards V, VI and VII formed three classes for these lessons with Miss Badcock instructing. Summer holidays July 29–August 30.

A Domestic Subjects Centre had been set up to instruct the girls in laundry work. There was a new student teacher – Miss Margaret Reeves. The netball team visited Cookham Rise School on September 19 with the result a draw of four goals each. In the return match (on home ground) on the 26th Cookham Rise won five goals to nil. Standard II and III were involved in nature walks to the Thicket on the 20th and 26th. The annual Harvest Festival (as last year) was on the 28th and all girls assembled in hall on the 29th for 'A half-hour with Beethoven'. A hymn and vesper was sung by all, Standards VI and VII sang two pieces, Miss Badcock gave two pianoforte solos and two items were given on the gramophone (to mark the centenary year of his death).

Closed for the Educational Conference on October 3; a short course of lessons with older girls on 'The Care of Baby' took place on the 5th, 19th and 26th; two teams played netball matches at Cookham Rise School on a Saturday afternoon, the first team lost, the second won, and Standard VII had lessons at the Public Library on the use of a directory, a railway time-table and books of reference on October 25 and November 15.

The Headmistress attended a meeting of the Rotary Club to consider the establishment of a clinic for cripples on November 7. Thirty eight girls of Guides and War Orphans left to attend the service at the War Memorial on the 11th. The rest observed the two minutes silence in school. On the 24th all assembled in hall to show what they had learnt this term on Shakespeare. A long programme of songs, recitations and scenes from plays was given with all classes taking part. Essays on his life and works were read, Standard IV performed three old country dances.

Owing to very slippery conditions of the roads on December 21, only 95 pupils were present in the morning. The number increased to 133 in the afternoon. Christmas holidays began on the 22nd.

1928

Poor attendance for the re-opening on January 10 due largely to measles and mumps. Two teachers were away with mumps. The Headmistress was at a conference in Windsor on 'Medical Inspection in Schools' arranged by the British Medical Association on February 17.

£31. 2s. 4d. was realized at the sale of needlework on March 1 while the following day figures recorded show that with N.O.R. 207, average attendance 200.7 and percentage of attendance 96.98 this was the highest weekly percentage ever reached since the school opened nearly twenty-one years ago. All classes had organised games in the playground for the last half-hour on the 5th to celebrate the good attendance. Miss Badcock who would be teaching Standard II in April visited the Infants' School to see the teaching of eurythmics on March 14 and returned on the 16th to see the work of Standard I girls in the chief school subjects. The twenty-first school year ended on the 30th.

Forty-two new admissions on April 2. Empire Day May 24 included one hour's secular instruction given in school after which the girls proceeded to Kidwells Park where other schools assembled. A procession was formed to the Rialto Cinema where Empire films were shown and a short address given by the Mayor, Alderman Cox. At the examination held during the month for Free Places at the County Girls' School, six of the twelve places were gained by scholars from the school, all Gordon pupils being successful.

The following scholars were successful in the Empire Film Essay Competition:-

Class I	(under 10)	Marie Flint	2nd prize
Class II	(10–12)	Violet West	2nd prize
Class III	(12–15)	Marjorie Keen and Eva Church – Highly Commended.	

Three large boxes of flowers were sent to an Infant School in London on June 11.

Standard VIII visited Ockwells Manor on July 14; Standard IV (in two divisions) to the Museum 11th and 18th and Standard VIII on the 19th. Summer Holidays August 3–September 4.

Nature walks to the Thicket to collect berries for Standard II on September 11, Standard III on the 18th, and on the 20th in connection with music teaching, upper standards assembled in hall for an 'Half-hour with Handel'. Girls sang songs, Miss Badcock played pianoforte solos and four gramophone records played. Standard VIII visited Reading Abbey and Museum on the 22nd.

The Educational Conference was on October 1, the Harvest Festival (arrangements similar to last year) on the 4th. Miss Goody who was Secretary of the National Savings Association of the school gave a lesson in every class resulting in twenty-two new members being enrolled.

Housewifery classes had to be suspended until after Christmas owing to illness of staff. Miss Partlo the Headmistress, had been absent since October 30. She was suffering from glaucoma in both eyes and entered hospital for an operation. Her resignation was submitted to the Managers on December 12 and would take effect from March 31, 1929.

In connection with the Schubert centenary Standards IV–VIII assembled for a programme of the composer's music on December 13. Songs were sung by the upper girls, Miss Badcock and a former scholar gave pianoforte solos and various gramophone records were played. Three short plays were performed on the 20th:-

(1) a scene from 'A Winter's Tale' by Standard II
(2) a scene from 'The Taming of the Shrew' by Standard III
(3) a Schubert play by Standards VI and VII.

'Christmas Fun' with each class preparing songs and plays ended the term on the 21st. During the years 1926–28 several teachers were on sick leave and it would appear that the same three teachers on supply, Mrs. Carter, Mrs. Mead and Miss Blay, who left to get married, covered in their absence.

1929

The new term commenced on January 8. A sad entry in the School Log Book for January 15. 'Owing to defective eyesight I am unable to continue my school duties till my engagement terminates on March 31. I finish work today after nearly twenty-two years of service in this School. B. Partlo'. A testimonial in appreciation of her services was granted under the seal of the Council. Miss Goody was temporarily appointed Acting Head Teacher after that date.

By order of the Sanitary Authority acting on the advice of the Medical Officer of Health the school closed on February 14 until the 25th owing to the prevalence of influenza. The number present on re-opening was still only 180.

There were forty-one new admissions for the new school year on April 9. Miss Dorothy Irene Parfitt commenced on the permanent staff on the 22nd. Medical inspections for eight and twelve year olds was on the 30th.

All girls assembled in the hall on May 6 to listen to 'The Trial Scene' from the 'Merchant of Venice' given by Standard VII. On the 10th they celebrated a half-day holiday granted to the boys because the football team had been successful in winning two Shields. (see BOYS). Empire Day was on May 17.

Two pupils gained places to the County Girls'. The whole school spent the last half-hour on July 26 listening to the music and songs composed by Schumann and sung by Standard VII. At the Swimming Gala on August 1 the team of three girls were successful in winning the Davies Cup. Summer holidays August 2–September 3.

A nature walk to the Thicket for berries on September 17 for Standard II. Closed for the Educational Conference on the 27th and Miss Lobb who had served the school for twenty-two years resigned to take an appointment as Head Teacher under the Wiltshire Education Committee at the end of the month. She was replaced by Miss Phyllis M. Trott who left at the end of December to take an appointment with Hendon Council.

Standards VI and VII visited the Town Hall on October 17 to listen to a lecture on 'Musical Instruments' illustrated by gramophone records supplied by His Master's Voice Gramophone Company.

November included medical inspections, the Armistice Service in the hall and Miss Parfitt being absent to attend the Bristol Eisteddfodd festival in which she was taking part.

The Christmas concert was on December 19, holidays beginning the following day.

1930

Re-open on January 7 with Miss Dorothy Quaintance replacing Miss Trott. The sale of needlework was on March 6 and there were twenty-seven admissions for the new school year on April 1.

A sub-committee of councillors met on May 7 to discuss the staffing of both the Girls' and Boys' Schools. Empire Day was on May 23 and there was one free place awarded to the County Girls' School.

In July Miss Parfitt had to consult a throat specialist and, following advice, had to take a three month rest on the hope of avoiding an operation. On the 21st an Inspectress of Physical Instruction from the Board of Education visited and saw drill lessons given in Standards II and IV. Again three girls were successful in winning the Davies Cup at the Swimming Gala on the 31st. Summer holidays August 1–September 2.

Miss D.M. Franklin was appointed at the commencement of the new term and Miss Parfitt returned on October 1. School closed for the Education Conference on October 6.

November saw medical inspections and the usual Armistice Service.

Miss Parfitt was absent on December 15 to attend an audition arranged for her by the Royal College of Music. Part of the programme arranged for the breaking up concert was given in the Boys' School on the 18th, the girls assembled the following day for their informal concert each class contributing an item. Christmas closure.

1931

The school re-assembled on January 6. The dentist examined every girl on January 28, heads being examined on February 5. Miss Franklin resigned on February 27. The needlework sale was on March 5.

At the commencement of the new school year the N.O.R. was 248. Miss Beryl Scott-Jones replaced Miss Franklin. Medical and head inspections during May with Empire Day on the 22nd. Miss Quaintance left to take a post with London County Council on June 26. One Free Place to the County Girls'.

The school closed on the afternoon of July 23 for the Elementary Schools Swimming Gala. Competitors from Gordon were successful in nearly all events winning the Davies Cup for the girls relay race and the girls 100 yards championship. In conjunction with the boys they also won the Richardson Cup and the Mayor's Cup which was given to the school obtaining the highest number of points. On the 30th the Mayor (Councillor Norris) accompanied by Mr. Biggs visited to present the prize gained by Gertrude Montague in the Essay Competition held in connection with Empire Shopping Week.

Summer holidays July 31–August 31. Education Conference September 28. Miss Doris Smith was appointed on October 1 to replace Miss Quaintance. Medical inspections and the Armistice were the main events in November. Miss Badcock resigned on November 30 pending her forthcoming marriage. Her place was taken by Miss H.I. Thomas who left the school on March 23 (1932). The Christmas concert was on December 23.

1932

School opened on January 11, N.O.R. 230. The needlework sale was on February 25. At the end of the school year the N.O.R. was 229, average attendance 214.6, percentage of attendance 93.7. The final entry in the Girls Log Book reads 'March 23, Owing to the amalgamation of the Girls and Boys Departments I have today finish three years work as Acting Head Teacher of the Girls' Department. A.B. Goody'.

8

Gordon Road Senior Mixed Council School

1932

Gordon Road became a senior mixed school as from April 1. The new school (Ellington) had been built but would not be open until August 30 and would be known as a junior and infants mixed school. Juniors under the age of eleven would be transferred but would have to remain at Gordon Road for the first term. Staff details:-

Senior School:	Mr. E.A. Bell (Headmaster), Miss A.B. Goody (Senior Girls' Assistant), Messrs. R.W. Murray, J.E. Cluff, F.G.W. Hammond and L.E.J. Adderson, and the Misses K.E.F. Phillips, D. Smith and A.L. Lillystone.
Junior & Infants:	the Misses H.M. Cook, I.K. Warburton, D.I. Parfitt, V.B. Scott-Jones, J. Jones (transferred from Infants' Department at King Street to Junior School at Gordon Road).

Re-open after the Easter holidays on April 5. Fifty-six had been admitted from the King Street Infants' plus nine others making the first number on roll 507. Average attendance 488.1 (96.2%). An experimental time-table was being worked. Empire Day was celebrated on May 24. The Headmaster had been invited to attend Educational Sub-Committees on May 31, June 20 and June 28.

Dental inspections on June 1, hair on June 30. Registers closed at 9.00 a.m. on the morning of June 7 the school at 11.00 a.m. In the afternoon 191 children attended the rehearsal of the Military Tattoo at Aldershot accompanied by two helpers and seven teachers. Two parties of 43 girls visited the Furze Platt Laundry on the 8th and 9th. For boys there were four Junior County Scholarships, one Spoore Scholarship and two Free Places; three Free Places for the County Girls'.

A half-day holiday for the Elementary Schools Swimming Gala on July 21 when the school was, once again, successful in winning the Norris Cup and Curtis Shield. The Headmaster and Mr. Murray attended the formal opening of Ellington School on July 26, the Mayor (Councillor E.B. Norris) distributed the prizes and certificates won by children who wrote essays on the films shown during Empire Shopping Week on the 27th and in order to enable staff to carry out the transfer to Ellington satisfactorily in time for August 30, Gordon Road and King Street Schools closed for the summer holiday on the 27th instead of mid-day on the 29th.

Final figures for the end of the first term. N.O.R. 509, average attendance 449.8 (88.3%). 190 children were transferred to Ellington Junior School and 17 to other schools in the town. Teachers transferred to Ellington, Miss Warburton, Miss Scott-Jones, Miss Jones, Miss Cook and Miss Parfitt. Gordon Road now became a Senior School.

Re-open August 30. During the holiday some of the floor blocks in the hall which had become loose were reset and an accelerator was fixed to the heating apparatus. Miss D.E. Wheeler commenced as a student teacher. With the opening of Ellington, King Street Infants' School closed.

On September 2 the N.O.R. was 284. Average attendance 245.6 (86.4%). Poor attendance as many children were still away on holiday. Miss Lillystone transferred to Ellington on the 12th. The Educational Conference was on the 30th.

Thirty four girls and twenty-eight boys, all twelve years old, were medically examined on October 19 and 20. There were two special cases and four re-examinations. Fourteen elder boys with the Headmaster went to the Guildhall on November 9 to see the election of the Mayor. Mr. Bell visited the Art, Woodwork and

Cookery classes at the Technical Institute in the afternoon.

By November the first H.M.I. Report of the Senior Mixed Department was issued. It read 'Very great credit must be given to the Headmaster and his staff in the tactful and efficient way in which they carried out the various details on the change, acting in co-operation with the Headmistress of the new Junior School (Ellington).

The school now has 280 children arranged in 7 classes, all of which except the lowest class contain either boys or girls separately. The school is therefore being conducted as a 'duel' rather than a mixed school a course which has a number of advantages.

There are altogether 12 classrooms which on a modern basis have an accommodation of 480. At the moment the school contains a good number of spare places. These spare places are however likely to be very valuable in the future; for any extension of the Borough boundary would no doubt include a re-organisation into a Junior School of the Alwyn Road Council School where pressure of numbers is increasing owing to the growth of new houses towards Pinkneys Green, and such re-organisation would involve a transference of the seniors to Gordon Road. Allowing for the possibility of such an extension the scheme of Council Schools in the Borough would be very sound, viz. a centrally situated Senior School of about 480 places with two Council Junior Schools (Alwyn Road and Ellington) each close to important housing estates on the outskirts of the town. The number of Junior School places would be about 1,000 which is about the correct number to feed a Senior School of 480.

The school is in the charge of the former Headmaster of the Boys' Department. An excellent report on it was sent some years ago in which the school was described as one of the best boys schools in the County. Several subsequent inspections showed that it has continued to deserve this high reputation'.

Instead of the usual lessons on the afternoon of December 23, an entertainment given by the children themselves, was held in the hall. School closed for the Christmas holidays.

1933

Re-open January 10. N.O.R. 265. Average attendance 237.6 (89.6%). There was poor attendance due to colds and influenza. The Headmaster was absent for half-an-hour on the 19th to attend the funeral of the caretaker's wife. He was also absent for part of the afternoon session on February 6 to attend the Education Sub-Committee meeting at Ellington. Heads were examined on the 9th and all the 12 year old group had a medical on April 5. In the competitions for the N.E. Berkshire Football Association on April 7 the school won the League Shield, the shield for the knock-out Competition and also the Junior Cup.

Empire Day was on May 24, head inspections the following day. Twenty-seven boys and girls attended the sports of the N.E. Berkshire Schools Athletic Association at Wargrave as competitors on June 1, and on the 29th Mr. Adderson was absent in the after-

Swimming Team circa 1933.

noon owing to injuries received in a motor accident.

There were six awards of special places at the County Boys' and two at the County Girls'. The annual exhibition and sale of work was on July 13 and the swimming team travelled to the County Sports at Reading on the 26th. The Mayor also visited the school on that day to present the prizes won in the Essay Competition arranged by the Maidenhead Chamber of Commerce. A holiday was granted on the afternoon of the 27th for the Elementary Schools Swimming Gala. The school gained:-

1. The Norris Cup for the highest aggregate of points
2. The Davies Cup (relay race for girls)
3. The Association Cup (100 yds Championship for boys)
4. The Thomas Cup (100 yds Championship for girls).

The boys' running team won a challenge cup at Cookham Flower Show on August 3. The Managers noted with great pleasure the success of the scholars at these events and sent their congratulations to the school and in particular to Mr. Adderson who was responsible for their training.

Attendance had not been adversely affected so much as usual this year by Sunday School Treats as St. Mary's and the Wesleyan were held during Whitsun Week and Boyn Hill and the Drill Hall treats on Saturdays.

Maidenhead Sports were held in Kidwells Park during the summer holidays, the boys' running team winning the Pitcher Shield for the relay race.

Autumn term commenced on September 5 with the first batch of seventy-eight children from the new school Ellington. Mrs. Paterson gave the elder girls a talk on Poland on the 20th and to the elder boys on the 27th.

A demonstration by the British Wire Broadcasting Service was held in school on the afternoon of October 17. It was attended by members of the Education Committee, head teachers and others. The Headmaster visited the Art, Handicraft and Domestic Science classes at the Technical Institute on the 26th. By the end of the month the purchase of the land adjoining the school for the use as a playing field had been completed.

Medical, dental and head inspections were carried out. Elder boys and girls attended the Mayor making ceremony on November 9, closing for the Christmas holidays on December 21.

1934

The new term commenced on January 9, N.O.R. 272. The first week's average attendance was 256.1 (94.1%). Wireless lessons would be taken this term by the four higher forms as an experiment making it necessary for some temporary variations to the time-table. Head and medical inspections during February and March.

Six girls in Class C were practising folk-dancing at Alwyn Road School in preparation for Empire and Civic Week and on May 4 the Headmaster visited Ellington, North Town and St. Mary's Roman Catholic Schools to rehearse music for this occasion. He also visited Braywick, Alwyn Road, Boyn Hill and the Church of England Schools. On the morning of June 1 all children were taken to Grenfell Park for the rehearsal of folk-dancing, physical exercises, singing, etc. in readiness for the afternoon's Civic Display. Forty-five children took part in the District Championships of the North East Berkshire Schools Athletic Association at Wargrave on June 6, and at the request of the Mayor a half-day holiday was granted on the 8th. The Headmaster visited the Baylis Court Senior School at Farnham on the 19th and the Boys' and Girls' Modern Schools at Newbury on the 27th. Stanley Child won the 220yds. (under 14) in the Berkshire School Sports (beating the record) and Edward Shervill was 2nd in the 220yds. (over 14) on July 3. They were both chosen to represent Berkshire in the Inter-County Sports to be held at Blackpool on July 15.

A fire took place on the evening of July 8. It broke out in the caretaker's cupboard but was extinguished before the arrival of the brigade. The door, shelf and contents of the cupboard were destroyed, a good many panes of glass cracked and damage done to the ceiling and woodwork. The school carried on as usual the following day. A half-day holiday for the annual needlework sale and exhibition of school work on the 19th and also for the Swimming Gala when the school won the Norris Cup on the 26th.

Summer holidays August 2–September 4.

The managers considered the steps to be taken in connection with the transfer of senior scholars to Gordon Road from Alwyn Road in September. It was recommended:-

1. That two staff be transferred – Mr. A. Viveash and Miss M.M. Claydon,
2. That Mr. F.H. Harmsworth, Handicraft Instructor at Alwyn be appointed Assistant Master on the staff of Gordon Road from September 1.

Upon the re-organisation of the schools after the summer holiday, the senior scholars were transferred, Alwyn Road becoming a Junior Mixed and Infants School.

On September 4 with:- 152 from Alwyn Road
62 from Ellington
9 others

the number on the roll had risen to 410. There was also a new member of staff, Miss Nancy M. Darvill. School closed for the Education Conference on the 28th. Medicals took place in October and head inspections in November. During the next three months the afternoon session commenced at 1.45.

Eight boys and eight girls witnessed the election of the Mayor on November 9. All schools were granted a holiday on the 29th, the wedding day of H.R.H. the Duke of Kent to Princess Marina of Greece. Dental inspections were on December 7 and Christmas holidays began on the 21st.

1935

Re-open January 8, head inspection again on the 31st. Form 5a attended an Infant Welfare Centre lecture on March 1. Medicals again on the 14th and 15th. Mrs. Downer from the League of Nations union addressed children on the 15th and Miss Leighton-Rust of the National Milk Publicity Council gave the first of a series of four lectures on Health and Cookery.

The school won the Junior Cup in the North-East Berkshire Football League on April 1.

The Board of Education approved the site for the practical instruction centre, comprising a science room, manual instruction room, combined cookery and laundry room and dining hall on August 1, 1934. Nine tenders were received for the building thereof, Messrs. Cripps & Green Ltd. being the successful firm. Work commenced on April 23 in order that the building could be completed and put into use after the summer holiday. The final cost was £2,970 14s. 2d. (£2,970.71p.) plus about £350 allowed for furniture and equipment. It would be necessary to appoint an additional cookery mistress when the new centre was completed.

It was King George V's desire that schools should in some appropriate way share in the celebrations in connection with the Silver Jubilee. A special event was arranged for all schools in Braywick Park on May 6 and the Jubilee Committee met the expense of the mugs presented to the children, teas provided, cost of transport and the several costumes that were made for the occasion. Empire Day was still celebrated on the 24th.

Thirty-one boys and girls took part in the North East Berkshire School Sports at Wargrave on June 5. The boys were successful in winning the championship. Three boys and two girls were awarded Special Places at the County Schools. There was one Spoore Scholarship.

The top class of boys visited the Electric Light Station on July 4 and was shown over by the Electrical Engineer. This same group of boys had been taking a course of lessons on J. Wesley Walker's 'A History of Maidenhead' and on the 16th visited the Guildhall and was shown the original charters, regalia, etc. by the Town Clerk. The exhibition of school work and sale of needlework was on the 18th and the swimming gala the 25th.

Close for the summer holidays on August 2. N.O.R. 340, average attendance 313.4 (92.1%). Miss N.M. Darvill transferred to Ellington.

Re-open September 3. During the holidays the exterior of the school had been painted, the hall and corridors whitewashed, distempered and varnished. Transfers from other schools:- Ellington 37, Alwyn Road 32, others 5. N.O.R. 359. Student teacher Miss D.E. Smith joined the staff and the mistress at the Technical Institute Centre, Miss E.M. Booth was now attached to Gordon Road as teacher of domestic subjects. Though all the furniture had not arrived for the practical instruction centre the rooms were being used. All the boys would be taking handicraft and all the girls domestic subjects. In addition twenty boys who would bc lcaving shortly would take twelve lessons in cookery and a similar class of girls twelve lessons in handicraft. The Education Conference was at Reading on the 27th. Medical inspections October 23/24/25.

A whole day's holiday was granted in all schools on November 6, the wedding day of H.R.H. the Duke of Gloucester to Lady Alice Scott, daughter of the 7th Duke of Buccleuch.

Head inspections November 7; Close for Christmas holidays December 20.

1936

The new term commenced on January 7, N.O.R. 314. Average attendance for first week 303.3 (96.6%).

On the day of the funeral of H.M. King George V (28th) the children assembled in the hall, a short service was held and then they were dismissed. The Mayor (Councillor Redfern) and Chairman of the Education Committee (Alderman Chamberlain) were present.

Many Headteachers attended the funeral service of Miss Bertha Partlo on February 17. Miss Partlo was appointed Headmistress of the Girls' Department when it was officially opened on April 4, 1907. She gave devoted and loyal service to the school until ill health forced her to resign in March 1929. On the afternoon of the 20th Forms 5 and 5a attended a lecture at the Town Hall given under the auspices of the National Association for the Prevention of Tuberculosis. Dentist on the 25th, heads March 5.

Mr. E.A. Bell tendered his resignation as Headmaster to take effect as from June 30. The managers were reluctant to accept and used every effort to persuade him to reconsider. He felt the school would be better served by a younger man and would not change his mind. A testimonial was granted to him under the seal of the council. The post for Headmaster was advertised and one hundred and sixty three applications were received. Seven candidates were selected to attend for interview on March 23, and by a unanimous decision, Leonard Edward James Adderson, already a

Football Team 1936.

member of staff at the school was appointed to commence duties on July 1.

The school was successful in winning two shields (for league and knock-out competitions) given by the North East Berkshire School Football League on April 8. The football team defeated Tonman Mosley School, Slough in the final match for the Grenfell Shield on May 9. They had won four football trophies during the season. The boys gained 1st place and the girls 2nd in the North East Berkshire School Sports at Wargrave on the 27th. Medicals and heads were inspected during the month. The 22nd was kept as Empire Day. Before taking over as Headmaster, Mr. Adderson visited Redlands Senior, E.P. Collier and Caversham Senior Schools in Reading, Ellington and Didcot Senior.

June 30 was Mr. Bell's last day as Headmaster, July 1 Mr. Adderson's first. Mr. F.A. Denzey joined the staff on July 6. There was a holiday on the 16th for the annual exhibition and sale of work in connection with which a drill and country dancing display was given. A great number of parents took the opportunity to visit the school. Among those present was Mr. Archer (Chairman of Managers) and the Revs. Clissold and Lewis. At the Maidenhead Swimming Club Gala on that day the boys won the team race for elementary schools. At the Schools' Swimming Gala on the 23rd the school won the following events:-

Norris Cup	:-	Highest aggregate of points
Curtis Shield	:-	Boys team race
Edwards Cup	:-	Boys diving (S. Broadbent)
Thomas Cup	:-	Girls 100 yards (M. Hargreaves).

The three senior classes boys and girls went to the Plaza Theatre for a film performance of 'A Midsummer Night's Dream' on the 24th.

Mr. F.G.W. Hammond who had been at the school since 1912 resigned with effect from July 31 owing to ill-health. Miss Booth also resigned as Domestic Subjects Mistress, her successor being Miss Joan Quoran Briggs. Summer holidays July 31 to September 1.

The new term saw the following admissions:-

Alwyn Road	36
Ellington	56
National	5
Boyn Hill	7
Others	4
	108

Mr A.D. Matthews joined the staff and Miss Davies as a student teacher. A busy September.

On the	9th	The Organiser of P.T. visited. In the morning all the boys P.T. classes were seen. A demonstration of modern methods was given by Mr. Alexander in the afternoon.
	10th	A violin recital by a Mr. Curnock of Slough in the afternoon.
	23rd	Miss Davis the P.T. Organiser saw all the girls classes at work.
	24th	Miss Claydon and Miss Phillips attended a demonstration of P.T. at East Street Junior School.

25th Closed for Education Conference at Reading University.

30th The caretaker spent a good deal of time on the playing field now in excellent condition for football. The goal posts damaged by the gale had been repaired.

Permission was given to the British Wire Broadcasting Service to erect a pole on the playing field at a charge of one shilling (5p) a year payable in advance. Gardening was also introduced as a subject for boys with tools being purchased to the value of £4. 15s. 0d. (£4.75).

As a result of close co-operation between the Handicraft Centre and the Science and Art Departments, many useful pieces of science apparatus had been constructed and the scope of the art lessons considerably broadened.

During November, December and January the afternoon session would begin at 1.45 p.m. 1001 lbs. of groceries etc. were collected on Pound Day, November 6 and sent to Maidenhead Hospital. Six girls and six boys witnessed the election of the new Mayor on the 9th. At the invitation of Baylis Court Senior School, Slough the girls and boys were successful in their respective netball and football team games. They were entertained to tea before leaving. An extension had been made to the wireless to enable the Armistice Ceremony broadcast from the Cenotaph heard by the whole school assembled in the hall.

Four groups of girls took part in competitions organised by the Berkshire Branch of the English Folk Dance and Song Society held at Reading on November 14. Three first places and certificates were gained – viz. Country Dances, Morris Dances, Folk Dances and Accompaniment. The girls were trained by Miss M. Claydon.

An Exhibition of Work took place between 3–4 p.m. on December 17. Selections were given by the choir and there was a dancing display. In the meanwhile the school carried on its normal work. In spite of wretched weather a good number of parents and friends were present. School closed with an end of term concert on the 23rd.

1937

Re-open January 11. N.O.R. 302. 261 heads inspected on January 28, dental inspection February 9. Milk Marketing Board films were shown to top classes on March 3.

'Keep Fit' classes for ladies was granted free use of the school hall for a period of six months after a demonstration was held on February 15.

On the evening of March 11 a concert and display of dancing and physical exercises was given to an audience of some 200 parents.

Miss Briggs resigned as Domestic Subjects Mistress at the end of March and her place was filled on April 6 by Miss Margaret Watson. A framed portrait of H.M. King George VI was presented to the school by Mr. E.A. Bell the former Headmaster on April 9. The school won the North East Berkshire League Shield, the Knock-Out Cup and the Junior Cup. The football team reached the final of the Grenfell Shield Competition but were defeated by 3 goals to 2. They were trained by Mr. F.A. Denzey.

A very effective Coronation decorative scheme had been carried out by children under the direction of Miss Phillips. The Coronation of King George VI was on May 12 and all schools closed at the end of lessons on the 11th for the remainder of the week. Many activities were arranged and the Council approved expenditure on flags and spoons, children's tea, entertainment and sports, decorations and the Maidenhead Pageant. Three days after the Coronation (the 15th) the Mayor Alderman Arthur Upson opened the newly built swimming pool on Cookham Road which replaced the former baths in East Street. At the Coronation Sports on the 25th the school won both boys and girls relay events and scholars were placed first in nine other events.

Miss Claydon and Mr. Denzey attended swimming instruction classes at Reading during the last week in May and physical training courses arranged by the County Organisers on Wednesday evenings at Windsor and Reading during June.

School closed on the afternoon of July 15 for the annual exhibition and sale of needlework. It was preceded by displays of dancing and physical exercises on the sports ground. The

Chairman of the Education Committee, several managers and a large number of parents were present, showing much interest in the childrens work. Success was the result of much hard work on the part of staff outside school hours. The annual Schools Swimming Association Gala was on the 20th. Three boys under Mr. Denzey went to Reading on the 29th to swim in the Team Championship of Berkshire.

Summer holidays July 30–August 31. N.O.R. 274. Average attendance 256.6 (93.6%). Miss Davis resigned. During the holidays lockers were fitted in lobbies, shelves in classrooms and the floor levelled in the new Art room.

On re-opening the following admissions were revealed:-

Ellington	57	
Alwyn Road	41	
National	12	
Boyn Hill	5	
St. Luke's	2	
North Town	2	
Others	4	
	123	Total number on roll 351

The Headmaster applied for permission to use the school on two evenings a week for social purposes for the benefit of teachers and scholars, but only one occasion per week was granted up to the Christmas holidays.

The school closed for the annual Teacher's Conference at Reading on September 23 and furniture for the new Art room was delivered making it usable for the 29th.

Separate medical inspections, girls October 4, boys October 7, heads on the 21st. The girls netball and boys football teams were entertained by Baylis Court School, Slough on the 13th. Both teams were successful.

From November 8 a change of time for the afternoon session – 1.45 until 4 o'clock. Prefects and house captains were present at the Town Hall on the 9th to witness the election of the first Lady Mayor in the history of the Borough of Maidenhead. All assembled in the hall on the 11th to receive the broadcast service from the Cenotaph. 622 lbs. (of groceries) was collected on the 12th and sent for Hospital Pound Day.

November 23, 24, 25 and 26 entailed a complete inspection of the school by Mr. Rayner, H.M.I. It was continued on the 30th by two more H.M.I.'s Miss Summers and Mr. Reynish. On December 3 an inspection of girls physical training by another H.M.I. Miss Grey. Lombardy poplars were planted on either side of the playing field and flowering trees in front of the school on the 13th. Christmas holidays began on December 23.

1938

The new term commenced January 11. On the 15th Maidenhead A.C. made the arrangements for the Inter-house Cross Country race over 1½ miles held on the Moor. The afternoon session reverted back to a 2 p.m. start from the 20th.

The H.M.I. report on the inspection of November last recalled the previous report of 1932, of how the school was re-organised from separate Boys' and Girls' Departments into a Senior Mixed School. It was forecasted in that report of an extension of the Borough boundary. Inclusion of Alwyn Road School was fulfilled in April 1934 and in September of that year re-organisation was completed by the transferring of the senior children from Alwyn to Gordon Road.

In the following year facilities for practical subjects as an integral part of the school were provided by the erection of a block of buildings of excellent design with spacious and well equipped rooms for Domestic Subjects, Handicraft and Science together with dining accommodation.

The Headmaster who had been in charge of the Boys' Department since its opening in 1907 and had given invaluable service to education in Maidenhead retired in 1936. His successor was promoted from the assistant staff and the Authority was fortunate in having in their service one in whose hands the conduct of this important school could be placed with confidence.

The number of senior children in attendance is 341 and the school is organised on a three-stream basis. The staff is a useful blend of older and experienced teachers with young and fresh assistants and good use is being made of those members who have special aptitudes in Art, Music and Physical Training. All support the Headmaster, the teaching throughout is sound and often enterprising and the general high standard of work and discipline traditional to the school is being fully maintained.

'Creditable standard is reached in all branches of English. Children write lucid exercises in Composition with good command of vocabulary, reading clear, recitation of poetry intelligent. Written work well set out and adequately corrected, care taken to see corrections are followed up by the children'.

'The three classes tested in written Arithmetic produced very satisfactory results, classes tested orally also did well. Algebra and Geometry were included in curriculum for more advanced scholars'.

'Oral work in Geography and History reaches a high level generally, good mapping is done. In many subjects judicious use is made of wireless broadcast lessons'.

It went on to say 'Instruction in music includes sight-reading, ear training and theory: choice of songs is good, singing pleasant in tone. The School Choir undertakes out of school activities in giving performances for deserving causes. Arts and Crafts are being developed on wider lines; crafts of local interest and historical origin can now be introduced and colour and design more closely related to needlecrafts and home furnishing'.

'In Needlework standard of stitchery is high, but girls experience in garment construction is limited. There is a carefully planned scheme of woodwork with some metal work. An interesting experiment is being made in giving instruction in what may be termed Domestic Handicraft to a class of older girls in the last term before they leave school'.

'The Boys Gymnastic scheme is limited to free standing exercises and playground games. A mistress is responsible for all P.T., games, dancing and swimming of the girls. Four weekly periods are allotted to subject with additional period for swimming during the Summer Term. A satisfactory standard of performance is reached in all branches of the subject. Particular mention is made of netball and swimming in both of which the school holds a good record. A happy and willing response is obtained from the classes in physical education. It is proposed to introduce Shinty as a field game as soon as equipment is obtained. Meanwhile winter play is confined to netball in the girls playground where there is sufficient space for one court; usc is also made of the boys playground when available.'

'The corporate life of scholars is fostered by the system of "Houses" and Inter-House Competitions in music, dramatics, folk-dancing and physical training displays encourage initiative in leadership and team spirit. The Headmaster keeps in close touch with parents, his record cards of progress and detailed terminal reports being means to this end'.

'The school should continue to do well'.

A theodolite (a portable surveying instrument for measuring horizontal and vertical angles) was given to the school by the Borough Surveyor's Department on January 24 and a letter press by the Town Clerk's Department on the 31st.

Miss E.G.B. Rogers was appointed Domestic Science Teacher commencing on February 28, Miss M. Watson having resigned to take an appointment in Staffordshire. Medical inspections February 22 and 23, dentist on the 28th.

On March 5 a party journeyed to Oxford to take part in the Festival of Folk Dance, Folk Song and Pipe Playing. Three first class and two second class certificates were gained. They were trained by Miss Claydon and Mr. Matthews. Afterwards they visited Oxford Colleges under the leadership of Mr. E.A. Bell the former Headmaster. On that day twenty-three teams competed in the Cross-Country Championship of Berks., Bucks. and Oxon. The school was unplaced finishing in seventh position. A concert and display was held in the hall on the evening of the 17th in aid of the Sports Fund. Nearly 200 people attended including the Chairman of Managers, Alderman Archer with Mrs. Archer.

414 eggs were sent to the Hospital on April 8. Lectures on the care of teeth were given to the entire school on the 11th. The Senior Football XI won the Grenfell Shield, the North East Berkshire League Shield and the North East Berkshire Knock-Out Shield after playing twenty-one games without defeat. They were trained by Mr. Denzey.

A teacher from St. Luke's Senior School was transferred to Gordon Road for the first week in May to allow Miss Claydon and Mr. Denzey to attend swimming classes each morning. The First

School Athletics Championships were held on the Sports Ground on May 19, the usual time-table being suspended. Empire Day was on the 24th.

At the North East Berkshire Athletics Championships on June 2 the school won the Boys Championship and second in the girls section. Individual successes:-

100 yards	1st;	440 yards	1st;	High Jump	1st;
Boys' Relay	1st;	Girls Relay	1st.		

On these results one girl and two boys would represent Berkshire at the All-England Sports to be held at Derby on July 9.

The first Inter-House Swimming Gala was held on the evening of July 7 at the East Street Baths. The annual Swimming Gala was on the 19th; Exhibition and Sale of Work on the 21st. Mr. Denzey attended a P.T. course at Aberystwyth during the week of the 25th. Miss Claydon took a team of four girls to Reading on the 27th to take part in the School Girl Team Championship of Berkshire. Summer holidays July 29–August 30. There was one County Scholarship.

For the commencement of the new term the following admissions were recorded:-

Alwyn Road	59	
Ellington	43	
Boyn Hill	6	
National	3	N.O.R. 351
St. Luke's	1	
Others	4	
	116	

During the holidays two rooms had been adapted to form a special practical room; additional lockers had been provided; both playgrounds re-surfaced, and the north side fence of the playing field painted. A party of thirty boys under Mr. Matthews and Mr. Denzey were in camp during the last week of holiday at a site near Swansea. Mr. Matthews had officially resigned at the end of July and his place had been filled by Mr. John Gordon Lunn from Huddersfield.

Miss Rogers and the Headmaster attended a two-day course in 'Organisation of Domestic Subjects' at Reading University on September 20–21.

With the threat of war looming, several schools were closed for three days (September 26–29) for the purpose of an emergency exercise. A number of teachers gave valuable assistance in A.R.P. (Air Raid Precautions came under the control of the Home Office and included anyone engaged as air raid wardens, auxiliary firemen or decontamination and first aid workers), and the distribution of gas masks and finding billets for London school children who were expected in the event of war. A very poor attendance was recorded for the 30th as children were uncertain about the re-opening date.

All forms assembled in the hall on October 30 to hear a lecture given by Capt. Cannon of the R.S.P.C.A. Senior children were present at the Guildhall on November 9 to witness the Mayor making ceremony. All heard the Armistice Day broadcast from the Cenotaph on the 11th. Pound Day raised 641 lbs. for Maidenhead Hospital on the 25th.

Severe weather during December. School work suffered during the term owing to the prolonged illness of three members of staff. Christmas holidays began on December 22.

The Headmaster made an application for the use of the hall to be made available free of charge for the purpose of whist drives at selected intervals on evenings during the winter months in aid of the School Sports Fund and for teachers social evenings once weekly. Free use was granted on October 21 for a P.T. class displaced from the Drill Hall owing to the County Girls' Speech Day. Consent was also given to the Workers' Educational Association using a classroom on Tuesdays and Fridays at a cost of one shilling per night remuneration to the caretaker for additional duties.

Owing to insufficient space for cycles in the girls' playground a restricting area was to be imposed so provision could be made for children coming from longer distances.

1939

205 children attended a pantomime at Chiswick on January 5. First day of term was the 10th, N.O.R. 317. From Thursday 26th

Miss Claydon and Mr. Denzey attended courses arranged by the P.T. Organiser.

Mrs. Rust from the Milk Publicity Council gave a lecture to senior girls on February 6. The school visited the Rialto Cinema on March 3 to witness a display of films on 'Tea'; a party of children visited Oxford on the 4th to take part in the Festival of Folk Dance and Song, and in the Cross-Country Championship of Berks., Bucks and Oxon on the 5th, F. Brooker was placed second out of 160 competitors. Medicals on 14th and 15th and a whist drive on the evening of the 15th in aid of the Sports Fund.

The Headmaster was away for part of the afternoon on May 3 taking part in an A.R.P. exercise and the school closed at 3.30 p.m. on the 4th for the official opening of Desborough Park. Ninety children visited Whipsnade Zoo on the 20th Empire Day being on the 24th.

The North East Berkshire Athletic Championships were held on June 13 both boys and girls being successful. The girls relay team beat the existing record by 1⅕ seconds and Joan Bedborough beat the County record for 150 yards. Other successes:-

100 yards Boys	FIRST
100 yards Girls	FIRST
High Jump Girls	FIRST
High Jump Boys	FIRST
Long Jump Girls	FIRST
440 & 880 yards	FIRST
220 yards Boys	FIRST
Boys Hurdles	FIRST
Boys Relay	FIRST
Girls Relay	FIRST

On the 29th three girls were members of the winning relay team at the Berkshire Championships Meeting held at the Royal Military College track, Sandhurst. Other successes:-

Girls 100 yards	3rd and 4th
Boys 220 yards	3rd and 4th
Boys 880 yards	3rd

On July 6 the Girls' Relay Team won the Hooper Shield while

competing against eleven schools from the Slough, High Wycombe and Maidenhead districts. Joan Bedborough and Edwin Coxhead were chosen to represent Berkshire at the All England Athletics meeting to be held at Loughborough College Stadium.

A large number of parents were present at the Inter-House Swimming Gala on July 13, while in spite of heavy rain throughout the afternoon attendance was good for the Exhibition and Sale of Work on the 20th. Athletic sports had been arranged but were cancelled because of the bad weather. With the permission of the Chairman of Managers a half-day holiday was granted. The school was successful in the Inter-Schools contest at Maidenhead Swimming Club Gala on that day winning both boys and girls team races. The time-table was suspended for the Inter-House Athletic Sports on the 25th and the School Swimming Gala on August 1. Close for holidays on the 4th.

When war appeared imminent, it was emphasized that school buildings and staff would be required for other purposes in the event of a national emergency. Authority was given for the closing of schools for two weeks should it arrive.

When the school did re-open on September 18 and the arrival of the evacuee children, a two shift system came into operation – mornings 8.45 a.m.–12.30 p.m., afternoons 1.00p.m.–4.45p.m. Children would attend morning/afternoon alternate weeks. Gordon Road shared its buildings with Avondale, St. Stephen's and Barking Castle Schools. Figures show that the number of children on the roll of all schools in the Borough came to 4,744 of which 2,189 were 'visiting children'. The word 'evacuee' was not often used in educational purposes. It was agreed though that in the event of an air raid warning during school time, children should be kept on school premises. A Drill Organiser had been appointed for schools and visited with Air Raid Wardens to inspect and fit gas masks.

For the first term of the war admission numbers were:-

from	Ellington	72	
	Alwyn Road	39	
	Boyn Hill	15	
	East Street	9	N.O.R. 373
	St. Mary's	1	

North Town	1
Others	9
	146

Mr. Denzey joined the R.A.F. on September 25, Mr. C.H. Bellamy commenced as his replacement on October 2. Medical inspections took place on November 14, 15 and 16 and with the dark evenings the afternoon session terminated at 3.45p.m. from the 20th.

To ease pressure on schools the Education Committee sought other venues and during a greater part of the term lessons had been conducted in the Toc H. Hut, the Masonic Hall in High Town Road and the Drill Hall in Marlow Road. These were frequently used even outside official school hours if the need arose. Attendance at these 'outside' lessons had been excellent.

The Christmas holidays were curtailed to cover the unavoidable loss of school time which had taken place during the term. Visiting children were given a much shorter holiday for two reasons:-

1. To prevent them returning to their homes in London,
2. To avoid increasing the burden upon those with whom they were billeted.

All schools closed on December 22, visiting children returned on December 27, Maidenhead children, January 9, 1940.

1940

January 9. N.O.R. 344, average attendance 319.75 (92.8%). Fire extinguishers and boxes of first aid equipment were fitted and four classrooms were protected against flying-glass. Head inspections on the 18th. Three classrooms were now only being used during the London session resulting in five rooms being placed at the Headmaster's disposal on various days by Avondale School. 110 children were absent on January 29.

Bad weather during February with influenza rife. The morning session commenced at 9.00am from the 26th. Medical inspections on the 27th and 28th.

Class IIB in the 1940's.

Forty children attended a musical appreciation concert at the Drill Hall on March 1. Approval was given for classrooms to be used for lectures in connection with the Women's Land Army on the 3rd, 10th, 17th and 24th April. Charge one shilling per night plus one shilling to the caretaker. Two staff were away during April with German measles.

The school visited the Drill Hall on May 10 to see a film show organised by Cadbury Bros. Whitsun holidays began on the 10th but were curtailed by order of the Government, school re-opening on the 14th. Although a full day's holiday was granted on Empire Day (the 24th) the visit of the Mayor was cancelled owing to his illness. Dental inspection on the 27th and 212 children received diphtheria immunization on the 28th. The second injection was on June 26.

Windows of lobbies received anti-splinter treatment during June and the school closed on the 14th and 15th for the second evacuation scheme exercise. Mr. Lunn was called up for military service on June 28 his place being taken by Mr. E. Williams on July 1. Two boys and two girls were awarded special places and four boys won Spoore Scholarships.

Mr. R.W. Murray ceased duties on August 1. He was one of the original teachers from when the school opened in 1907, and was granted a testimonial under the seal of the Council. Mr. C.W. Richardson who had carried on working well into his seventies, resigned as caretaker at the end of August and Mr. E.A. Cartland was appointed as from September 9.

The new term commenced on September 3 with Miss V.E. Lynam appointed to the staff.

New admissions from:-

Ellington	69	
Alwyn Road	34	
Boyn Hill	12	N.O.R. 382
East Street	6	
Roman Catholic	1	
Others	3	
	125	

School closed mid-day on September 11 in order to receive evacuee children from Canterbury. Re-open on the 16th. Mrs. Truman was appointed to the staff on the 23rd. Again school closed mid-day on October 3 for the evacuation of additional children. Staff billeted 52. Medicals on the 8th, 9th and 10th, while on the 10th a group of 48 Mitcham children started with their Miss Jones in charge who became attached to the staff at Gordon.

Alderman, Councillors, Mr. Bell former Headmaster and the Town Clerk were all present at an official ceremony to mark Mr. Murray's retirement also on the 10th.

As there was a possibility that there could be an air raid warning before school commenced and whilst a great majority of the children have assembled in the playground, the Headmaster requested the staff to be at school at least 15 minutes before 9 o'clock although most had made the practice of so doing for some years.

Summer time continued throughout the winter months and from November 18 the morning session for all schools commenced at 9.30a.m. instead of 9.00a.m.

Mr. Bellamy joined the Royal Artillery early in December and his place was taken by Mrs. Hobday. 120 woollen garments for the Forces were knitted by the children from wool supplied by themselves. Mr. Williams was absent on December 12 as his house had been damaged by enemy action. Christmas holidays began on the 20th, school re-opening on the 31st. A Punch and Judy show was given to evacuated children in the hall on the 31st.

1941

A party for the Mitcham children from Alwyn and Gordon Schools took place on the afternoon of January 9. There was no school for Maidenhead children. Miss Rogers resigned as Domestic Subjects Mistress from the 31st.

Mr. Williams joined the R.A.F. on February 21 his successor being Mrs. Blay. Stanley Henry Hawes, an old scholar was awarded the D.F.M. during the month. Medicals on the 12th.

Miss H. McIntyre was appointed the new Domestic Subjects Mistress from March 1. A Nutritional Survey carried out by Dr. Bell (Deputy Medical Officer of Health) resulted in the number of children having milk under the scheme had considerably increased. Protective blast walls had been erected on both sides of the Domestic and Handicraft rooms, a pit having been provided all dangerous acids had been removed from the Science Room. Sixteen bags of sand was delivered for fire fighting purposes.

As a result of a War Savings Drive the amount taken during the term totalled £370 as compared with £22 in the corresponding period for last year. Although the school closed for the Easter holidays on April 9 it opened on Easter Monday to receive National Savings.

Empire Day was not celebrated in the customary manner, but the Mayor visited schools during the functions being arranged for War Weapons Week. A greater part of the week was devoted to displays and exhibitions and the time-table adjusted accordingly. The first day's takings was £515, total for week £1,701. This excellent total was the result of a co-operative effort on the part of the staff in combination with great enthusiasm on the part of the children. Again although the school closed for the Whitsun Holidays on May 30 it still opened for War Weapons Week contributions.

The following figures may be of interest. In June 1941 the number of evacuees in Maidenhead were:-

Unaccompanied children	1,734
Accompanied children	1,615
Teachers	106
Helpers	11
Other adults	933
	4,399

Three boys and three girls gained special places at the County Schools. Miss D. Smith resigned at the end of term. Summer vacation – August 1–26. The school opened on Mondays the 4th, 11th and 18th for National Savings.

Miss H. Newall commenced on the 26th and Miss Kemp joined as a student teacher. There were 122 admissions from Junior Schools bringing the N.O.R. to 387.

National Savings takings since January 1 amounted to £2,566 14s. 0d. compared with £77 for the corresponding period last year. The loose surface of the playground which had resulted from the tar spraying caused accidents in P.T. lessons.

The War Agriculture Executive Committee advised that subject to certain safeguards children between twelve and fourteen years of age could be released from school attendance 'as would best suit the seasonal agricultural operations of each locality'. This particular year potato picking at Mr. J. S. Findlay's farms at Pinkneys Green was the venue. Twenty two boys were released from October 2. 800 tons of potatoes were lifted during that season.

Permission was given to erect a corregated iron shed in the grounds to be used for the training of Fire Guards in association with the A.R.P. (Air Raid Precautions) in extinguishing of incendiary bombs. The Local Battalion of the Army Cadets also made use of the school. The school was also recognised as a Rest Centre and the Headmaster had to call the attention that large quantities of stores were being delivered by the Public Assistance Department. A Sub-Committee was appointed to consult with the P.A.D. on this matter with powers to act if need be.

The War Savings Group aimed at a target figure of £300 for September but this was exceeded by £23.

Medical inspections October 7–9; cash of £3. 5s. 2d. and 170 lbs. in goods was sent to the Hospital Pound Day. Attendance figures and percentages were low during October as each attendance the boys made at a farm was shown as an absence from school.

1941 saw the Board of Education pressing for the establishment of school feeding centres where scholars could remain for mid-day meals. The Borough Surveyor and Electrical Engineer visited on November 7 in connection with these arrangements. Mrs. Blay and the Headmaster attended the County Girls' School Speech Day on November 21.

Maidenhead held a Waste Paper Week during December when a competition open to all schools in the area for the best essay on the saving of waste paper received the support of the Town Council. The author then in his last year at Gordon Road was chosen to submit his entry which was awarded third prize (a five shilling National Savings Stamp) in the competition.

The issue of Clothing Cards was completed on December 10. Seventy-two children qualified for the extra coupons. Forty toys constructed from odd pieces of wood were handed to the W.V.S. for distribution, Mr. Harmsworth being responsible for the idea. National Savings for the term amounted to £850. Christmas holidays began on the 19th but the school opened on the 22nd and 29th for Savings. Mrs. Hobday ceased duties. Approval was given for Miss Claydon to attend a course of Folk Dancing at Shrewsbury from December 30 to January 6.

1942

Re-open January 6. Mrs. Sara appointed to the staff. The hall was used by Avondale School for an entertainment on the 7th. Miss Lynam ceased duties on the 30th having been appointed to Middlesex teaching staff.

The school attended a film show at the Rialto Cinema on the afternoon of March 10 and on the evening of the 12th 240 parents and friends were present at the Exhibition and Display when the Mayor, Councillor and Mrs. Harrison, Mr. Bell and the Rev. Canon CEM Fry were in the audience. Total receipts including a raffle raised £60. Third prize in Class I of a Poster Competition was won by Bryan Cutler of Form IVA.

The National Savings grand total for Warship Week was £1,280.

Savings invested for the year ending March 31 amounted to £5,017.

Empire Day was held on May 22 when the Deputy Mayor, Councillor Maudsley made the customary visit.

Permission was given to the National Fire Service to erect a dam (subject to being covered) on the waste land in front of the school, but alterations had to be made to the entrance gates to admit vehicular access. A shed was erected for the training of Fire Guards and the Home Guard (formed in 1940 as the Local Defence Volunteers) was granted use of the school three nights a week.

Under the directions of the Ministry of Supply, a County Salvage Drive for Berkshire was organised from June 20 to July 4. Although larger bones were already being salvaged on the screen at the pulverising plant the Borough Surveyor was concerned about the collection of smaller bones which were lost if placed in dustbins. Teachers were approached as to the possibility of having an organised collection of these bones in schools, and that the Education Committee be recommended to offer a prize to the school with the largest collection. Large quantities of salvage was brought in by the children, two bins of bones being collected and three large sacks of dried nettle leaves which were dispatched to the County Herb Centre. A considerable consignment of foxglove leaves were also collected.

Safety First lectures was given by a Police Officer on July 7. Miss Kemp ceased duties as a student teacher when holidays began on the 31st. The holiday had been curtailed (back on August 25) in order that a further period (October 2–13) could be granted at a time when children could assist with the harvest.

The Board of Education asked for arrangements to be made to open schools during the summer holidays for care and occupation of children whose parents might be engaged on war work. All teaching staff were prepared to play their part in carrying out these proposals. Schools opened for any children wishing to attend, but Head Teachers had the discretion in consultation with the Clerk to close any school if circumstances did not warrant the continuance of the schemes. Gordon opened on August 4 with 1 girl and 6 boys present. The following day 4 girls and 7 boys attended. The school closed for the remainder of the holiday period.

97 children were admitted from junior schools on August 25 bringing the N.O.R. to 330. Mrs. E.D. Scott joined the staff. A party of girls went blackberrying with Miss McIntyre on September 1. This was made into jam for use in the domestic science lesson. A National Day of Prayer was held on the 3rd (third anniversary of the war) when the whole school assembled in the hall to receive the broadcast service. 3½ cwts. of rose hips were collected by children in the evenings during September and dispatched to the centre. From Wednesday the 23rd 30 boys in the morning and 30 in the afternoon were helping with the potato harvest.

The school closed for the agricultural holiday on October 2 re-opening on the 13th. During that time boys helped clear 50 acres of potatoes and gathered nearly 450 tons.

Under a Government scheme a depot was established at the school and by October 15, 3½ tons of horse chestnuts ('conkers') had been dispatched together with a further ¼ ton of rose hips.

1942 had seen a big decrease in the evacuee population of the town. By July 11 the total was 2,306, September 14, 2,143 (less than half the total of June 1941), and by October 12, it had fallen to 2,063.

Medical inspections on October 20 and 22; the Headmaster attended a Juvenile Delinquency Conference at Windsor on the 28th and, for the first time, a telephone was installed on the 29th. The Headmaster was at the County Girls' School Speech Day on the 29th.

By bringing their own books and toys and selling them amongst themselves, the children raised £30 for the Red Cross Prisoners of War Fund. November and 12½ tons of 'conkers' value £93. 15s. 0d. passed through the centre, Gordon Road childrens' collection alone was valued at £26. 5s. 0d. Miss Phillips the Science Mistress was the organiser.

The Headmaster took a party of boys to see over the printing works of the Electrical Press Ltd. on the Cordwallis Industrial Estate. One boy agreed later to be apprenticed. The Headmaster attended the County Boys' School Speech Day on November 18, the dentist visited the school on the 25th.

Thirty-five senior girls visited the Fuel Exhibition and heard a lecture on Wartime Cookery on December 9 while on the 14th the whole school heard special broadcast health talks from 11.00–11.15 each day that week on:-

Eating and drinking
Teeth
Coughing and sneezing
Keeping warm
Questions answered.

Mrs. Sara resigned when the school closed for the Christmas holidays on December 23. Owing to the difficulty in obtaining the services of a teacher with a qualification in teaching art approval was given to a proposed scheme for attending of classes at Maidenhead School of Art, subject to the approval of the County Authority.

1943

The new term commenced on January 12. N.O.R. 289, average attendance for week 271.8 (94%). School meals commenced on the 13th with 86 children staying for dinner. On the 18th dinners had increased to 112. On the 29th a third contribution of £10 making £47 in all since September 1 was paid to the Prisoners of War Fund. The money was received in payment for the herbs collected by the children.

February 1 and Mr. T.G. Thomas replaced Mrs. Sara.

Proposals outlined by the Ministry of Supply (Salvage Department) to hold a Book Drive from March 6–20 was referred to the Recovery and Salvage Scrutiny Committee. The books would be sorted into four categories – those suitable for troops, those suitable for restocking blitzed libraries, books which should be preserved for national interest and those available for salvage. School buildings were to be used as receiving depots. It proved a very successful campaign, as no fewer than 78,146 books were collected throughout the Borough. Gordon Road's contribution to the total was 2,600 books and 750 magazines.

Medical inspections took place on March 23 and March 24.

Some colleagues joined in the presentation ceremony on April

20 to mark the retirement of the Headmistress of Ellington School, Mrs. C.G. Day. Miss Newall ceased duties on the 21st having accepted a teaching post with Gloucestershire.

Empire Day was on May 21. 'Wings for Victory Week' was held in May. The school set its target of £1,000 but the final total reached £2,166. In the Poster Competition 2nd prize went to Gordon, Highly Commended to M. Lake. In the Essay Competition, Class C, 1st prize went to Maureen O'Donnell.

To combat the need to deal quickly with incendiary bombs, static water tanks holding hundreds of gallons of water became a familiar sight at strategic points all over the town. It was considered essential that N.F.S. (National Fire Service) officers should visit schools and address children on the dangers of these tanks. One of these was given on June 3, subject 'Importance of Static Water Dams'. Miss E.N. Griffiths commenced in early June. Swimming instruction began on June 22.

Miss Claydon was a judge at the County Girls' School Inter Form Folk Dance Competitions on July 20. The Cambridgeshire Syllabus for Religious Instruction having been introduced at Ellington School both the juniors and seniors at Gordon took sections of the same course. Summer holidays July 29–August 24.

116 children were admitted for the new term on August 24 when Miss H. Rowsell began as a student teacher. N.O.R. 327. Mrs. Scott ceased duties on the 31st her successor being Mrs. S.N.S. Hobbs.

It had been announced that Mr. F.A. Denzey, a member of staff now serving with H.M. Forces, had been granted a commission attached to the Parachutist Wing of the R.A.F.

When the school leaving age is raised the playing field accommodation would become inadequate. The Headmaster asked that this matter be borne in mind when the Council deals with post-war plans. It was passed to the Post-War Development Sub-Committee to consider together with the needs of other schools.

120 scholars attended the showing of Anglo-Soviet films on September 14; medicals on the 23rd; potato picking at Mr. Findlay's farm from the 24th until October 1. An additional 50 children were also working on Lord Astor's farm during this week. Approximately 800 tons of potatoes were lifted during the period. October 15 and 32 were working at Gardner's Farm each morning. The County Girls' Speech Day was on October 28.

Twelve senior children attended the Mayor making ceremony on November 9. Influenza was prevalent during December with many children and up to five staff away. Another Book Drive was held during the month the school's contribution amounting to 1,134 books. Civics Prizes kindly presented by one of the Managers were won by E. Maidment, J. Silver, Fowler and Blumfield. Profits from the sale of toys made by boys through Mr. Harmsworth amounted to £13 and receipts from the Herb Committee for herbs collected by children through Miss Phillips amounted to £4. 15s. 0d. – £17 15s. 0d. being sent to the Red Cross. School closed for the Christmas holidays on December 22, Mrs. Hobbs ceased duties.

Reception and service in schools resulted in inspections and visits particularly in connection with school meals. The price of a school meal in 1943 was 5d. (old money). 1943 still saw a reduction in the number of evacuees. During the summer months the number had dropped to 1,615.

1944

Re-open January 11 N.O.R. 298.

An extract from a letter received from the County Herb Committee read 'I am writing to express the thanks of my Committee for the untiring work done by your pupils in Herb Collections. I have no hesitation in saying that your school has a record unbeaten in the County'.

Mrs. J.M. Allan commenced duties on February 7. The Ministry of Information's 'Safety First' and other films were shown during the month. The dentist visited on the 17th, medicals for the girls on the 28th, boys March 2. Dr. Griffiths gave a series of lectures in connection with sex education to both parents and children on March 27 and 28, and Mrs. Hughes ceased duties on the 31st having secured a teaching post with L.C.C.

A Savings Film performance was given on April 3; Mrs. Sybil Baker commenced duties as from May 1. Empire Day celebrations was on the 24th. Further to Dr. Griffiths' lectures parents of children had contributed £9 towards the establishment of a Sex Education Library.

Head Teachers and teaching staff were asked to co-operate with the Ministry of Labour and National Service in the setting up of local Juvenile Employment Bureaux. They would work closely with the Ministry's officers in ensuring the smooth running and maintenance thereof.

Approval was granted for teachers' Physical Training Classes organised by the County Council to be held on one evening a week during the summer term.

The number of evacuees on June 12 had dropped to 1,394, but with the launching of the German V-1's and V-2's, the first long range guided missile rockets commonly known as the 'Doodle-bug' aimed at London and the South East, evacuee numbers began to increase. By July 10 the number had risen to 1,526, by September 11, 1,792 and by October 16, 1,873.

A letter from the National Savings Committee asked for every possible support and assistance from schools in making the 'Salute the Soldier' Week a success. On June 15 damage was caused to the entrance by the tank which came to the school in connection with the event. In the Essay Competition, Class C, First Prize went to G. Sherley.

Miss McIntyre the Domestics Subjects Mistress was granted one week's leave of absence to get married and returned as Mrs. Bailey.

The success of the Book Drive in 1943 prompted the 'Books for the Forces' Drive to be held from July 3–8. The main collection would be done once again by schools, and by the end of the week, 25,590 books were collected in the Borough. On July 11 and 12 Ministry of Labour Juvenile Employment Officers visited to interview school leavers. Children from Ellington and Alwyn Road who would be entering next term came for classification tests on July 25–27.

An H.M.I. on a recent visit commented on the cleanliness of the school building. Re-open after the summer holidays on August 29, new children from:-

Alwyn Road	30
Ellington	46
Boyn Hill	24
Others	3
	103

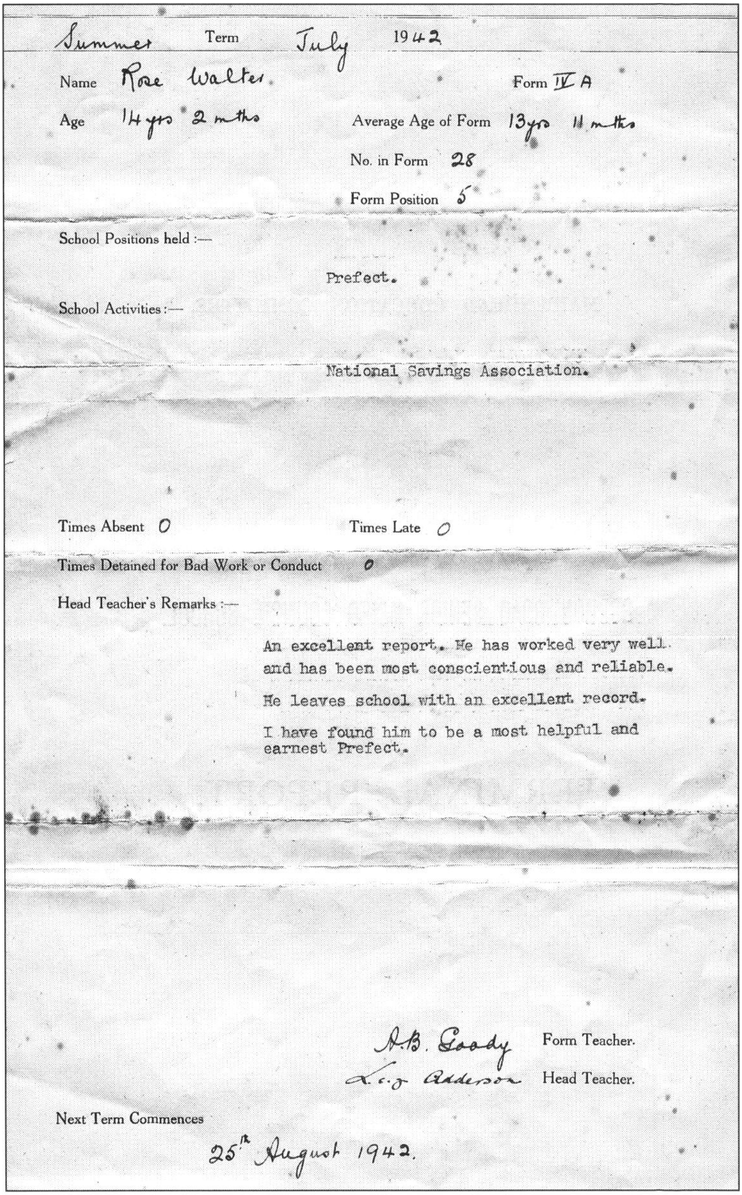

Summer Term July 1942

Name Rose Walter. Form IV A

Age 14 yrs 2 mths Average Age of Form 13 yrs 11 mths

No. in Form 28

Form Position 5

School Positions held :—

Prefect.

School Activities :—

National Savings Association.

Times Absent 0 Times Late 0

Times Detained for Bad Work or Conduct 0

Head Teacher's Remarks :—

An excellent report. He has worked very well and has been most conscientious and reliable.

He leaves school with an excellent record.

I have found him to be a most helpful and earnest Prefect.

A.B. Goody Form Teacher.

L. C. J. Adderson Head Teacher.

Next Term Commences

25th August 1942.

School leavers report.

Subject	Maximum Marks.	Marks Gained.	Teachers' Remarks.
Arithmetic ...	20	14	Very good results. He works steadily and well his work being accurate and neat.
Mental Arithmetic ...	20	14	
Speed and Accuracy ...	20	16	
Literature ...	20	16	A good steady worker. Has tried hard the whole term. Poetry and oral reading are very good.
Composition ...	20	16	
Oral Reading ...	20	18	
Silent Reading ...	20	13	
Poetry	20	18	
Handwriting ...	20	15	
Spelling	20	14	
History	20	14	A very conscientious worker
Geography ...	20	15	Very good indeed.
Arts and Crafts ...	20	16	A steady worker.
Woodwork ...	20	15	Makes steady progress.
Metal Work ...	20		
Mechanical Drawing ...	20	14	Very good. - making progress
Science	20	15	Quite good
Domestic Science ...	20		
Needlework ...	20		
First Aid	20	14	Does good work - and is very helpful
Music	20	13	A fairly good result.
P.T. and Games ...	20		
Religious Knowledge ...	20	11.	Very Fair

Many older Maidonians will remember Dr. J.J. Paterson, the School Medical Officer and Medical Officer of Health for the East Berkshire Combined District, who retired on June 30. His sudden death in Italy was recorded at the Town Council meeting on October 31 and came as a great shock to his many friends and colleagues in the area. (His successor, Dr. William Brodie Moore was appointed as from August 1).

A circular from the Ministry of Education called attention to the additional work falling upon teaching staff arising from school meals, national savings, clothing coupons, salvage collection, etc. which could prejudice their primary duty of teaching. Authorities should make every effort with the assistance of local officers of the Ministry of Labour to obtain secretarial and domestic help on the basis of suitable payment wherever such assistance was required. If paid assistance could not be secured, the help of the Women's Voluntary Service could be obtained on a strictly temporary basis. The first part-time clerical assistant to deal with this work commenced duties on September 4.

Medical inspections were on October 12, 13 and 16. 140 children began potato picking during this period reflecting low attendance figures. (N.O.R. 315, average attendance 267.3, 84.8%). The Headmaster attended the County Girls' School Speech Day on the 27th.

Seventeen girls from Braywick School were admitted on November 21 and H.M.I. visited and inspected the work of retarded children on the 30th. An application was made to the owner of Maidenhead College for facilities for girls to play hockey on the playing field adjoining his school. This was offered for one afternoon each week free of charge. Christmas holidays began on December 22.

1945

An immersion heater had been fitted in the tank which supplied hot water to the Domestic Science Room. When school re-opened on January 9 six Holyport boys were admitted. (N.O.R. 296, average attendance 271.5, 91.7%).

The Maidenhead Branch of the English Folk Dance Society was

granted permission to use the hall in aid of the Red Cross on January 13. A fee of 5 shillings (25p) plus remuneration to the caretaker for the extra work was charged.

Flight Lieut. F.A. Denzey of the Parachutist Training School and a member of the staff had been mentioned in Despatches for his work with the 6th Airborne Division in Normandy. School closed at 3.40p.m. on February 10 to permit a small celebration of Mr. J.E. Cluff's 65th birthday and 38 years service in the school. Major A.S. Hooper gave a lantern lecture on life in Soviet Russia on behalf of the Anglo Soviet Friendship Society on February 20.

Physical Training classes by the Girls' Section of the Youth Centre was held on four evenings in February. The Headmaster was elected to serve on a Joint Advisory Committee of Berkshire Teachers comprising five secondary and five other teachers.

Medical inspections on March 14 and 15 and a Juvenile Employment Officer interviewed school leavers on the 19th.

Under the provisions of the (Butler) Education Act, 1944, schools were transferred from the Maidenhead Borough Council Education Committee to Berkshire County Council on April 1. Records show the last meeting of the Council School Managers as being held on March 14. The Town Clerk reported that Berkshire County Council had asked Managers to act for the time being until the new arrangements had been made. Any decisions taken by the Managers were passed to the County Authority for recommendation.

It is to be noted that the three schools in Maidenhead which provided exclusively for pupils over eleven years of age became, under the Act, Secondary Schools. They were Gordon Road Senior, the Church of England Senior Boys' and the Boyne Hill Church of England Girls'.

Re-open April 10.

In accordance with the Government's announcement of VE (Victory in Europe) Day celebrations, the school did not open on May 8 and 9. Children under 11 years of age were to have teas followed by sports at their individual schools, while older children were to take part in a Victory Display and Sports Gala to be held at the York Road Football Ground on July 26. Empire Day was celebrated on May 18. During the month the Headmaster requested the removal of blast walls, fire sheds and other emergency and rest centre equipment.

The Victory Display scheduled for July 26 had to be cancelled owing to rain. It was eventually held on the 30th with the childrens sports taking place in the school grounds the following day.

The Juvenile Employment Officer interviewed school leavers on August 1. Summer holidays began on the 2nd when Mrs. Allen and Mrs. Bailey resigned. During the holidays the Domestic Science block had been re-decorated, loose blocks in the main building re-set and a concrete strip laid in the north lobby.

The new term commenced on September 11, Miss Gordon being appointed the Domestic Science Mistress. Admissions:-

from	Alwyn Road	24
	Boyn Hill	23
	Ellington	41
	Braywick	9
	Holyport	8
	Others	13
		118

Potato picking commenced on September 24 ending on October 19. Medical inspections on October 9 and 15. In a response to the Help Holland Appeal 800 garments were collected. There were still 711 evacuees in the town on October 15.

Thanksgiving Week began on October 19. The Freedom of the Borough of Maidenhead was conferred on Field Marshal Sir Bernard L. Montgomery 'as a tribute to his military genius and inspiring leadership in which he led the British Armies and their Allies from El Alamein to Luneburg which culminated in the unconditional surrender of the German Armed Forces on May 7, 1945'. A holiday to mark the occasion was granted on October 19 when children assembled on The Moor and later lined part of the route so as to have the opportunity of seeing him. The Mayor Alderman L.R.F. Oldershaw and the Field Marshal were both scholars at St. Paul's School, Hammersmith.

October saw the suggestion of a pre-fabricated dining hall which was approved. The Maidenhead Scientific Film Society used the school at a fee of 7s. 6d. for each evening plus 5s. 0d. for the caretaker.

Flight/Lieut. Denzey was awarded the Croix de Guerre for training paratroopers at Ringway. He had been closely associated with men of the French Resistance movement and had taken part in hazardous flights to drop these men into heavily defended territory.

Twenty pupils attended the Mayor making ceremony at the Guildhall on November 9. Mr. J.G. Lunn returned to the school on the 12th after having served 5¼ years in the Army.

A new gas cooker and boiler had to be installed in the Domestic Science Room during December. Christmas holidays began on the 20th. 170 children visited a pantomime in London on the 28th. Dutch children who accompanied the party were guests of children attending the school.

1946

The new term commenced on January 9. Mr. Lunn pointed out that he was finding it difficult to get accommodation in the town and unless the situation improved he would be seeking an appointment nearer his home. The school was broken into during the night of January 29. £50 worth of savings stamps were stolen and several bunches of keys (later recovered by the police) were taken away. Doors and desks were forced and damaged.

Mr. Bellamy returned on February 11 after serving in the Royal Artillery for five years. Mr. Denzey returned on March 1 after six and a half years in the R.A.F. A party of boys visited the Anti-Attrition Metal Co. Ltd on the 26th. Mrs. Truman transferred to Alwyn Road School during the month.

A member of the Schools Broadcast Department of the B.B.C. visited on March 30 to hear a history broadcast, and a party of R.A.F. Officers who were intending to become teachers spent the afternoon at school.

A party of girls visited the Telephone Exchange and Sorting Office of Maidenhead Post Office on April 9. Mr. Lunn who failed to gain accommodation in the town ceased his duties on the 10th. Mr. Williams who had not yet returned from the Forces resigned for the same reason. He asked if his appointment might be determined on May 19 in order to take a post with the London County

Council on the 20th which would be near to his home.

The Town Clerk submitted a letter in connection with the County Authority Development Plan. It was the intention of the Education Committee to arrange a conference of all concerned in Maidenhead when the plan would be discussed. The purchase of gramophone amplifying apparatus at a cost of £8 was approved.

Empire Day was on May 24. Mr. Tomlin was appointed on May 20, Mr. J.W. Bird who specialised in Music and Art commenced on June 3 and Miss L. Clifford was appointed Joint Needlework Mistress of Boyn Hill Senior Girls' and Gordon Road.

In the North East Berkshire Sports the school won both the Senior Girls and Senior Boys Championships. Winners of events:-

80 yards	B. Wheeler (Record 10.6 secs.)
Long Jump	Barker
100 yards girls	J. Riddell
150 yards girls	J. Riddell
Relay girls	Gordon Road 'A'
440 yards Boys	Newbold
880 yards Boys	Newbold
High Jump	Slade
High Jump (14–16)	Egby
440 yards (14–16)	Saul

The Managers congratulations were conveyed to Gordon Road, Alwyn Road and Ellington upon the outstanding success secured by their competitors in these events.

Honours also went to an old pupil. Mr. A. Worth was appointed Head Postmaster of Windsor.

Dental inspections were held on June19; a party of 120 children visited Whipsnade Zoo on the 22nd (a further group on July 27) and at the Berkshire County Championships held at Palmer Park, Reading on June 27 June Riddell won the cup for the best individual performance. She put up the best time for the 150 yards recorded during the sixteen years the Championships have been held. She will represent the County in the All-England Championships. Sylvia Worth won the Long Jump Championship and will also represent the County. A half-day holiday was granted in honour of June Riddell's performance.

Application was granted for the use of the school playing field on Saturday August 24 for childrens sports in connection with Maidenhead Wardens Association and for use of the main hall in the event of unfavourable weather.

A presentation ceremony was held on July 30 to mark the retirement of Mr. J.E. Cluff after over thirty nine years service to the school. Alderman Archer took the chair and amongst those present was the Mayor, Alderman Oldershaw, Mr. H.E. Pickman, Mr. R.W. Murray and Mr. J. Kemp. He was granted a testimonial under the seal of the Council. During the month Miss Claydon attended a course on Local Studies at Somerville College, Oxford, four girls from Boyn Hill School were entertained to lunch, the meal being prepared and served by girls of the top form and police visited and examined all cycles, some of the trademen's cycles were found to be in a dangerous condition. Summer holidays July 31–September 11.

The lowest total of admissions for ten years (82) was recorded on the first day of term. New staff:- Miss Helen Rowsell, Mrs. Sweet, Needlework Specialist teaching for 2½ days a week and Mrs. Shaw, visiting pianist. Mr. C.H. Bellamy left on September 30. Approval was given for a series of lectures organised by the Workers' Educational Association on Tuesday evenings from September 24 to December 10. Mr. Denzey became First Assistant.

Potato picking commenced on October 11. Eight girls from Touchen End School were admitted on November 6. The top form were studying the development of the Pinkneys Green Housing Estate. The Borough Surveyor very kindly placed many plans and maps at their disposal.

Medicals took place on November 11, 13 and 14. Form IVA visited 'Britain Can Make It' Exhibition. In the afternoon (the 19th) the girls went to the Natural History Museum and the boys to the Science Museum, Miss Goody and the Headmaster being in charge of the party.

Mr. V. Ball commenced duties on December 2. It was the turn of IVB to visit the Exhibition and Museum on the 3rd, Form IV the Exhibition, St. Paul's and the Natural History Museum on the 10th. A display and exhibition (open evening for 280 parents) on the 11th was attended by the Mayor, three aldermen, Mr. Bell, Canon Fry and Mr. Pickman. The visit to the pantomime at Chiswick was on the 30th. Mr. Bird ceased duties.

1947

Mr. V. Griffin commenced duties on the first day of term – January 7. The school sent £25 13s. 2d. to the London Hospital for Sick Children on the 15th. Senior girls began attending Maidenhead Cricket Ground on Wednesday afternoons for hockey practice. Eighty children from the top forms visited the Young Vic at the Lyric Theatre, Hammersmith for a performance of the King Stag. January ended with a low percentage due to influenza and inclement weather.

Maidenhead was affected by severe flooding in March which resulted in low attendance at several schools.

The school Football Team won the North East Berkshire League Shield during April with an undefeated record and beat the County Boys' School by 3 goals to 1 to win the knock-out shield. The team trainer was Mr. Denzey. Dr. Bell gave lectures to two groups of senior girls on 'The Mother To Be' on the 23rd. Commencing Monday April 28 groups of girls visited Boyn Hill School for commercial subjects, Boyn Hill girls came to Gordon for Folk Dancing. Mrs. Keach from Boyn Hill took groups for music and Mr. Thomas attended Boyn Hill to take Spoken English and Debate, etc.

A May Day celebration for Form III which included an inter-house Nature Competition with parents entertained to tea. A film 'Instruments of the Orchestra' was shown to a combined group of Boyn Hill and Gordon Road children on the afternoon of the 2nd. Form IIIA visited the Science and Natural History Museum in the morning and Kew Gardens in the afternoon of the 6th. In connection with the Biology Scheme and a follow-on from Dr. Bell's talks three girls visited the Health Centre on Friday afternoons and two Burberry Hall on Tuesday afternoons. The Headmaster and Mr. Denzey visited the Royal Geographical Society's Exhibition on visual aids on the 13th. A Mr. W.A.G. Hardy, a Jamaican gave a lecture on his country to top forms on the 15th. Two groups from the top forms commenced a period of one hour each of cricket at the Bray ground. Empire Day was on the 23rd, and eighty children visited Whipsnade Zoo on the 28th.

Gardening films were shown to senior boys by a representative of the Plant Protection Society on June 3. Work commenced on the new Practical Buildings on the 5th. A small party of senior boys visited the County Planning Exhibition at Reading on that day. At the North East Berkshire Athletic meeting held on the evening of the 12th the school won both the Senior Girls' and the Senior Boys' Championships. On the morning of the 13th Form IIIA visited Hurley leaving at 10.45a.m. and returning at 5.30pm. In the morning they made sketches of objects of historical interest and spent the afternoon being conducted round Lodge Place by Col. Rivers-Moore. Sixty-six children visited Reading for a performance of 'Macbeth' on the 20th. Dr. Mary Bell lectured to senior girls on 'Post Natal Care' on the 23rd.

Ministry of Education films 'Beginnings of History' and 'houses' were shown to selected classes on July 4. Mr. Tomlin was playing cricket for Berkshire on the 16th and 17th while on the 17th the year's practical work was on view at the Parents Open Day. Summer holidays – July 30–September 12. All outside metal work had been painted and the hall and Headteacher's room re-decorated during the vacation.

143 children were admitted on the first day of term. Father Wright conducted a Roman Catholic group for Religious Instruction on the 15th. 160 children visited the Drill Hall for a performance of 'The Dumb Wife of Cheapside' on the 16th. Mr. V.R. Moll Maidenhead's Borough Treasurer gave a lecture to 4th year pupils on the 23rd and on the 30th seventy children (Va and V) visited the Playhouse, Henley for a performance of 'Quality Street'. Miss Gordon the Domestic Subjects Instructress left the school.

Mrs. Godfrey replaced Miss Gordon on October 1. During the Autumn Term many talks and lectures took place in the school and these are included in date order. On October 1 Mr. Apse the Deputy Engineer spoke to senior children. On the 7th Mr. H.E. Pickman the Deputy Town Clerk lectured senior forms on the responsibilities of his Department. The following day a member of the Imperial Institute (erected as the national memorial of the jubilee of Queen Victoria) gave a lecture on India. On the 14th Mr. Child the Consumers Engineer gave a talk to the senior group. On the 24th Dr. Brodie Moore the Medical Officer of Health spoke on the work of his Department to the 14–15 age group and Mr. Jones from the Sanitary Inspector's Department addressed the senior form on the 28th. The Headmaster attended the County Girls' School Speech Day celebrations on the 30th.

A lecture by the Sub-Postmaster on November 11. Form IVA visited Windsor Castle in connection with the history course on the 13th also the day of the Parents Evening. Miss Hornby gave a violin recital when ten children attended a concert at Reading Town Hall on the 14th. The Superintendent of Police lectured senior children on the 18th. All schools closed on November 20 for the wedding of H.R.H. Princess Elizabeth. Ten boys visited the automatic exchange at Reading on the 25th the day that Mr. North a Chartered Architect lectured in school.

Two lectures during December – Mr. Mansbridge the Deputy Station Master on the 2nd and Mr. Sutton Smith from Bonds Bros. on the 9th. Geographical films were shown on the 11th, Christmas holidays beginning on the 19th.

1948

Re-open January 7 with Miss Hornby commencing as part-time Music Teacher. A programme of geographical films to selected forms began on the 15th. A new schedule of Caretakers and Cleaners had been drawn up by the Divisional Executive but had not yet been implemented resulting in unsatisfactory cleaning in schools. The Sub-Committee visited Gordon in connection with these duties on the 16th. During Salvage Week the school collected 1 ton 7 cwts. of waste paper. Mr. Herbert the Director of Education lectured to senior groups on the 20th. Two representatives from the B.B.C. visited to observe History broadcasts on the 22nd. Councillor Loosen arranged a talk and film on a modern engineering firm on the 27th.

Mr. Naish the Manager of the National Provincial Bank addressed children on February 3. On the 4th forty girls went to Reading to see the Women's Hockey Match – North versus South. On the 5th a half-day holiday was granted for North East Berkshire v Bath.

A Juvenile Employment Officer addressed school leavers on March 2. Miss P. Adams commenced on the 8th. Medical inspections on the 10th and 11th. Mr. Jeavons and Mr. Shervell commenced duties on the 15th.

On April 22 for the Spring Competition a pre-view of film strips was produced by Miss Phillips.

A visit to Kew Gardens by Forms VA girls, V boys and IV on May 3. Miss Felden commenced duties on the 6th. Forms IVA and VA attended a performance of 'The Yellow Jacket' at the Playhouse, Henley on the 7th. Films on the gas industry were shown by the Maidenhead Gas Company on the 12th and Empire Day was on the 24th.

Another new member of staff on June 14 – Mr. Price. 150 children and 22 staff made the journey to Bath and Bristol on the 16th. The Mayor presented the Dunkels Cup to the Football Team winners of the North East Berkshire League on the 30th.

An exchange visit took place between June 24 and July 1. Mr. Denzey and thirteen children left for Sheringham, Norfolk and a teacher and twelve children spent the week at Gordon Road. Open Day July 1.

Summer holidays July 22–September 8. During the vacation two staff rooms and six classrooms were decorated. One room was adapted for Biology in the old building. In the new building the Science, Handicraft and Dining Rooms were decorated and a new Raeburn cooker installed. Wire was erected in the playgrounds to prevent balls damaging the windows.

142 new admissions (54 girls, 88 boys) were recorded on September 8 children coming from Alwyn Road, Ellington, Boyn Hill, Touchen End, Holyport, Braywick, Knowl Hill, White Waltham, St. Mary's Roman Catholic, East Street, County Boys' and County Girls'. N.O.R. 460.

Mr. V. Griffin resigned on September 30 and Mr. E Robinson commenced on October 1.

School Prize Day Awards were presented by Sir Graham Savage, Education Officer of London County Council on November 22. Christmas holidays began on December 22 but 160 children visited Bertram Mills Circus on December 31.

Posts of Special Responsibility for 1948–49:-

Mr. F.A. Denzey	First Assistant
Miss A.B. Goody	First Woman Assistant
Mr. F. Harmsworth	Teacher in charge of practical instruction.

1949

The new term commenced on January 11. The east side of the playground had been re-surfaced during the holidays. Sixty boys visited the Schoolboys Exhibition on the 14th. Form VB woodwork boys visited a factory in Slough during the afternoon of the 19th and fifty-two children visited the Royal Opera House to see 'Cinderella' on the 29th.

A small group visited Reading Art Gallery on February 9 and fourteen attended a concert at Reading Town Hall on the 11th. The Headmaster was at St. Luke's School Prize Giving on the 22nd; thirty visited Bisham Abbey on the 23rd and Form IVA the Bourne End Paper Mills on the 24th. Mr. A. Viveash's appointment was terminated during the month.

Although no mention was made in either the School Log Book or the Governors' Minutes in connection with the 1939–45 memorial board, the edition of the Maidenhead Advertiser of February 18, 1949 reported:-

Prize Day became an annual event after World War II.

'SCHOOL LOSSES IN WORLD WAR – Memorial at Gordon-rd.'
'The Mayor (Cclr. Dr. Osmund Frank) placed a wreath on the oak memorial tablet which he unveiled at the Gordon County Secondary School on Thursday of last week before an audience of scholars, relatives and friends'.

The board reads:-

In honoured Memory of the Old Boys of this School who gave their lives in The World War 1939–1945

K. Astbury
J. Attersoll
G. Axford
J. Badcock
M. Badcock
E. Ball
H. Ball
A. Blay
W. Brandon
A. Broadbent
D. Brooker
R. Brooker
E. Clark
A. Collins
A. Cousins
A. Dalton
L. Draghi
F. Edwards
J. Elms
R. Gardner
L. Griffin
E. Hulme-Jones
K. Hutley
G. Isaac
F. Lawrence
D. Lee
C. Levy
L. Mead
S. Meade
E. Norkett
G. Palmer
D. Ray
J. Rowell
L. Stacey
H. Trinder
T. Walker
R White
F. Wilson
A. Wilson
J. Yeulet

'Greater love hath no man than this that a man lay down his life for his friends'

Both of the School's Memorial Boards, 1914–1918 and 1939–1945, are held in the Royal Borough Collection (Royal Borough of Windsor and Maidenhead), and can be seen by appointment by ringing the Honorary Curator on 01753 525547.

Eight children sat the Slough Technical Examination on March 4 the day IVA visited the Brick Kiln at Knowl Hill. The school presented ‘Puck’s Post’ at the Drama Festival on the 21st.

A special meeting was called for March 21 as it was realized that the three schools of Gordon Road, Alwyn Road and Ellington were regarded as full. In the case of Gordon the Managers resolved that the intake for any academic year should not exceed 100 and these places should be allocated in the following order of precedence:-

(1) Suitable candidates for any definite courses offered by the school
(2) Pupils from the two County Primary Schools
(3) Pupils from other Primary Schools in the Division.

On the basis of intake for the next session the Managers agreed that the Headmaster should be assisted by a small committee consisting of Mr. E.A. Bell (former Headmaster of Gordon), Miss E.J. Slocock (School Manager) and the two Head Teachers of Alwyn Road and Ellington whose senior children would be eligible for transfer.

The Headmaster was at a conference at Broadcasting House on March 28; at the Open Evening the following day over 300 parents were present.

The Junior Team won the County Championship at the Netball Rally held in Wokingham on April 2. Medical inspections April 1–8 and Mrs. Godfrey attended a Domestic Science Course at Wargrave from the 4–8.

Three visits during May. Thirty boys with Messrs. Denzey, Jeavons and the Headmaster saw H.M.S. Vernon at Portsmouth on the 13th and on the 16th IIIA toured St. Martin’s Jam Factory and Form V Bray Church.

The school was very successful at the Slough Festival of Folk Dance on the 17th. In the UNDER 12’s IIIA were 1st with Haste to the Wedding and Form II 2nd with Long Eight. In the 12–15 YEAR GROUP 1st was IVA with Picking up Sticks and 2nd IIIA with Cheerily and Merrily. The teams were trained by Miss Claydon. They were awarded a cup for the best performance of the evening.

The Mayor, two Aldermen, three Councillors, the Town Clerk, Mr. Sutton-Smith, Mr. E.A. Bell, Mr. H.E. Pickman and the Divisional Officer were present for the Empire Day celebrations on May 24. A school meals and a P.E. inspection was carried out during the day.

Miss Claydon and Mr. Tomlin were in charge of a party of twenty-eight children visiting Keswick for a week from May 26. Miss Phillips and Mr. Ball were in charge of fifty-six children from the senior forms who visited the Chelsea Show also on the 26th. The usual hair inspection by the nurses was on the 30th.

Miss Claydon attended a conference on History at the B.B.C. on June 10.

A general inspection of the school was carried out by seven His Majesty's Inspectors from June 13–16. A special meeting of Managers took place on the 16th to receive a verbal report on this inspection although this was not published until January 1950. It was of a highly commendable nature and was received by the Managers with pleasure. The Headmaster and staff were complimented on the high standard of education reached and special words of praise was given to the caretaking staff.

In the North East Berkshire Athletic Sports on the 16th the school won the Girls' Championship. Robey broke the record in the boys 100 yds. and 220 yds.

Posts of Responsibility:-

Mr. F.A. Denzey –	First Assistant (Deputy Head)
Miss A.B. Goody –	First Woman Assistant for Summer and Autumn Terms 1949 only (she would be retiring at Christmas)
Mr. F.H. Harmsworth –	Master in charge of Handicraft (Metalwork and Woodwork Rooms).

The school journey to Wells, Wookey and Cheddar took place on July 4. On the 7th Form IVA visited Watson's Farm. The Open Afternoon on the 13th was well attended. Mr. Denzey attended a Ministry Camping Course from the 13th until the end of term. Dr. Bell lectured to Forms IV and IVA on the 21st, the day that Mr. Viveash ceased duties. Summer holidays July 21–September 7.

100 children were admitted on the first day of term bringing the N.O.R. to 429. Mrs. Cox became a new member of staff. During the vacation the boys and girls lavatories had been reconstructed and six form rooms decorated.

The Deputy Director of Education stated that in accordance

with Clause 4 of the Instrument of Government it was necessary to appoint four co-optative governors for three years from September 1, 1949. These were Alderman J.B. Maudsley, Mr. Pickman, Mrs. Christie-Rae and Mrs. Flew.

The girls playground was re-surfaced on September 28.

The Headmaster attended a County Film Meeting at Theale on October 12 and the following day a course for Headteachers at the Royal Hotel, London. Subject:- Developments in Housecraft. On the 19th Miss Claydon attended an afternoon Historical Conference at Reading University. The first meeting of the Governors was held at the school on the 20th.

A party of thirty children went to the Ernest Read Orchestral Concert for Children at Central Hall, Westminster on the 22nd while on the 24th eighty-five from Forms VA and IVA saw a performance of Hamlet at the Plaza Cinema.

It was agreed that the word 'Road' should be deleted from the title of the school. It became known as Gordon County Modern School (Secondary). Perhaps a brief review would be appropriate. At the end of September 1949:-

N.O.R. 431. 244 Boys. 187 Girls. (1948 – 460).

The fall was due to the fact that for the first time the intake was limited to 100 children (50 boys and 50 girls). Approximately 30 were refused admission and some confusion resulted on the first morning of term when a number of children had to be turned away.

Staff

Headmaster	L.E.J. Adderson
Deputy Headmaster	F.A. Denzey
First Woman Assistant	Miss A.B. Goody
Assistant in charge Handicraft	F.H. Harmsworth

Men assistants	*Women assistants*
Mr. V. Ball	Miss M.M. Claydon
Mr. T. G. Thomas	Miss K. Phillips
Mr. E. Shervell	Mrs. H. Appleton
Mr. E. Robinson	Mrs. P.B. Blay
Mr. J.K. Price	Mrs. I. Cox
Mr. R.H. Tomlin	Mrs. R. Godfrey
Mr. C. Jeavons	Miss P. Adams
	Part-time Needlework Mrs. H. Sweet

TOTAL	1 Headmaster
	9 Men assistants
	8 Women assistants
	18
	1 Part-time

Number of Forms	13.	A Stream	4 mixed
		B Parallel	4 Boys
			4 Girls
		Retarded	1 Boys

Hours	Clerical Assistant	25	
	Caretaker	30	cleaning assistance
	Meals	6	women daily

November 15 – Prize Day. These were presented by the Town Clerk, Mr. S. Platt, deputising for Prof. H.C. Barnard. Among those attending Alderman Archer (in the chair), Alderman Neve, Rev. R.W. Cleaves, Mrs. Flew, Mr. E.A. Bell, Mrs. Hearne, Mr. Sutton-Smith, Mr. Pickman and many parents and friends.

The Headmaster visited Easthampstead Park College on December 1 for a visual aids meeting. A special meeting of Governors on the 5th to appoint a successor to Mr. Denzey who had been appointed Headmaster of a new Woodley Primary School. Three candidates were selected for interview, Mr. D.A. Read appointed although he reversed his acceptance. Geography films were shown on the 6th and the Christmas concert was on the 16th.

A presentation to Miss A.B. Goody to mark her retirement after 42½ years service to the school took place on December 19. It was recorded that in all those years she had only been absent for 7½ days. The Mayor presented her with a testimonial under the Borough Seal on behalf of the Council. Her last day was the 21st when the Christmas holidays began. 102 children attended Bertram Mills Circus on the 27th and a party of children with members of staff went to a pantomime at the London Casino on the 30th.

1950

The report of the H.M.I. inspections which took place from June 13–16, 1949 was received from the Ministry of Education on January 7. Running into several pages (too long to include in full) it was divided into six main sections, the principle points made being:-

1. HISTORY, NATURE AND SCOPE OF SCHOOL

Of the five secondary schools in Maidenhead, Gordon was the only County School taking boys and girls from 11–15 plus years of age. This section dealt with its history from when it opened in 1907 as separate departments for boys and girls through to its amalgamation to form one Senior Mixed School in 1932; the building in 1935 of a block of practical rooms and the addition of H.O.R.S.A. practical rooms to meet the needs of the school when the leaving age was raised to 15.

Mention was made of the last inspection in 1937, a three stream basis until September 1948 when an unusually large number of entrants from the primary schools led to the formation of four First Year Forms. Effective organisation was made difficult due to the recent excess of boys over girls (1948, 52 girls 90 boys).

Staff photograph from the 1950's.

Over three years 127 girls and 121 boys left, 30% of girls to posts in offices as receptionists or telephonists, 18% to factories, 17% to shop assistants, 16% to domestic work in homes, hospitals and laundries, 9% to hairdressing and 9% to needlecraft trades. Boys were more varied – metalwork, electrical, building, printing, upholstery, motor engineering and plumbing trades. Some became clerical workers, postmen, shop assistants, factory and farm workers or gardening. There was a Fifth Year Course of shorthand/typewriting for a small number of girls.

2. PREMISES AND EQUIPMENT

There were twelve FORM rooms, five for Art, Needlework, Music, Biology and History. There was a serious shortage of space for Physical Education equipment. Another possibility was the provision of warm water might be considered. The life and work of the school was limited by the lack of a school kitchen and dining room, playing fields and library.

3. STAFF

The Headmaster was credited for setting good standards of work and was supported by a thoughtful and vigorous First Assistant Master. Mention was made that the Senior Mistress would be retiring shortly. There were 16 full-time teachers (10 men, 6 women) and 2 part-time women.

4. ORGANISATION AND CURRICULUM

There were four Parallel forms of first year pupils, three at second, third and fourth year. Entrants were tested rather elaborately. Those who do well were put into a mixed 'A' Form, the remainder separated into single sex forms.

A four year course in English, Arithmetic, History, Geography, Religious Education, P.E., Music and Art was planned for all pupils. Girls had a four year course in Homecraft and Biology – boys, Handicraft and General Science.

5. SUBJECTS OF INSTRUCTION

Religious Instruction – two or three periods weekly
English shared by six teachers
History
Geography
Arithmetic – four masters and mistresses share this subject with the help of the Headmaster.
Biology (Girls) – one of form rooms had been adapted.
Gardening (boys). A small meadow of about two acres adjoining the school

was being converted to a school garden. A comprehensive plan was drawn up for the use of the ground bringing one acre under cultivation and leaving the remainder as a lawn which could be used for P.E. and other activities. Part of the meadow would be used for growing vegetables. Due to staffing difficulties it was not possible for all forms to receive instruction. *Commercial Subjects.* 11 girls join 17 from two other schools one half-day per week at the Technical Institute for Shorthand/ Typewriting. It would be better served if post 15-year olds could receive a full-time secretarial course at the Technical Institute.

Art
Handicraft – Woodwork – separate masters
Homecraft and Needlecraft – Shared by two fully qualified mistresses.
Needlecraft shared by two mistresses.
Music
P.E. Activities for girls – weekly gymnastics, also included hockey, netball in winter, tennis, rounders and swimming in summer.
boys – football, cricket, swimming in summer, second winter game recommended might be coached in tennis. Some badminton played by both sexes. The formation of a Rambling Club would open up great possibilities which could well include experience in camping.
girls – Negotiations were in progress for the appointment of a specialist teacher in English Folk Dancing to be included for all girls classes. It was hoped to include other forms of dancing.

6. GENERAL SCHOOL ACTIVITIES AND CORPORATE LIFE

A dignified assembly sometimes conducted by the Headmaster or pupils from other forms gave a good reverent beginning to each school day.

Varied inter-house activities, clubs, school journeys. visits and camps provided opportunities for wider experiences, self discipline and development of personal tastes giving older pupils scope for responsibility and leadership.

Parents were invited to open afternoons and evenings. The school takes its place in inter-school games, dancing, athletics and local music and drama festivals.

Approximately 200 children take advantage of the meal which is served in three sittings under staff supervision.

CONCLUSIONS

Pupils find themselves in a society which sets clear standards of work and behaviour and which makes from demands. There is a prevailing atmosphere of security and stability created over many years by the older members of staff which eases the absorption of less experienced teachers and new pupils.

This accounts for the measure of poise which most pupils develop during their school life and for the quiet confidence with which they meet visitors. It would be unfortunate if overcrowding of the school was allowed to undermine a good tradition or to cramp the healthy spirit of enterprise which now shows itself in many school activities.

Mrs. Christie Rae presented Beethoven's Symphony No. 9 in D Minor on gramophone records to the school on January 7.

The first day of term was January 10 with a new member of staff Miss A. Johnson. On the 27th senior boys visited the Morris Motor Works at Cowley and the following day a group of children attended the Ernest Read Concert at Central Hall, Westminster.

Posts of responsibility for 1950:-

Miss K. Phillips	First Assistant
Mr. F.H. Harmsworth	Teacher in charge Handicraft
Mr. R.H. Tomlin	Teacher in charge of boys discipline and activities.

Medical inspections were held on February 8.

Mr. Noble the Schools' Music Organiser lectured on February 17. A small party of children with Miss Claydon attended the Police Court to witness proceedings on the 20th. Dental inspections on the 20th, 21st and 22nd. A film was taken on behalf of the Domestic Science Organiser of a boys cookery class and of a special display of advanced cookery by the senior girls. The school was closed on the 23rd for the General Election so the 22nd was a good day to hold a mock election. The 28th was Mr. Denzey's last day after 13½ years as a member of staff. He became Headmaster of a Woodley Primary School. (A presentation was made on March 13).

The Juvenile Employment Officer visited on March 7.

In his report of March 9 the Headmaster stated the N.O.R. was 394 (boys 222, girls 172). Leavers at Christmas 1949, 27. Subject to the approval of Governors, thirty children would make an informative survey of the Keswick area from May 19–26, the entire cost to be borne by parents.

The Slough Technical Examinations took place on the 10th and at the Drama Festival on that day the school presented 'The Dyspeptic Ogre'. Mr. E. Standbrook-Evans joined the staff from the 13th. A metalwork course held at the school under the direction of Mr. Windle, an H.M.I. took place from the 22–25. Mr. Sutton-Smith (a Governor) made a gift of timber for library shelves on the 24th. At the Open Evenings and Displays on the 28th and 29th over 400 parents and friends raised £110 for the sound film projector fund. Mr. Tomlin and Mr. Shervell attended a cricket course at Didcot on the 29th and 30th.

A programme by the Berkshire Singers arranged by Mr. Noble was on April 3. Medical inspections April 27, May 3 and 4. The Drama Organiser conducted a programme with first year children on May 8 the day that the school gained 1st, 2nd, 4th and 5th places in the Folk Dance Section at Slough Arts Festival. The Choir was placed 2nd, one point behind the winners. The cup for the best performance was won for the second year in succession. A party of boys in charge of Mr. Harmsworth visited Swindon Locomotive Works on the 11th.

The Governors met on May 11 to appoint a P.E. specialist. Miss Barbara Nelson was successful but did not accept the post. Empire Day was the 24th and Mrs. I. Cox resigned on the 31st.

A party of boys with Messrs. Tomlin and Robinson in charge visited H.M.S. Vernon at Portsmouth on June 5. A Mr. P. Blackman of the Imperial Institute lectured on the West Indies on the 13th.

The school received a Municipal Charities Grant of £75 for Drama, Library and School excursions.

The school closed on July 5 to enable a large party to visit the Dress Rehearsal of the Farnborough Air Pageant. The Open Day and Exhibition of Work attracted a very large number of parents and friends on the 13th. Among those present was Mr. Oldershaw and Mrs. Jarvis, Chairman and Vice-Chairman of the Education Committee and Governors of the School. A party visited the Natural History Museum on the 18th. Summer holidays commenced the following day.

Re-open September 7. N.O.R. 424 (boys 232, girls 192). Leavers in July, 39. 6 pupils decided to stay on beyond the leaving age. 106 children applied for admission but only 104 could be taken. During the vacation the floor of the hall had been planed, lighting in lobbies renewed and the Domestic Science Room (1) redecorated. Miss P.H. Lanchbury commenced as P.E. specialist and Mr. H.V. Chelsom as Assistant Caretaker. A sound projector was purchased after voluntary effort by the school. School closed at mid-day for the annual conference on the 29th.

Mr. E.A. Bell, Governor and former Headmaster generously presented a piano to the school on October 2. The first attendance of hop picking began on the 8th and continued for 11½ weeks. Medical inspections on October 25, November 1 and 2.

Forty-eight children attended a performance of 'The Black Arrow' at Reading on November 15 and a second party of sixty were present at The Merchant of Venice on the 18th. Library Week commenced on the 20th and parties attended talks at the Town Hall during the week. Prize Day was on the 22nd and the Right Reverend the Lord Bishop of Oxford consented to distribute these. The Youth Employment Officer was present for interviews on the 28th.

The school gave a Carol Service at St. Peter's Church, Furze Platt on December 7 and repeated it at the Congregational Church on the 12th. Christmas holidays began on the 19th being the last day for Mrs. H.E. Appleton (Art) and Miss A.E. Johnson (Drama).

1951

New term January 9 – new member of staff Mr. B.P. Jones (Art and Craft). During the vacation the hall floor surface again had to receive attention. Ten pupils sat the Slough Technical Examinations on the 19th.

Mrs. W. Cherry was appointed English and French mistress from February 1. Mr. Thomas and the Headmaster attended the funeral of Alderman L.R.F. Oldershaw, Chairman of Berkshire Education Committee and a School Governor on the 6th. A small group attended an orchestral concert at the Town Hall, Reading on the 8th and an Ernest Read Concert on the 17th. The greenhouse was completed and in use, Messrs. Jeavons, aided by Harmsworth, Ball and Cartland all worthy of commendation. N.O.R. 391 (boys 216, girls 175). Leavers at Christmas 1950, 30. A visit was made to the Imperial Institute on March 5; parents were interested in the practical work on display at the Open Evenings on March 13 and 14; Mr. Jones was at a course of the School of Art on the 15th and Mr. Price at a Music Conference at Reading on the 19th. A complaint of the unsuitability of the dress of some of the senior form was made and a circular to all parents of pupils mentioned the desirability of quiet dress.

Posts of Responsibility:
First Woman Assistant in charge girls activities and discipline – Miss M.M. Claydon
First Man Assistant in charge boys activities and discipline – Mr. R.H. Tomlin
Other posts –
Woman Assistant in charge welfare, meals and milk – Miss K. Phillips
Man Assistant in charge, handicraft – Mr. F.H. Harmsworth.

Special Governors Meetings were held on April 23 and May 9 to appoint staff for the Autumn Term.

Mr. V. Ball ceased duties on April 30 having been appointed to the Headship of a school in Cheshire.

Empire Day was on May 24 with the usual half-holiday in the afternoon. Twenty-eight children in charge of Mr. Evans and Mr. Jeavons left for the Isle of Arran (May 25–June 1). Medical inspections on the 30 and 31st. At the Music Festival Form IIIA received favourable comment at the audition.

The Festival of Britain commemorated to coincide with the centenary of Prince Albert's Great Exhibition of 1851 combined national exhibitions of arts and sciences with Britain's outstanding advancements prevailing since the end of the war in 1945. Visits to the South Bank Exhibition was made by pupils on June 8, 15, 22 and 29. Maidenhead had its own local Festival of Britain celebrations when a Schools' Combined Display of P.E. and Dancing was held in Grenfell Park on July 12, a Pageant of Maidenhead written by Maidenhead's own authoress Dorothy B. Upson took place in the Park on the 19th and 21st.

N.O.R. 360 (boys 197, girls 163). Leavers at Easter 27. The admission number was being increased to 120 (60 boys and 60 girls), the present limit was 100. It was agreed that Ellington and

Alwyn Road children should have priority. It was also agreed that a Pre-Nursing Course be instituted for girls between the ages of 15 and 17. The Headmaster was allowed to initiate the scheme with an interim report at the end of one year, a more decided one at the end of two years with a decision at the end of the third year as to whether the course should continue or not. There would be no segregation before the age of 15. Application for permission had to be awaited from the Nursing Council and the Ministry of Education.

The Rev. C.G. Gardner (left district in 1952) and Mr. P.A.J. Hammett were elected to the body of Governors.

Mr. Robinson was absent during the afternoon of July 4 to play cricket for Maidenhead. At the Schools' Swimming Gala the school won the Norris Cup for the highest aggregate of points, the 100 yards Championship for Boys (E. Badcock: Record Time in the event) and the Diving Championships for both boys and girls (S. Goom and D. Badcock). At the North East Berkshire Sports Meeting the girls won the Senior Championship and – Lewington broke the record for the 220 yards boys. The first Inter-House Gala since the war was held during the month, Gordon House gaining the Championship.

The Mayor and Mayoress, H.M.I.'s, Governors, Rev. and Mrs. Morcom Harnies, Rev. Lowman and many parents attended the Open Afternoon on the 19th. Miss Lanchbury left at the end of term to get married.

The new term commenced on September 4 with Miss Margaret E.V. Witts (Physical Education) and Mr. Frederick Curd (Gardening). 126 new children were admitted. During the vacation the main building had been re-wired, a physical education store shed erected in the girls playground and the H.O.R.S.A. hut decorated externally and the Domestic Science Room internally. Twenty four boys visited H.M.S. Vernon at Portsmouth on the 21st Mr. Shervell and the Headmaster being in charge. Evening school commenced on the 24th. Closed on the 28th for the Reading Conference. Potato picking again on the agenda.

October saw two male teachers absent with mumps.

N.O.R. 430. (boys 230, girls 200). Visits to the National Exhibition of Children's Art and the Ernest Read Orchestral Concerts were made. Fifty children from the senior forms attended a performance of La Boheme on November 5. Mr. J.F.

Wolfenden, Vice-Chancellor of Reading University distributed the prizes on Prize Day, November 16. A Carol Service was presented at St. Luke's Church on the 20th.

A special Governors meeting was held on December 3. From September 1952 it would be unable to accommodate children seeking admission unless the new two-classroom block approved in current estimates is completed as scheduled. This decision was taken after considering the numbers of children who will require places in secondary schools in the years 1952–55.

The choir sang at the Bible Society Annual General Meeting on December 3. Mrs. Godfrey with two pupils Brian Lambourne and John Kittles visited the B.B.C. to record a programme for Lionel Gamlen's Younger Generation.

– Dean and – Badcock were selected to play for Berks. Bucks. and Oxon. Christmas holidays commenced on December 20. Leavers 34.

1952

Re-open January 8. Wallace Film Promotions made a short film of boys doing domestic science on the 16th.

Medical inspections took place on February 13 and 20. The school assembled for a memorial service on the morning of the 15th for the funeral of H.M. King George VI and for a broadcast service in the afternoon.

A concert and display was given at the Open Evenings on March 26 and 27. These were very well attended Governors, the Mayoress and the Deputy Director of Education being amongst the guests. A generous grant from the Maidenhead Municipal Charities made it possible to curtain the hall and purchase a new edition of Chambers Encyclopedia.

Thirty-eight children and three staff left for the school journey to Alston, Cumberland returning on May 31. Empire Day was celebrated on the 24th.

A small party visited the Fire Station on June 12. The girls won the Senior Championship at the District Sports held at the County Boys' Grammar School on that day. The Rev. J.H. Cook was appointed a Governor on June 30.

Form VA in charge of Mr. Tomlin visited Reading automatic exchange on July 1. A large number of parents and friends attended the Open Day and Annual Exhibition of Work on the 17th; the Inter-House Folk Dance Competition was the following day; the Inter-House Swimming Gala on the 20th, summer holidays commencing on the 22nd. A very favourable comment was received by the school at the Music Festival.

Fifty-five girls and sixty-nine boys were admitted on the first day of term – September 9.

It was agreed that as there were sufficient places available all applications for admission of girls in September would be granted. Seventy-four applications from parents for admission of boys were considered having previously decided on information from the Headmaster as to the number of places available. At least sixty-five should be granted, the Divisional Education Officer writing to parents whom it was not possible to accommodate. It was left to the Headmaster to write to the parents of those offered places.

Although five staff attended, the school did not this year close for the annual conference. The Headmaster attended a National Savings Conference at Southsea on October 3.

Mrs. P. Flew, Mr. J.B. Maudsley, Mr. H.E. Pickman and Mrs. V. Christie Rae were appointed co-optative Governors for a further three years. Should any decline the vacancy would be offered to Mrs. N. Bromley.

N.O.R. 437. Boys 232, Girls 205.

Her Majesty's Inspectors advised that a class of forty was rather large for the successful teaching of French. As the Pre-Nursing Group (approval had been given by the Ministry of Education and the General Nursing Council) would not be a complete form it would assist organisation if an additional member of staff could be appointed in September 1953. (This was allowed for in the estimates for 1953/54). It was also felt that maintenance staff for the playing field should be on the establishment of the school. Nine girls had been following the Commercial Course this year. Two of last year's students passed their first typewriting examination with distinction. Potato picking commenced on October 13 with the usual disruption of work in the third and fourth years. The Gardening Master lost all his strongest boys at a most important time of year when it is desirable to complete digging and reconstruction.

Prize Day November 18 this year distributed by Mr. R.P. Bell, M.A., F.R.S., Bedford Professor of Physical Chemistry, Oxford University, son of the first Headmaster of Gordon and an old boy. Also present:- the Mayor, Mrs. Jarvis and the Deputy Director.

A Carol Service took place at the Congregational Church and at Bray on December 4. – Lambert was chosen to play for Berks. Bucks. and Oxon against Bedfordshire. Christmas vacation began on the 16th the last day for Mr. Jones. Leavers twenty-two, nine eligible to leave decided to stay on.

1953

The new term began on January 6 with Mr. Lacy as the new Art Specialist. In an endeavour to improve the standard of English and Arithmetic in Form IIB Geography and History had been suspended for a term experimentally. A Cadbury's film show was shown on the 28th.

The Youth Employment Officer interviewed pupils on February 23 but there was a low attendance during the month (84.9%) due to influenza.

March – N.O.R. boys 215, girls 194, total 409. At the Area Cross Country Race on the 13th the school team was placed 2nd, and won the Schools' F.A. Trophy and League Cup on the 19th. 250 people attended the Open Evening on the 18th. One girl and three boys were eligible for transfer to grammar schools in the 13 plus examinations.

A number of children attended Art classes at the School of Art on Fridays from 4.45–6.30p.m. A course of Painting and Decorating was being considered. The response to the flood relief from children and parents was remarkable. Over 1000 garments, £10 in cash and a large box of sweets was sent to the W.V.S.

Mrs. Cherry resigned on April 30.

A school party of forty-one left at 5.15p.m. on May 15 for Ballachulish with Miss Claydon, Mr. Tomlin and the Headmaster in charge. Their knowledge of the history and geography of Scotland gained considerably. Unfortunately owing to illness two members of the party and the Headmaster had to return early. On the 28th the school received a visit from the Mayor when a programme appropriate to the Coronation was presented. A pleasing decoration scheme for the hall was carried out by the Art classes under the direction of Mr. Lacy. The County Education Committee presented a set of books suitably inscribed to mark the occasion. The Coronation holiday took place from June 1–8. The Authority intended to make a communal gift to secondary schools of books for the library. A suggestion that the School would like the gift of a wireless set and record player in preference was agreed. The Old Boys Association presented the School with an attractive new flag pole and the Old Girls gave a new Union Jack.

Dental inspections were held on June 8, 17 and 18 and medicals concluded on the 11th.

The Coronation Display actually took place on the beautiful afternoon of July 2 when a large crowd witnessed the physical education performed on the lawn.

Mr. R. Bristow was appointed French Specialist commencing on July 6.

The Headmaster drew attention to the anticipated heavy intake of children in September. It was agreed that in determining which children should be admitted preference should be given to those coming from the Borough Primary Schools and after that consider such representations as are made by the parents. All girls applications were granted as there were sufficient places. Ninety applications from parents of boys were received but only sixty-one granted. In detail from:-

Alwyn Infants	25	
Ellington Primary	22	
White Waltham	1	
Bisham Church of England Primary	1	
St. Mary's Roman Catholic	1	
Holyport Church of England Primary	3	Previous family connection
Knowl Hill Primary	2	Previous family connection
All Saints Junior	5	4 family association, 1 from Redriff Hostel
Waltham St. Lawrence	1	
	61	

Written arrangements to parents were the same as last year.

Open Afternoon was well attended on July 23 and the Inter-House Swimming Gala was at the Corporation Baths on the 27th. The School was placed second in the Area Cross Country Championship, the Football XI won the District League Championship and Knock-Out Shield, one boy being chosen to play for Berks. Bucks. and Oxon. The one act play 'The Stolen Boy' was presented at the Youth Drama Festival and received favourable comment from the adjudicator. Summer holidays began on July 28. Leavers 60. During the vacation the exterior of the Practical Block and interior of the woodwork room was re-decorated.

120 new pupils were admitted on September 8. Two staff attended the Secondary Modern School Conference at Reading University on the 21st while the school closed for the annual Reading Conference on the 25th.

Forty boys commenced potato picking at Findlay's Farm on October 5. Mrs. Godfrey and Miss Adams attended a course at Abingdon on the 20th and Messrs. Harmsworth and Jeavons visited Didcot to judge handicraft competitions on the 28th.

N.O.R. boys 229, girls 222 total 451. Mr. T.G. Thomas who was very seriously ill whilst a patient at St. George's Hospital during August appeared to be making progress and returned home but would need a long period of convalescence. He was granted six months sick leave.

Twelve girls were taking the Commercial Course which was the maximum number of places available at the East Berkshire College of Further Education. Eight children joined the Friday Evening Art School class but only one boy elected to go to the Painting and Decorating Course. Six girls completed the Pre-Nursing Course. A wrought iron gate constructed by boys under the supervision of Mr. Harmsworth was erected in the garden adding greatly to the general appearance of the ground. Provision of an Art and Needlework block had been approved by the Executive and sent up to the Authority as first priority under the Minor Projects for the year 1954/5.

Mrs. E.N. Lancaster-Jones, a supply teacher, became a member of the permanent staff on November 1. Mr. D.C. Robbins from the Imperial Institute lectured on Kenya on the 6th. Senior girls visited the Electrical Appliances Display and Demonstration on the 11th and the Headmaster attended Boyne Hill Girls' School Speech Day on the 12th.

The most pleasant Prize Day to date was on the 18th. The awards were distributed by Mrs. B.A. Bennett, O.B.E., D.M., Principal Nursing Officer, Ministry of Labour and National Service in the presence of the Mayor and Mayoress, Education Officials, H.M.I.s, representatives of local churches and a large number of parents. Youth Employment interviews took place on the 24th and 28th and Form IVA visited a Missionary Exhibition at Reading on the 25th.

A half-day holiday was granted on December 4 to mark the success of Prize Day. Carol Services were held in the Baptist Church and St. Mary's Church on the 3rd and 10th and a large choir of 100 boys and girls were specially asked to sing at the new Methodist Church in St. Mark's Crescent. Collections amounted to approximately £15 which was devoted to the funds of the individual churches. A film was shown in the hall on the 17th and Miss Adams resigned after six years service on the last day of term. Leavers 34.

1954

Defence Regulations Nos. 29 and 30 under which arrangements had been made by local authorities for exempting children from school attendance to help with the gathering of crops had been allowed to lapse on December 10, 1953, therefore no such exemptions would in future be granted.

Re-open January 7 with Miss M.J. Fowler as the new Domestic Science teacher. Mr. Thomas returned after his long illness.

A severed water pipe as a result of subsidence interrupted water supplies on January 12.

N.O.R. 418, (boys 214, girls 204). The Executive recommended the Authority should approve that a pavilion be purchased for the playing field and that the school should raise half the estimated cost. Owing to the impending closure of the Central Schools Meals Kitchen the Authority considered a project for providing certain schools with canteens and under this scheme it was proposed to erect a new kitchen together with dual purpose dining accommodation at Gordon.

March 1 and the death of Mr. E.A. Bell, the School's first Headmaster, a position he held for twenty-nine years. An entry in the School Log Book reads:- 'Beloved by his pupils, his staff and by colleagues in all schools of the Maidenhead District. A fine Christian gentleman, he was greatly respected by all sections of the community'. The school closed on March 5 to enable staff and senior scholars to attend the funeral.

Youth employment interviews took place on March 19 followed by a youth employment talk on the 23rd. A talk by Lt. Phillips of H.M.S. Vernon was on the 25th.

The school presented 'The Eye of the Beholder' at the Drama Festival on April 2. 220 parents and five Governors were at the Open Evening on the 6th, Mr. Shervell completed his duties as P.E. Instructor on the 7th, the evening that the Headmaster attended the opening of Courthouse School. The assistant caretaker also resigned.

Mr. K.R. Horne joined the staff as P.E. Instructor on May 1. The Headmaster gave a lecture to Ministers Fraternal on the 10th; Forty-two children in charge of Mr. Evans and the Headmaster commenced the school journey to Glasbury-on-Wye (near Brecon Beacon) on the 22nd. The health visitor accompanied the party. The Deputy Mayor visited the school on Empire Day, the 24th.

Medicals on June 9, youth employment interviews on the 10th and 11th and a talk by Flying Officer Steinforth on the 27th. In the County Athletic Sports on the 28th, M. Beckett was first in the long jump and represented Berkshire in the All-England Championships and Brian Webber third in the 880 yards. Medicals again on June 30 and July 1.

Eighty children visited the Royal Show on July 9 and on the last day of term, the 27th, Miss Fowler left to take a post in Tanganika, Mr. Price transferred to Ellington and Mr. Thomas completed his duties on retirement. Leavers 43.

The school opened on September 7, 128 children being admitted out of 175 applications. Miss W.A.M. Lawrence commenced as Domestic Science and Mr. H.A.T. Johnson, English, Mrs. Bailey was taking Music on a part-time basis on Tuesday and Wednesday. N.O.R. 473 (boys 241, girls 232).

Four girls gained Pitman's Shorthand Theory Certificates and six the London Chamber of Commerce Typing Certificate. Roger

Garrett was selected to attend a week's course at Ryecotewood College of Rural Crafts and Sylvia Woodruff attended an intensive course in cake decoration at a College in London. Raymond J. Allaway was under training as a boy seaman in H.M.S. Ganges.

A number of parents expressed a desire for their children to stay on at least an extra year in order that they may sit their G.C.E. It was proposed as an experiment to allow selected children to follow the syllabuses laid down by the new Examining Board. The first group of candidates to take examinations would sit in 1957.

Service before Self prizes awarded by Maidenhead Rotary Club went to Barbara Mason and Kenneth Robbins who were both invited to the weekly lunch.

A Simplicity Pattern Show was held on October 5 and a Simplicity Pattern Fashion Show for parents on November 11.

Much to the appreciation of Governors, parents and friends of the school the Prize Fund had been very generously supported. Held on November 24 prizes this year were distributed by the Rev. A.V. Hopkins, B.A., Principal Chaplain to the R.A.F. With the Rev. Cleaves in the Chair, other guests included the Mayor and Mayoress, Alderman Archer, other Governors and Ministers of Religion. A half-day holiday in respect of the day was granted on December 3.

A Carol Service took place at St. Mark's Church on December 15, this being relayed to the Hospital wards. School closed on the 17th when Mrs. R. Godfrey completed her duties on retirement and Miss V. Witts and Mr. E. Robinson resigned. Leavers 39.

1955

School re-opened on January 11 with the following new staff:-

Miss F.M. Higgins	–	Domestic Science
Miss C.A. Johnson	–	Physical Education (Temporary until March 4)
Mr. G.H. Lewis	–	History and Science
Mr. F.G. Albon	–	Music.

Mrs. N. Lancaster-Jones was granted unpaid leave of absence for the duration of the Spring Term to visit her husband in Iraq.

At the Governors meeting on February 7 a considerable discussion on the criteria to be adopted for admissions took place. It was finally agreed that children from Ellington Primary and Courthouse Junior should be given special consideration and that children of former scholars priority if vacancies remained. Numbers had increased for the last five years:-

N.O.R.	1951	391
	1952	399
	1953	409
	1954	418
	1955	433

A small committee representative of the School and the Old Gordonians fixed a target of £100 for the E.A. Bell Memorial Library Fund. This amount was easily exceeded.

Beside the usual games the following activities were in weekly operation:-

Country Dancing Club (mixed)
Gymnastics Club
Drama Club
Art Club
Gardening Club
Stamp Club
Rugby Club
Italic Writing Club

Members of staff gave generously of their leisure time.

There was a possibility that the Headmaster would become a member of the Berkshire Education Committee as Teacher Representative. Absences would bring additional responsibility to the First Assistant. It was suggested that Mr. R.H. Tomlin should be appointed Deputy Headmaster and this was approved as from the Summer Term.

The Old Gordonians 'Boys' Association expressed their desire to erect a club room and to work in this respect with the school towards the provision of a pavilion on the playing field in Courthouse Road. Approximately £400 had been collected and it was hoped that this could be owned jointly by the School and the Association.

As he would be leaving the district the Rev. R.W. Cleaves tendered his resignation as a Governor.

A party of children visited Morris Motors at Cowley, Oxford on March 4; youth employment interviews took place on March 7 and 8 and a party of girls visited the Ideal Home Exhibition on the 18th.

The open evening, concert and display was held on April 5. Nine girls and eight boys with Mrs. Blay, Mr. Bristow and Mr. Lacy visited Paris from April 10–17. Mrs. S.J. Lowe became the new P.E. Specialist on the 26th but found the journey to school too difficult and left on July 22. Leavers at Easter 30.

Forty-nine children accompanied by Mrs. Sweet, Mr. Horne and the Headmaster and school nurse began the journey to Ballycastle, Northern Ireland on May 20 returning June 1. Empire Day celebrations May 24.

At the District Sports meeting held on the afternoon of June 9 the school won both the boys and the girls championships. Patricia Pugh broke the record for the girls 100 yards and P. Baldwin broke the record for the long jump (boys).

N.O.R. 404 – boys 204, girls 200. The school meals accommodation had commenced at the beginning of term and was making good progress. The number of admissions for September again exceeded places, pupils from Courthouse was extremely high. It was evident that very soon Courthouse and Ellington would fill all vacancies. 89 boys and 70 girls had made applications and after admitting 56 boys and 47 girls from the above two schools, 4 boys and 12 girls who appeared to have special grounds, this left a rejection of 11 girls and 29 boys.

The school participated in the Drama and Music Festivals. A recorder group had been formed and padder tennis became an additional summer game.

Posts of Responsibility were the same as 1951 but with:-

Deputy Head	Mr. R.H. Tomlin
Domestic Science Mistress	Miss F.M. Higgins.

There were now three vacancies on the Board of Governors caused by the resignations of the Rev. R.W. Cleaves, Mrs. Hearne and Mr. S. Sutton Smith.

Mr. H.E. Pickman, M.B.E., Deputy Town Clerk, School Governor and a distinguished old scholar died very suddenly on June 15. He had attended a Governors meeting the previous evening.

Miss Higgins and Miss Lawrence attended a course at Didcot on June 17.

Medical inspections June 6, 8, 15 and 16th.

In the County Sports held on June 25 the following pupils were placed:-

100 yards (boys)	P. Baldwin*	2nd
100 yards (girls)	P. Pugh	4th
Long Jump	P. Gaskins	4th
Hurdles (15–17)	A. Jones	4th

*selected to run for Berkshire at the All-England Championships at Manchester.

At the Area Athletics on July 7:-

880 yards	D. Crossman	2nd
100 yards	P. Pugh	1st (equalled the 100 yards record)

Mr. Tomlin attended a week's Science Course at Reading from July 4–8. A very large number of parents and friends visited the school for Open Day on the 21st. Mr. Lacy was responsible for the presentation of exhibits which were effectively displayed. Summer holidays commenced the following day. Leavers 48.

Two pupils were entered for the G.C.E. as an experiment and in order to gauge standards. Both were successful. Next year some of the Pre-Nursing will take the examination and two boys will offer practical subjects. The first group will sit in 1957. Results:-

A. Mitchinson (English Language, Needlework, Domestic Science)
A. Harvey (Craft – Wood).

The new term commenced on September 6 with Mrs. A.H. Price as the temporary P.E. Specialist (until December 20). New admissions 120. School closed for the annual conference at Reading on the 30th.

Recommendations for a new Art Room was included in the Divisional Executive's Minor Projects for 1956/7 together with prepared plans for an extension of the lobbies.

Mr. Hewitt, Mr. Mudd, Miss Marsh and Mr. Firth were nominated as co-operative Governors for the period 1955/8. Mr. E. Stanbrook Evans gained his B.Sc. after five years of evening study.

At the Maidenhead and District Swimming Gala the school won:-

Norris Cup for the highest aggregate of points	
Boys Team Race	First
Girls Team Race	First
Boys Diving Championship	
Girls Diving Championship.	

The results were due to the enthusiastic work of Mr. K.R. Horne.

The Headmaster informed the Governors of his disapproval of the wearing of jeans in school and of the style of hair cuts of various boys.

Miss H.S. Kermode, M.A., J.P., gave an interesting talk to the children following the distribution of awards at the annual Prize Day on November 9. The Mayor, Town Clerk, Divisional Officer, Governors, Parents and Old Scholars were present and thanked for their generosity and support. A party of children visited the Town Hall, Reading to attend the St. Cecelia Day concert on the evening of the 22nd.

A Christmas collection for Dr. Barnardo's Homes totalled £21 3s. 0d. chosen possibly to commemorate the 50th anniversary of the death of its founder Thomas John Barnardo. An innovation was the attendance of the whole school at the Methodist Church for the annual Carol Service on December 14. On the following day a Carol Service for parents was held at St. Peter's Church, Furze Platt. School closed on the 20th. Leavers 32.

1956

Serious leaks in the roof of the main building caused damage to equipment after a heavy snowfall. First day of term January 10. A party of boys in the charge of Mr. Tomlin visited the automatic exchange at Reading on February 1. Mrs. P.A. Monaghan was appointed to the full-time staff until the end of the Summer Term. Youth employment interviews were held on February 29.

The death occurred of Alderman W. Archer, Chairman of Governors from 1925–55. It was recorded that 'his real interest in our (school) affairs, his wise counsel, his unfailing support and his kindness to the staff and children influenced, to a high degree, the development of Gordon School'. He was greatly respected by the Headmaster and staff.

N.O.R. boys 224, girls 222 = 446 an increase of 13 on the previous year. With new classrooms becoming available and an increasing number of children staying on beyond leaving age consideration was being given to the appointment of an additional teacher for the Autumn Term. A new groundsman was responsible for the Courthouse and Gordon playing fields.

The Headmaster received donations of suitable books for the

A day at the docks!

School Library and the first consignment of 200 books from the County Library was a most welcome addition to the stock.

Due to the valuable work being performed by Mr. K.R. Horne assisted by Miss W. Lawrence on behalf of both the older scholars and those who had recently left school, an average of 60 boys and girls attend each Friday evening for Old Time and Modern Dancing. This was known as the Under Eighteen Club.

A remarkable scheme had been put forward by the Old Gordonians Association for the provision of a pavilion to be erected on the Gordon School playing field to mark the 50th anniversary of the opening of the school. The thoughtfulness and generosity of this well organised body was commended to the Governors. The provision of an Art Room had been included in the list of Minor Projects 1956–7. This should bring relief to the pressure on accommodation and make possible the establishment of a fully equipped library. When completed there would be room for a further intake of sixty pupils. The dining room and kitchen was now nearing completion.

It was agreed to adopt the following principles:-

(a) those children with family connections should have a prior claim of entry
(b) those children from primary school of the area should normally be admitted as a matter of course
(c) girls from Ellington should have preference to places
(d) remaining applicants should be considered by House Committee on their merits.

Mr. L.T. Lee was nominated as the Authority Representative in place of Alderman Archer.

At the well supported Concerts and Display Days on March 19 and 20 visitors included the Vice-Chairman of Berkshire Education Committee, the Director of Education and the Chairman and most of the Governors. £36 was added to the Pavilion Fund.

'The Seventeenth Highwayman', a one-act play, was presented at the Town Hall for the Drama Festival and received praise from the adjudicator.

Forty-eight children and eight staff made the journey to Aeschi, Switzerland during the period April 8–17 and had a glorious holi-

School trips during the 1950's.

day in the Bernese Oberland. Costing £21 per head they stayed at Pension Friedegg a well-equipped hotel of 45 rooms which was fully taken up by the school. Visits planned included:-

(1) Col des Mosses-Aigle Montreaux, Vevey Bulle Jaunpass
(2) Brunigpass-Luzern-Entlebuch-Schallenberg-Thun
(3) Jungfraujoch by the Wengernalp and Jungfrau Railway
(4) Lauterbrunnin-Trummelbach-Grindelwald
(5) Interlaken.

The new dining room opened on April 18; dental inspections took place on the 30th.

Classes commenced in the new needlework room on May 6. Girls were working under very pleasant conditions and enjoyed lessons on the veranda in warm sunshine. Although the new dining arrangements were working smoothly and the quality of meals invariably excellent, 200 meals were being served daily. If the total exceeds 240–50 overcrowding will result and it may become necessary to draw up some ruling to restrict the number staying to dinner. Each case would be considered on its merits and left to the discretion of the Headmaster. It was hoped the Music classes would commence in the second room on May 27. Two new bays had been added to the cycle shed on the boys side and boundary fences of the garden had been painted. 300 books in very good condition had been presented to the Library by members of the school.

Nine children took part in the inspiring programme of the National Music Festival at the Albert Hall which was joined by Maidenhead children for the first time. A second year group entered by Mr. Albon for the Local Schools Festival performed very creditably. During the year small groups had attended the Saturday morning Ernest Reed concerts at the Festival Hall.

Six children took G.C.E. and one sat Part I of the General Nursing Council Preliminary State Examination. She was the first candidate to enter, was successful, and continued her training at Maidenhead Hospital. The first girl in attendance at Gordon to pass the G.C.E. exam worked for the Australian Embassy at The Hague at a salary of £550 a year.

The Simplicity Pattern Show was on June 1. A special train conveyed the majority of the school to Southampton on the 5th. They visited the Graving Dock, had a 2½ hour cruise around the harbour and then went to the Terminal Building from which was obtained a magnificent view of the 'Queen Elizabeth'. The Headmaster, Fay Norris and Charles McCullough attended the Rotary Club luncheon in connection with Service above Self prizes on June 18.

Sporting Successes:- the girls won the Championship and the boys were placed second. Patricia Pugh broke the 150 yards record which had stood for 20 years. She later ran for Berkshire in the National Championships at Plymouth and reached the semi-final in the 150 yards. In the Berkshire County Championships results were:-

Patricia Pugh	1st	150 yards
Sara Mealing	2nd	Long Jump
David Crossman	3rd	880 yards
Clive Moses	3rd	80 yards hurdles

Awards in the Maidenhead and District Swimming Championships:-

Norris Cup for the highest aggregate of points		
100 yards championship		John Bell
Diving championship		Jill Sanders
Team Race	1st	Gordon Girls

Berks. Bucks. Beds. and Oxon. Championships at Luton:-

100 yards	2nd	J. Bell
Diving	3rd	J. Sanders

At the Maidenhead and District Chrysanthemum and Dahlia Society Show the school won the Inter-School Challenge Trophy for the best exhibit of chrysanthemums.

A special meeting was called to consider 185 (98 boys, 87 girls) applications for September. After admitting all applicants (26 boys, 39 girls from Courthouse and 9 boys, 14 girls from Ellington) 25 boys and 10 girls whose applications appeared to have special grounds for admission were selected.

It was proposed to inform parents of future entrants that it was the wish of the Governors and Headmaster that school uniform should be worn.

The siting of the new classroom block would be on the opposite side of the lawn from the new kitchen-dining room and at right angles to the existing two-classroom block.

Open Day (afternoon and evening) was on July 19. The school closed for the summer holidays on the 20th the following staff leaving – Mr. G.H. Lewis, Mrs. E. Lancaster-Jones and Mrs. P. Monaghan (who was temporary). Leavers 61.

The following candidates gained success in the G.C.E. examinations of the Associated Examining Board:-

C. Weeks	–	Human Biology; Household Cookery; English Language; English Literature
F. Stanmers	–	Human Biology; Household Cookery
A. Blackman	–	Household Cookery
D. Crossman	–	Handicraft – Wood
P. Baldwin	–	Handicraft – Wood.

School re-opened on September 5 with the following new members of staff:-

Mrs. C.M. Butler	–	Physical Education
Mrs. A.M. Fleming	–	English
Mr. L.J. Monk	–	Science
Miss M. Jackson	–	Geography and Mathematics
Mr. J.F. Mayhew	–	temporary for one term only.

126 new children were admitted. Closed for the annual Teachers Conference on September 28.

The Headmaster attended Reading Abbey School Speech Day on October 10 and the County Girls' Grammar School Speech Day on the 25th.

The Right Reverend the Lord Bishop of Reading distributed awards for Prize Day on November 14. Guests included the Chairman and Vice-Chairman of Berkshire Education Committee, the Deputy Director and Ministers of Religion. Again the Prize Fund received generous support.

A Carol Service for the entire school was held on the afternoon of December 14 at St. Luke's Church. An evening service for parents took place at the Congregational Church on the 17th. There was a generous response to the Hungarian Relief and Dr. Barnardo's Christmas Fund Appeals.

School closed on December 20 being the last day for Miss Higgins. Mr. A.C. Firth had also resigned from the Governing Body. Leavers 28.

1957

First day of term January 8. Medical inspections on the 15th. Approval had been obtained from the Ministry of Education to erect a pavilion on the playing fields. A formal agreement was being drawn up and building would commence as soon as planning permission had been received.

The Authority proposed to erect two classrooms in addition to the Art and Craft Room. Work should commence soon permitting the intake of an extra 30 children each year.

A Jubilee Concert of music and singing devised and conducted by Mr. Albon was held on the evenings of March 13 and 14. There was a very good attendance on both occasions. The Headmaster was absent on the 22nd to attend the Convocation at the University of Reading and to be present at the opening of the new Faculty of Letters building by H.M. the Queen. In the District Cross-Country on the 23rd the school won the Open Championship and the Closed District Championship. At the Drama Festival on the same day the one-act play 'What do you think' was presented.

The Open Evenings on April 2 and 3 consisted of one-act plays, a French play, displays of country dancing and separate boys and girls physical education. Again the events were very well supported adding money to the Pavilion Fund.

On the beautifully sunny day of April 4 the school celebrated its fiftieth birthday. A commemoration service was held at St. Mary's Church conducted by the Rev. E. Barnes, the Rev. G.H. Cook and the Rev. J. Mudd. The address was given by the Rev. J. Leslie Webb. A truly memorable service with inspired singing. Mrs. Sheasby and members of the Board of Governors attended. It was intended to compile a commemoration magazine. Among the 82 guests at the Celebration Dinner was the Mayor, Mrs. B. Sheasby (Vice-Chairman of Berkshire Education Committee), the Town Clerk, Director of Education, Mr. E. Preston, Dr. Bell together with former and present members of staff with their wives and husbands. Old Gordonians were also represented. A special day's holiday to mark the occasion was granted for the 5th when Easter holidays began. Leavers 21. It was Mrs. Fleming's last day.

Under the direction of Mr. C.E. Jeavons an excellent lectern had been constructed and a special table made for the Mayor's parlour.

In accordance with the new Burnham Report posts of responsibility were:-

Deputy Head – Mr. R.H. Tomlin, master in charge Arithmetic

Heads of Department
Mr. E. Stanbrook-Evans, master in charge Mathematics and Geography to 'O' level and with responsibility for co-ordination with Science
Miss M.M. Claydon, mistress in charge of English and History and with responsibility for the Library

Mr. F. H. Harmsworth, master in charge of Handicraft.

Graded Posts
Miss K. Phillips, mistress in charge of Pre-Nursing, Biology and Girls welfare
Mr. E. Lacy, master in charge of Art and Crafts throughout school
Mr. R. Bristow, master in charge of French throughout school
Mr. K. Horne, master in charge of Physical Education and Games
Mr. L.J.C. Monk, master in charge of Science
Vacancy, mistress in charge of Domestic Subjects.

Miss H.M. Baldwin was appointed on April 30 as Assistant Mistress (Domestic Science) for the Summer Term. The Rev. M. Paterson addressed the school on May 9 and a Y.W.C.A. talk during the month. A small group attended the Mayor making ceremony on the 22nd.

29 girls and 19 boys together with Mr. and Mrs. Tomlin, Mrs. Sweet, Miss Taylor, Mr. Horne and the Headmaster left for Strathpeffer, Ross-shire, on May 31 returning on June 9. They visited Inverness, Culloden Moor, John O'Groats and explored the rugged area in the west of Ross and Cromarty. Weather permitting it was hoped to ascend Ben Wyvis (3,429 feet) from which the view embraces the Ord of Caithness, the Moray Firth and the coast of Aberdeenshire, Ben Nevis and the varied forms of countless hills.

St. Cloud (Maidenhead's twin town) ceremonies was held on June 4. A mobile nursing exhibition on the 7th and youth employment interviews on the 17th and 18th. Medical inspections on the 19th and 20th, G.C.E. examinations commencing on the 21st.

Mr. W.A. Roberts was nominated as a co-operative Governor in place of Mr. A.C. Firth.

June 26 was the school journey to the Isle of Wight.

Six boys Peter Doe, David Church, Anthony Corbett, Robin Furlong, Roger Rackley and Robin Brooks were selected for the pilot scheme of the Duke of Edinburgh Award (registered charity founded in 1956). At a week-end camp at Avon Tyrrell they gained first certificates, David Church was one of only two boys out of 37 to get an 'A' award.

The Whit Monday Fete held by the Old Gordonians Association raised £150 for the Pavilion Fund.

On July 1 Mr. Adderson celebrated the 21st anniversary of his appointment as Headmaster, the Governors granting a half-day holiday to mark the occasion.

Sports Day was on July 5. The Governors attended the school on the 16th to present an electric clock as a Jubilee Year gift. The following day was the Schools' Swimming Gala when Gordon won the Norris Cup for the highest aggregate of points, the Curtis Shield for the Team Race, the 100 yards boys championship and the boys Diving Cup. Jubilee Open Day was on the 18th when an extremely large and appreciative number of visitors included the Chairman of Governors, other Governors, the Deputy Mayor and the Divisional Officer. The Inter-House Swimming Gala was on the 22nd. School closed on the 23rd the last day for Miss Baldwin and Mr. Curd who left to take up primary work with a view to obtaining a Headship. He had given good service to the school for the past six years.

The Education Officer stated the Authority had been requested to carry out the adaptation of the second cloakroom into changing rooms and showers at the same time as the first cloakroom so that the advantage of a single piece of work by one contractor might be derived.

The Rev. J. Mudd resigned from the Board of Governors following his new appointment.

School re-assembled on September 11 with the following new staff:-

Mrs. A.C. Morton (Domestic Science)
Mr. H.E. Jones (General Subjects)
Mrs. P. East (English) now full-time
Miss P.E. Cook (English)
A new Cook Supervisor and a new Assistant caretaker.

N.O.R. Boys 257, Girls 268 = 525 the school now equal to a Group X establishment. Previous figures for October 1954 473; 1955 479; 1956 480.

The experimental period ended with four candidates gaining the following G.C.E. successes:-

John Goddard – English Language; Mathematics (76%); Geography (68%)
Clive Penney – English Language; Mathematics; Geography
Margaret Smith – English Language
Jennifer Markham – Household Cookery.

John Goddard had been transferred to the County Boys' Grammar School to take his Advanced Level subjects.

Two girls, Janet Jones and Susan Ward gained the Royal Society of Arts Stage I Elementary Typewriting Certificates. A full group will, next year for the first time, take a wide range of subjects.

During the summer vacation the practical block was re-decorated internally and externally. New exit doors were provided in the Science and Metalwork rooms. The small hall was now used as a form room.

Four teachers of English in French schools spent the day observing on September 19. The school closed on the 25th due to an outbreak of influenza. It was agreed that there would be no half-term holiday during the current term.

The Simplicity Pattern Show was on October 10; nurses examined heads on the 17th; dental inspections on the 23rd and 24th; a performance of Oliver Twist on the 31st.

With the introduction of examination courses, capitation rates for books and stationery were proving inadequate. There was now no reason why secondary children of equivalent ages should receive equal allowances. A Grammar school boy of 12 years had an allowance of 53/- but a Secondary Modern pupil only 29/- (It was eventually hoped to bring the level of secondary modern pupils capitation allowances in line with Grammar pupils over a period of three years).

It was fitting that the awards on Jubilee Prize Day should be distributed by the Director of Education, Mr. T.D.W. Whitfield in the presence of the Chairman of the Education Committee on November 13. A Prize Day holiday was granted for the 27th. Opening of the new pavilion by Mrs. Barbara Sheasby to mark the Golden Jubilee occurred in December. The Director of Education, Chairman of Governors and representatives of the Old Gordonians were present.

A carol service was held at St. Mary's Church on December 16 and at the Methodist Church on the 18th. Christmas holidays began on the 20th. Leavers 28.

1958

Re-open January 7. An 'all clean' hair inspection took place on the 16th.

Work commenced on the new art-room block and on the enlargement of the junior girls' lobby. The Governors were informed that the proposed alterations to the County Girls' Grammar School which will eventually become an annexe to Gordon School had been approved as a minor project and work would commence during the summer holidays. It was anticipated it would be ready for occupation in January 1959.

Mrs H. A. Rourke commenced on February 1 and Mr S. Platt was elected to the Governing Body.

The Open Evenings on March 31 and April 1 were both well attended. Mr Horne left on April 2.

N.O. R. 494 (boys 245, girls 249). A likely build up of pupils was forecast as:

1958	intake	215	Roll	615
1959	intake	215	Roll	730
1960	intake	215	Roll	845
1961	intake	215	Roll	940

It was unlikely to be affected to any extent by the opening of the Furze Platt Secondary Modern School.

A party of eighteen pupils in the care of Mr Bristow and Miss Jackson left for an 8 day trip to Paris on April 10. It was hoped to visit: Ile de la Cite, Notre Dame Cathedral, Flower Market, Conciegerit Revolution Souvenirs, Port Neuf, Parc de Vincennes and Zoo, Latin Quarter, Local Market, a boat trip on the Seine, the Eiffel Tower, the British Embassy Church, Versailles via St Cloud, the Arc de Triomphe, Champs Elysees and Gobelins, the manufacture of tapestries and carpets, large Parisian stores, Montmartre, Louvre, Tuileries Gardens and Rue de Tivoli.

Mr R. H. Tomlin the Deputy Headmaster and a member of staff for eleven years had been appointed Headmaster of Wallingford County Modern School and left on April 30. It was Mr C. Ganz last day too. Leavers at Easter 24.

It was not possible to ascertain the number of children who would require dinners in September. It did seem certain that three shifts would be necessary and some adjustment in school hours would have to be made to lengthen the dinner period. In spite of the difficulties involved it would still be wise to accept the large intake of 215 into the main school for the new term.

Mr T. J. Richards (English) took up his appointment on May 1 and Mrs Lancaster-Jones commenced on the 2nd. Medical inspections on May 3, 14 and 15 and three scholars visited the Mayor making ceremony on the 20th. The Commonwealth Day visit by the Mayor Councillor T. Bailey, an old boy of the school and the first former pupil to hold that office was accompanied by Alderman Neve, the Town Clerk, Mrs Bromley, Mr Hammett and Mr Hewitt. Youth employment interviews were on the 29th and 30th, the French oral examination at the Technical College, Reading on the 31st. The school supported the Drama and Music Festivals during the month.

Mr E. H. Stanbrook-Evans became the new Deputy Head.

A parent presented the school with a second-hand milling machine which Mr. Harmsworth repaired and painted.

In the District Athletics a new record for the long jump was set up by R. Holland and in the Cross Country the team won the Maidenhead Closed Championship and was placed second in the Area Championship. Ten boys participated in the Duke of Edinburgh's Award tests for bronze and silver medals and a party with Mr Lacy in charge visited the Royal Tournament.

N.O.R. boys 235, girls 233 = 468. The intake for September decided by the Divisional Executive was 215 and already 280 applications had been received.

The school closed on July 11 when the Examination Form and six staff visited West Wittering and Guildford Cathedral. A large number of parents and friends together with the Mayor and Mayoress, Mrs. Jarvis and School Governors supported Open Day on the 17th. Holidays began on the 23rd, Mrs. C.M. Butler (P.E.) deciding to give up teaching. Leavers 65. In view of the coming expansion of the school, the lack of applications from men teachers was disturbing. Three vacancies remained to be filled.

Twenty pupils took G.C.E. Examinations analysed below:-

6 subjects	2 pupils
5 subjects	3 pupils
4 subjects	7 pupils
3 subjects	5 pupils
2 subjects	2 pupils
1 subject	1 pupil

including English Language; English Literature; French; Religious Education; Geography; History; Household Cookery; Needlework; Metalwork; Human Biology; Mathematics and Art. Results:-

3 candidates gained five passes
4 candidates gained four passes
9 candidates gained one to three.

Two successful candidates transferred to the Girls' High School for advanced work and two boys obtained posts which would not be open to them without passes in the appropriate G.C.E. subjects.

In swimming the boys gained the Norris Cup for the highest aggregate of points at the Maidenhead and District Gala. John Bell won the 100 yards championship for the third successive year and the boys won the team championship and the diving. Parties have visited the Ideal Homes Exhibition, the Planetarium and Science Museum in addition to the Ernest Reed concerts at the Festival Hall.

School re-opened on September 9, 205 eleven plus children being admitted. Six Form Rooms, the Hall and the Domestic Science Rooms were re-decorated during the holidays. N.O.R. boys 305, girls 295 = 600 (1955 479; 1956 480; 1957 528). In view of the greatly increased numbers the Education Committee decided that the new group number should be XIII (IX). This affected the number of special allowances and made provision for a new post of Senior Mistress.

Posts of Special Responsibility:-

Deputy Head
Mr. E.H. Stanbrook-Evans, Master in charge of Mathematics and Geography

Senior Mistress
Miss M.M. Claydon

Heads of Department

Mr. R. Bristow	Master in charge of English and French
Mr. L.J.C. Monk	Master in charge of Science
Mr. F.H. Harmsworth	Master in charge of Handicraft

Graded Posts

Mr. E. H. Lacy	Master in charge Art and Craft
Mrs. A.C. Morton	Mistress in charge Domestic Science
Miss K.E.F. Phillips	Mistress in charge Pre-Nursing and Girls Welfare
Mr. C.E. Jeavons	Master in charge Woodcraft
Vacancy	Master in charge P.E. and Games
Vacancy	Mistress in charge Needlecraft
Mr. F.G. Albon	Master in charge Music
Mr. H.A.T. Johnson	Master in charge English and Drama.

New staff:-
Mrs. S. Bowditch (P.E.)
Miss S. Moore (Art & Craft)
Miss J. Rees (English & History)
Miss G. Williams (Mathematics & English)
Mrs. P.R. O'Neill (Needlecraft)
Mr. D.J. Hunt (Mathematics)
Mrs. P. Johnson (Commercial Work & Supply Teaching).

The Art and Craft room came into use for the first time as did the new junior lobby and changing room.

It was the intention to transfer first year pupils (206) to the annexe. They would assemble and dine at the annexe but report to the main school for practical subjects and games. Every effort would be made to avoid movement during sessions.

Dental inspections took place on September 16 and school

closed for the annual Conference on the 26th.

Lieut D.M. Davies spoke to the Naval Cadets on October 22; six boys with the Headmaster attended a United Nations service at Southwark Cathedral on the 26th, Peter Doe and Robin Brooks going on to a reception given by Sir John Hunt; a group visited the Christian Council Exhibition on the 30th.

Lady Helen Smith, member of Berkshire Education Committee and Chairman of Berkshire Association of Mixed and Girls' Clubs distributed the awards on Prize Day, November 5. The Mayor (a former pupil) and Mayoress were present. Maidenhead Music Club gave a Dancing of Spain on the 27th.

The Rotary Club Lunch for 'Service above Self' prize winners Jacqueline Denmark and Robin Furlong was on December 1; the Carol Service at St. Mary's Church on the 16th; the Prefects' Party on the 18th, school closing on the 19th. Leavers 36. The removal of equipment and furniture to the Annexe was made on the 31st.

1959

The new term commenced on January 6. First year children did not attend as it was found necessary to grant them an extra day's holiday in order that the move to the Castle Hill Annexe might be effected more smoothly. The careful arrangements made were seriously affected by much staff illness. This combined with bad weather and the reconstruction work being carried out strained staff to the limit. (Staff illness on an unusual scale continued throughout the term).

New part-time teachers:- Miss S. Oberman, Mrs. M. Binder, Mrs. M. Stafford and Mrs. B. Freeth (both left in July). Miss Chalmers commenced duties as pianist. The request for additional member of staff was approved as two part-time teachers, a less satisfactory arrangement of the matter. An increase in the establishment of three additional teachers had been approved from September 1959.

A group visited the Ideal Home Exhibition on March 2; a member of the Christian Council Crusade addressed children during morning service on the 11th and a party attended a concert at the Festival Hall on the 21st.

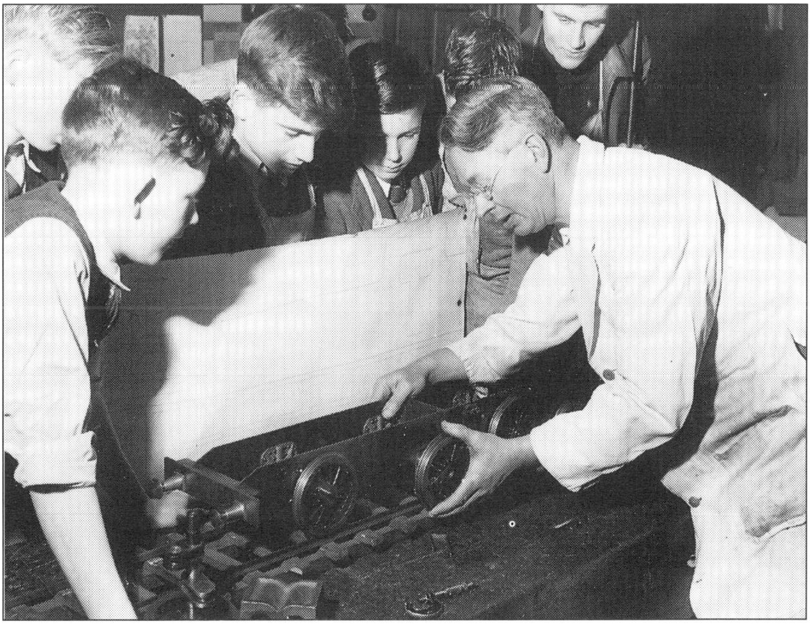

Mr. Harmsworth Master in Charge of Handicrafts.

Even before showers came into operation objections were raised by some parents. The aim was in taking showers customary rather than compulsory. The Governors were informed that a meeting was to take place during the month between certain parents and representatives of Governors to discuss the use of girls showers. Dr. Calder the Assistant Schools Medical Officer and Miss Court the Organiser of P.E. were invited to attend. Although the excuses advanced were not at all reasonable the problem was solved.

N.O.R. Boys 282, Girls 278 = 560. (1956, 446; 1957, 448; 1958, 494). Leavers at Easter 26.

Mr. F.H. Harmsworth tendered his resignation as master in charge of Handicraft and retired on March 25. He had given outstanding service to the school for twenty-four years. Mr. Jeavons would take over as teacher of Metalwork and master in charge of Handicraft and Mr. M.B. Kinch (commenced April 15) would be in charge of Woodwork. It was also recommended that

Mrs. F.B. Blay be given the graded post as Mistress with responsibility for Needlework and for the welfare of the senior girls.

It was interesting to note that Mr. F.A. Denzey formerly Deputy Head had been appointed first Headmaster of the new Crowthorne and Sandhurst Secondary Modern School.

A party of twenty-seven children and five staff spent 10 days in Copenhagen starting on April 2. The route took them via Dover, Ostend, Brussels, Cologne, Dusseldorf, Essen, Munster, Osnabruch, Breman, Hamburg, Kiel, Flemsburg, and Odense was full of interest and especially the journey from Jutland across Funen and Zealand. Visits were made to the Royal Danish Porcelain factory, to a State Dairy Farm, the great Carlsberg Brewery, the National Museum, the Resistance Movement Museum, the Danish Ballet, the busy dock area, Copenhagen Zoo, Elsinore, Frederiksborg Castle, the Royal Palace, Helsingborg (Sweden) and, of course, the Little Mermaid.

The Rev. Sedgman addressed the school on April 23, the Concert and Display was on May 5, a group visited the Planetarium, Science Museum and Imperial Institute on the 8th, a Festival Hall Concert on the 9th, two senior pupils attended the Mayor making ceremony at the Guildhall on the 20th, the day of the French Oral examination, a group with Mr. Monk visited Reading Power Station on the 25th, the Music Festival on the 26th and the Matron of Mile End Hospital addressed children on the 27th.

The Headmaster attended the opening ceremony at Maidenhead High School on June 2. G.C.E. examinations in Metalwork on the 3rd and 4th and English Language on the 8th. The school won the Girls' Championship at the N.E. Berks. Athletics on June 4. – Clarke beat the javelin record, – Potter equalled the 100 yards record and – James beat the hurdles record. The 15–17 boys relay was also won by the school. Mrs. Birch lectured to the Duke of Edinburgh award girls. School leavers interviews were held on the 10th and 11th. A group visited the Royal Tournament on the 16th and parents enrolled new pupils on the 16th and 17th.

N.O.R. in June 535. Estimated intake for September 210, estimated roll 700.

The Headmaster and Mr. Stanbrook-Evans visited Brunel College on July 2 and Mr. Adderson and Mr. Jeavons Shoreditch Training College on the 7th. Mrs. Blay with six girls visited the College of Art Dress Show on the 8th. Inter-House Athletics was on the 10th and the Gala on the 20th. Governors together with a large number of parents took the opportunity to see the school, inspect the work on view and discuss children with staff at the Open Day on the 16th. Summer holidays began on the 22nd. Leavers 55. The following staff resigned:- Mr. T. Johnson (English), Mr. R. Monk (Science), Mr. F. Albon (Music), Miss Williams (English & Mathematics), Miss S. Moore (Art), Mr. Kinch (Woodcraft), Mrs. P. Johnson (Secretary & Commercial), Mrs. Sweet (Needlecraft) and Mrs. H. Rourke (Secretary).

G.C.E. results (with number of passes) came through in August:- Iris Marshall (4), David Church (3), John Clarke (3), Carole Smith (2), Patricia Squire (2), Christine Folland, Rosemary Plummer, Glenise Redding, Veronica Taylor, Peter Banks and Roger Woolcott (all one each).

Commercial Subjects:- Pitman Elementary Typewriting – Shirley Clarke, Patricia Penfold, Sandra Mitchell, Susan Norris, Barbara Evesden, Rosemary Plummer, Patricia Squire, Christine Nowell and Cynthia Smith. Shorthand Theory Stage I:- Shirley Clarke and Patricia Penfold.

It is interesting to record that John Goddard who was transferred to the Grammar School two years ago gained passes in three subjects at Advanced Level and one at Scholarship Level. He will continue his studies at the Brunel College of Advanced Technology. Former pupils Miss Josephine Huckle gained a Gold Medal in the Maidenhead Hospital Final Examinations – the first for some years – and also the Prize for Medicine. Miss Evelyn Hull won the Senior Nursing prize. One girl had been transferred to Maidenhead High School Sixth Form this year.

Mr. N. Hewitt had resigned as a Governor and was succeeded by Mr. A.E. Wheeler.

205 new pupils from primary schools were admitted for the new term on September 8. New staff:- Mr. A. Baker (Science), Mr. L.H. Piercey (Music), Mr. M.J. Reading (English and History), Mr. A.C. Barrett (Art), Mr. M.S. Organ (English), Mrs. D.M. Wilson (English and Mathematics), Mrs. P.M. Jones (General Subjects)

and Mr. T. Stone (Handicraft). Part-time:- Mrs. M.O. Brown, Mrs. W.M. Brown and Mrs. Lancaster-Jones.

Establishment:-

Head and full time staff	29
Part time staff	5
Clerical Assistants	2
Caretaking	6
Canteen	13
Groundsman	1
	56

Revised Posts of Special Responsibility:-

Mr. Lacy Master in charge of Art and Craft
Mr. Jones Master in charge of Science to 'O' Level G.C.E.
Miss Jackson Mistress in charge of Girls Geography, Junior School Mathematics and Girls Cloakrooms.

Four terrapin classrooms came into use. A party visited Mile End Hospital on September 29. N.O.R. 685.

An Extraordinary Joint Meeting of the Schools Management Committee was held at the Guildhall on October 13. A parent whose application had not been successful referred the case to the Minister of Education who requested the Authority to admit the boy as he had determined on the circumstances made known to him that admission had been refused on other than reasonable grounds. The Joint Committee unanimously supported the Governors action, declared their inability to comply with the Minister's request and asked that the Minister receive a deputation comprising of four Governors together with the Director of Education and the Divisional Education Officer. This took place at the Ministry on Thursday October 15.

A recommendation for the necessary development to bring the school up to a three-form entry standard had been included in the 1962/3 major building programme.

A Simplicity Fashion Display was held on October 9 and a talk by the Youth Employment Officer on the 12th.

The awards for Prize Day on November 4 were distributed by Sir William Mount in the presence of Mrs. Sheasby, Mrs. Jarvis

(Chairman, Education Finance Committee), the Director of Education, the Divisional Officer and members of the Governors. The following day a group in the charge of Mr. Bristow and Mr. Organ saw a performance of As You Like It at the Old Vic. Youth Employment interviews on the 9th and 10th, the Headmaster visits Blackstone School on the 11th and attends the Grammar School Prize Day on the 12th, a party was at the opening of the Junior Library on the 13th, a concert by the Berkshire String Players in the main school on the 17th and medicals on the 23rd, 24th and 25th.

Mrs. Erskine, Secretary and teacher of Commercial Subjects commenced on December 1. Dental inspections on the 1st, 2nd and 3rd. A cross country run on the 10th, the junior carol service at the Methodist Church on the 11th, the senior at St. Mary's Church on the 13th, the staff play on the 15th, a film show on the 17th school closing on the 18th. Leavers 27. In a period of three weeks £80 was contributed to the local World Refugee Appeal.

Five shifts were in operation to cope with the demand for school meals, six would be necessary in September 1960. Moderation of the main dining room was essential if sound social training was to be maintained and extension of the dinner hour avoided. Additional furniture for the Annexe Dining Room would also be required. Arrangements were being made to provide extra space in the main school dining room to accommodate 144 on each of three sittings by removing the partition and storage room.

1960

Re-open January 6. A W.R.N.S. lecture on the 11th and medicals on 19th, 20, 21, 26 and 27th.

After a year's experience of the Annexe it became clear that the divided school and the movement that resulted was affecting children adversely. The general standard of behaviour was not so high, they were much more restless and it took more time to settle to their work. Loss of time was not inconsiderable. It would help for a gymnasium to be installed at the main school together with additional hard playing surface. Playgrounds are now very crowded and the work of the P.E. specialists extremely demanding. The lobbies, now ready for occupation, brought welcome relief as cloakroom facilities had always been poor. It was hoped that two more terrapin rooms would be provided in time for the Autumn Term.

A youth employment talk occurred on February 11 followed by interviews on March 1 and 3rd. A lecture on Australia on February 25 and a W.R.A.F. talk on March 1. Form IVB visited the Handicraft Exhibition at County Hall on March 10, a party at the Ideal Home Exhibition on the 15th.

Because of the success of an old school boy (J.A. Madden) who had proved to be the best all round recruit at a naval school, Gordon was to be presented by the Admiralty with a set of four books for the School's Library. The presentation by Commander Wynne, R.N. took place on Thursday March 17.

Thirteen year olds had an eye inspection on March 18, a group of senior pupils with Mr. Bristow in charge saw a performance of The Importance of Being Earnest at the Old Vic on the 19th, police inspected cycles on the 21st and a Road Safety talk on the 24th.

Mr. Bristow gave a teaching demonstration with a group of children from IVA at a week-end course for teachers of modern languages at the University of Reading during the month.

No applications had been received for the vacancy for the Summer Term nor for the three additional posts for September. A serious situation could arise if they are not filled soon as there were already four unqualified members of staff.

Two plays were presented for the Drama Festival at the School Concert at St. Mary's Church Hall on April 5 – The Great Walk and The Man in the Bowler Hat.

After full consideration it was agreed to adopt the following policy regarding first year admissions:-

(a) those children with close family connections should have a prior claim of entry to the school.
(b) those children from primary school of the area (Courthouse) should normally be admitted as a matter of course.
(c) girls from Ellington County Primary School should have a preference to places.
(d) remaining applications should be considered by the House

Committee on their merits giving consideration to applications from every school.

(It was anticipated that the roll for September would be 770 plus). It was also agreed that the Headmaster should not interview parents of children until after it had been decided who would be admitted and that the information required by the House Committee should be incorporated in the return requested of parents of first year admissions. It stated in the letter that parents request for the school did not imply the right of admission and that personal applications to the school should not be made until the parent is advised in which school the child had been given a place (in consultation with other Secondary Modern School Head Teachers).

School closed on April 6, Mr. Baker's last day. Leavers 32. A school party with Mr. Bristow visited Amsterdam for one week. Re-open on the 28th with Mr. R. Wells for one term only.

The G.C.E. Cookery Practical took place on May 2; a talk by Major P. McDonnell of the W.R.A.C. on the 12th and on the 25th Sylvia Rackley gained first prize in the Children's Newspaper Handwriting Competition, age group 13–18 years. A cheque for £50 was awarded to the school, £10 to Sylvia. (The money was used to augment the library allowance).

At the District Athletics on June 2 the girls won the championship, the boys came third and D. Reynolds held the record in the 15–17 year age group high jump. French oral examinations took place on the 8th and youth employment interviews during the latter part of the month.

The Headmaster attended the funeral of Mr. J.E. Cluff, a master at the school from 1907 until his retirement in 1946, on July 4.

A party visited H.M.S. Vernon at Portsmouth on July 13, School Sports on the 14th, swimming sports and tests on the 18th and 20th. At the District Gala Peter Smith won the 100 yards championship. A very high proportion of pupils were able to swim and many gained certificates of merit during the season. Open Day between 2pm and 9pm on the 21st was extremely well attended.

The Divisional Education Officer reported that the Authority had submitted to the Ministry for inclusion in the Major Building Programme for 1962/3 extensions and adaptations to bring the school up to the required size for the three-form entry mixed secondary modern school, and in the event of this project not being included in that programme include in the 1960/61 a minor project consisting of a gymnasium and changing rooms. (It was not included but under consideration for 1961/2).

School closed on July 22 the following staff relinguishing their posts:- Mrs. A.C. Morton, Mrs. S.A. Bowditch, Mrs. P. Jones and Miss J.C. Rees. Mr. E.J. Furness and Mr. R. Wells held temporary appointments prior to entering training college.

G.C.E. results showed individuals gained the highest possible grade in Physics, French and Art. Two boys reached a sufficiently high standard to qualify for transfer to the Grammar School Sixth Form. In:-

5 subjects:-	Brian Clayden, Roger Hunneman
4 subjects:-	David Bates, Christopher Rush, Clive Andrews, Roma Wadhams, Janet Chamberlain
3 subjects:-	Michael Vogt, Ann Hubach, Gaynor Whitham
2 subjects:-	Susan Anlez, Josephine Castle, William Barnes, Ian Benson, Michael Jackson, Ian Seagrove
1 subject:-	Lawrence Frew, Dudley Reynolds, John Wilkey, Anne Ryalls.

Typewriting:- Pitman's Elementary, Mary Collins, Gloria Clarke, Ann Hatcher, Monica Pearce, Josephine Ranscombe, Janet Soden, Kristine Worlock, Mary Williams.

Jacqueline Denmark who was transferred to the High School Sixth Form on her 'O' level results in 1958 gained admission to a teachers' training college.

The new term commenced on September 7 with the following new staff:-

Mrs. L.Z. Halford	P.E. (became a graded post)
Mrs. E.M. Walker	P.E. (one term only)
Miss P. Williams	History and English
Miss M.J. Scott	Mathematics and Games
Miss S.E.A. Shayler	English and History
Mr. Hugo de Schanschieff	English and History
Mr. Ian Severn	Geography
Mr. D. Robinson	Science
Mr. V.E. Hurrion	General and Commercial Subjects

Two additional Terrapin classrooms had been erected, as a result no serious teaching space problem during 1960–61. The school continued to be seriously affected by lack of Physical Education, Science and Drama facilities on the main site. It was unable to compete on equal terms with other secondary modern schools at tennis, netball, cricket and athletics. The removal of the playing field improvement scheme from the estimates was a great disappointment to both the school and the Old Gordonians.

Experience showed it was not the best arrangement for the Annexe to be the base for all the first year children. Next session classes from the entire age range would occupy the buildings and an endeavour, though difficult, would be made to reduce movement between the two departments.

After many complaints staff and pupils regretted the felling of the poplar trees. Children worked on the garden site – as many as 250 at a time – and although trees were replanted, the area appeared much less attractive.

A graded post was granted to Mr. Organ as from September 1. School closed for the annual conference on the 30th.

The Headmaster and six pupils attended the twinning ceremony at the Town Hall and Skindles on October 5; a talk by Youth Employment Officers on the 10th; five staff attended a meeting to welcome new entrants to the profession on the 13th; a Nursing Recruitment Officer addressed senior girls on the 18th.

N.O.R. 694 which included 153 admissions from Primary Schools.

Youth employment interviews on November 7 and 16; Mr. Bristow and Mr. Organ visited the A.E.B. English Conference on the 12th; the McCall Fashion Display for older girls was on the 22nd.

The principal guest for Prize Day on November 25 was Mr. S.E. Goodall, M.Sc. (Eng.), F.Q.M.C., M.I.E.E., Director of Engineering, Associated Electrical Industries (Woolwich) Ltd. Also present was the Mayor and Mayoress, Councillor and Mrs. Abell, Mrs. E. Jarvis, the Divisional Officer and School Governors.

Sir John Hunt paid an informal visit to speak to the Duke of Edinburgh Award Group on December 1. (The three gold award boys who accompanied Sir John on the Greenland Expedition had a remarkable experience. One was chosen for a special and very demanding mission from which he emerged with real credit and high praise from Dr. Slessor).

A half-day's holiday was granted for December 2. No local church was now available to seat the entire school for carol services so 500 children attended St. Mary's and nearly 200 St. Mark's Crescent Methodist. Christmas vacation began on the 20th, Mrs. Walker and Mrs. Cadwalada leaving. Leavers 25.

Concern was raised over children who cycled between the Annexe and the main school because of a dangerous crossing. It was felt that if parents were agreeable then the responsibility was theirs. Mr. Bristow was responsible for the production of the first School Magazine.

1961

Re-open January 10 with two new members of staff; Mrs. E. Miller and Mrs A. Hill. A party visited the Mermaid Theatre for a performance of Emil and the Detectives on the 27th. Mr. Bristow attended a French Language course at the B.B.C. on the 30th.

The Pearce Hall became available at the beginning of the year. It was used on four mornings and one afternoon weekly. Although again, movement was involved, the pressure on P.E. accommodation was relieved. Ann Hubach was awarded the Berkshire County Pies Prize for Domestic Science.

Medical inspections were carried out on February 1, 2, 7, 8, 13, 14, 22, 23 and 28. Tuberculin testing and B.C.G. immunisation were offered to all thirteen year old children. A Commonwealth lecture on the S.W. Pacific by Mrs. E.S. Rutter was on February 6 and a lecture with coloured slides of outstanding quality on Ghana by Mr. Dennis Kemp of Kodak Ltd was on the 22nd. Groups visited the Old Vic to see "As You Like It", Orchestral Concerts at the Festival Hall and senior girls the Ideal Homes Exhibition.

Following the School Inter-House event a team took part in the Berks. Championships at Thatcham. The best performer was placed 20th in a field of nearly 200. A newly formed chess club had its first match when Borlase School were the visitors.

Youth employment interviews with parents and leavers took place on March 1 and 2; an A.C.F. lecture on the 13th; medicals on the 15th; Music Festival and a talk on the A.T.C. on the 16th; dental inspections 17th; an Ernest Reed concert 18th; the school presented a three act play "The Government Inspector" by Nikolai Gogal at St. Mary's Hall on the 21st and 22 (good audiences) and dental inspections again 24th. At the end of term Mr. de Schanschieff (History and English) and Mr. A.C. Barrett (Art) resigned. Leavers at Easter 29.

It was reported that Secondary School Heads proposed Gordon should concentrate on the development of the following courses as centres of interest for the general education of its pupils:-

Art and Craft course designed to cover design in its widest sense, and Craft including such things as printing.

Science course, the object of which would be to provide a general education based on scientific principles

In addition it may be possible to develop special facilities for Music at the school at which the more able instrumentalists in the area would gather on a certain number of occasions.

Re-open April 20 with two members of staff for one term only:- Mr. C.J. Ross and Mrs. John. Lawrence Frew and Susan Greaves attended the Rotary Club Lunch on the 24th.

A discussion concerning the development of the school with the Deputy Director and the Divisional Officer was held on May 1; a party visited the Aldershot Tattoo on the 3rd. The first party to travel by air flew by B.E.A. Viscount to Belfast and proceeded by rail and coach to County Donegal on the 5th. Thirty-eight pupils accompanied by the Headmaster, Mr. D. Robinson and Miss K. Taylor had a birds eye view of the Mersey, North Wales, the Isle of Man and the Belfast area. Five boys led by Mr. Robinson on one occasion covered thirty-two miles on foot including the ascent of Lough Salt Mountain. They made no attempt to take advantage of a lift on the way home. A most enjoyable week's journey. Three pupils attended the Mayor making ceremony on the 24th.

The School closed for the District Athletics on June 1 and G.C.E. examinations were in progress by the 12th. At the end of the month Mr. Adderson had completed twenty-five years as Headmaster and a full day's holiday was granted to mark the special occasion.

Because of the number of 'B' candidates who had been given

grammar school places the N.O.R. for admission in September was now 147 (76 boys, 71 girls). Four boys and three girls who had not been able to get at their second choice of school (Wargrave) should be admitted. Present roll 626, anticipated intake 152, applications for admission 240, anticipated roll 726.

A final schedule of accommodation had been drawn up and the Architect instructed to prepare an outline plan for the development of the complete school. The first instalment, a gymnasium with ancillary accommodation was to commence during the current financial year.

Concern was expressed over certain boys who dashed away from school in the evening in order to collect papers from the station at four o'clock. As children should not be employed after school until 5 o'clock according to Bye-Laws, the matter was reported to the School Attendance Sub-Committee with a request that action should be taken against the employers concerned.

Eight pupils with the Headmaster attended the Freedom of the Borough Ceremony honouring Alderman Neve, a Governor of the School on July 13. Good attendance for the Open Day on the 20th.

At the District Swimming Gala the school won the Norris Cup for the highest aggregate of points, both the boys and the girls being top of their sections. The school also won the 100 yards free style championship for girls, the 100 yards breast stroke championship and the boys diving championship. The inter-schools swimming sports held in glorious weather were very successful but bad weather caused the athletics sports to be cancelled.

Summer holidays began on July 26 the following staff terminating their employment – Mr. V. Hurrion (Commercial Subjects), Mr. M.J. Reading (History and English), Miss M.J. Scott (Maths and P.E.), Mrs. E. Miller (P.E.) returning with husband to Rhodesia, Mrs. A. Hill (Domestic Science, temp), Mr. P. Toseland (Art, temp). During the vacation Mr. D.H. Robinson was obliged to send in his resignation because of urgent family difficulties in Bermuda. Leavers 73.

Fewer candidates sat for G.C.E. examinations this year – eighteen compared with twenty-six in 1960. Results were extremely pleasing in some subjects but disappointing in others.

Quite outstanding was the standard reached in Mathematics – four candidates gained Grade I passes and two Grade II passes. No candidate failed in Physics and Human Biology and again candidates were much more successful in French than in their own language. Susan Greaves gained six passes and with two others was transferred to the Grammar School Sixth Form. A disturbing feature had been the unreliability of parents' promises. Having asked for their children to join a particular course they have removed them part-way through without adequate reason.

Names and number of passes:-

Susan Greaves	SIX
Susan Rackley, Richard Astley, Malcolm Hagen	FOUR
Jennifer Free, Derek Ingram, Ronald Stacey	THREE
Christopher Allaway, Richard Allen, Michael Bradley	TWO
Kaye Meredith, Jean Woodley, Roger Foster-Smith	ONE

Pitman's Typewriting Examinations (Elementary) passes:-

Jennifer Wilder, Valerie Tugwell, Diane Goulden, Christina Castell, Teresa Sawyer, Maureen Gould, Jean Woodley, Priscilla Layton, Penelope Hopgood, Barbara Croxford, Marion Bunce, Kaye Meredith, Rosalind Woodruff, Phyllis Holden, Sheila Campbell.

Autumn Term began on September 6 with the following new staff:-

Mrs. P. Pethybridge (History and English)
Mrs. R. Beech (P.E. and Maths)
Mr. R.H. Shadbolt (History and English)
Mr. T.L. Richards (Art) attended course at Reading Institute during term
Part-time:- Mrs. A.J. Good (History and English), Mrs. T.M. Miller (Dom. Science), Mrs. Binstead (Commercial Subjects)
Temporary:- Mr. P.N. Stallwood (General Subjects).

Under the system operated by the Ministry of Education Mlle Michele J.R. Sauveplane had been appointed as French Assistant for the period September 1961 to July 1962.

Mr. P.A.J. Hammett resigned from the Board of Governors and was succeeded by Mr. P.F. Murray. During the vacation Miss P.E.

Cook attended a month's course at Poitiers and Mr. Stone a fortnight's handicraft course. Mrs. Wilson and Miss Jackson completed a two year evening course in mathematics.

Miss J.F. Morgan (Science) commenced on October 2 until the end of term. Festival Hall concerts were on October 7, November 4 and December 2. Talks to school leavers took place on October 11, 19 and December 7 (interviews November 21 and 24) and a party visited the Minerva Ballet at Oxford on October 18.

It was found that a great deal of time could be saved if the girls' classes at the Annexe continued to use Kidwells Park for games three hours weekly.

The principal guest on Prize Day November 7 was Mr. W.R. van Straubenzee, M.B.E., M.P. for Wokingham and Parliamentary Private Secretary to the Minister of Education. The Headmaster attended Prize Days at Blackstone School, Wallingford on the 22nd and Boyne Hill School on the 23rd.

A Carol Service at the Congregational Church on December 13, St. Michael's Church, Bray on the 15th, a Christmas film show on the 18th school closing on the 20th. The following staff resigned – Mr. J.G. Wilkinson (P.E.), Miss Morgan, Mrs. Miller and Mrs. Potter (Domestic Science). Leavers 49. £62. 10s. 0d. was raised toward the upkeep of a twelve year old girl in the care of the Ockenden Venture. This pleasing total was reached largely as a result of activities planned by pupils.

Concern was expressed at the lack of liaison between Secondary Modern Schools and the College of Further Education. A letter was sent to the Governors of the East Berks College requesting there should be the same liaison as with Grammar Schools. (A meeting between respective Chairmen of Governors, the Headmaster, the Principal of the College and the Divisional Education Officer did take place during June 1962).

1962

Re-open January 10 with the following new staff – Mr. D. Warren (P.E. temp), Mr. J.W. Barnes (Science), Mrs. J.M. McQue (Homecraft), Mrs. C. John (Homecraft) and Mrs. J.H. Hovill (part-time for two terms only). Two parties from the Junior

School, one on the 16th, one on the 17th saw Toad of Toad Hall at the Saville Theatre. Medicals on January 23, 26, 30, February 2, 6, 9 and 13. Ernest Read concerts January 27 and February 17. Mr. Moreton left on January 31.

The Commercial Group visited the offices of Johnson & Johnson in Slough on February 8, the school teams won the East Berks Netball Rally on the 10th and Youth Employment interviews took place on the 14th, 15th and 16th.

The decision to remove a double unit to another school was a disappointment and a setback to plans for reducing movement.

Under the Beloe Report it appeared likely that the new Secondary Schools Certificate Examination would be introduced in the summer of 1964. This examination would provide an incentive for an additional 20% of the pupils and serve as a useful means of selection for further education courses. Discussions continued on a regional basis, exams would be teacher controlled and operated, groups of schools in the meantime undertaking experiments.

Her Majesty's Inspectors visited for two days during the term. Their comments were most encouraging, particular reference being made to the good standard of work in Mathematics, Physics and Metalcraft.

Members of staff attended week-end and evening courses on the "Use of English", "Primary and Secondary Transition" and on School Libraries.

Dr. E.M. Bell became the newly appointed Co-operative Governor.

Annexe children were given a talk on the N.S.P.C.C. on March 15, interviews for Summer Term leavers on the 19, 20 and 21 and Mr. Piercey attended a Music Course on the 28, 29 and 30. Senior girls visited the Ideal Homes Exhibition during the month.

The School was placed in Group XIV in April. The number of graded posts would increase to a total of eleven. Each Scale I post counted as one point, each Scale II post two points. The position in May would be:-

Mr. H.E. Jones	Scale II	Science
Miss K. Phillips	Scale I	Pre-Nursing
Mr. M. Organ	Scale I	Drama

Mrs. F.P. Blay	Scale I	Needlecraft
Mr. L.H. Piercey	Scale I	Music
Mr. D.C. Williams	Scale I	P.E.
Vacant		Domestic Science; Library
In abeyance		Girls P.E.; New Post.

The School participated in some of the functions connected with the New Town Hall Festival. Mr. Lacy spent much time in organising and arranging the School's Art and Craft display, performances of the children being of a high standard.

At the Drama Evenings on April 4 and 5 the school presented scenes from St. Joan (George Bernard Shaw) and The Little Man (John Galsworthy) at the Wesley Hall. The following day the Headmaster attended Prize giving at Edgbarrow School, Crowthorne. Close for Easter on the 12th when Miss M. Jackson, Mrs. A.J. Good, Mrs. T.Z. Halford, Miss S. Shayler, Miss P. Williams and Mrs. R. Beech all resigned. Leavers 40.

Re-open May 1 with new staff of Mrs. B.J. Evans (English) and Mr. J.K.C. Kemp (English) for one term only, Miss J.R. Hibberd (History, Geography and English) and Mr. D.C. Williams (P.E.). Mrs. B.M. Milne (P.E.) commenced on the 7th. G.C.E. examinations began on the 15th; six pupils attended the Mayor Making ceremony at the New Town Hall on the 23rd; Youth Employment interviews were on the 30th and 31st.

At the Maidenhead and District Athletic Club meeting which was open to schools in West Buckinghamshire and East Berkshire the boys trophy for the highest aggregate of points was won by the school. John Spratley set new records in the 100 yards (11 secs.) and 220 yards (24.7 secs.).

H.M. the Queen paid a visit to Maidenhead on June 25 to open the new Town Hall in St. Ives Road. The school was represented at the function.

Visits included the Science Museum and Planetarium, the R.A.F. Training School, Halton and to see "A Tale of Two Cities".

The school Swimming Gala took place on July 16. 416 pupils were able to swim and during the summer 23 boys and 25 girls gained their learner certificates. Summer holidays began on the 20th. Mr. E. Stanbrook-Evans, Deputy Headmaster, Head of the Mathematics and Geography Departments and a member of staff since 1950 left the school on his appointment as Headmaster of the Henderson School, Norwich. Mrs. P.R. O'Neill (Needlework Specialist) left as her husband was taking an appointment at Abingdon. Mr. J.K.C. Kemp (temporary) and Mrs. J.H. Hovill (part-time) also terminated.

Subjects taken in the G.C.E. examination included English Language, English Literature, French, Mathematics, Physics, Geography, History, Workshop Practice, Art and Crafts, Dress, Human Biology and Music. Results recorded:- Wilkins (6), Croxford (5), Foy, Vallis and Hopgood (4), Jennings, Saker and Wheeler (3), Britton, Thorne, Campbell, Layton and Morris (2), Dove, Bunce and Jarvis (1).

Outstanding individual gradings:-

English	Sheila Campbell*
	Thomas Vallis**
Art	Michael Foy*
	Thomas Vallis*
	Ronald Wilkins*
Mathematics	Thomas Vallis***
	Ronald Wilkins***
	John Wheeler***
Workshop Practice	Ronald Wilkins**

Grade I = *
Grade II = **
Grade III = ***

Typewriting Results – Intermediate:- Priscilla Layton, Marion Bunce, Angele Lelliott and Jennifer Wilder (2nd), Teresa Sawyer (1st). Elementary:- Valerie Andrews, Pat Wilson, Carol Mace and Angele Lelliott.

Members of staff attended courses on "The Teaching of Spelling", "Use of English", Domestic Subjects and "The Last Year at School". The vacant Scale I post was awarded to Mr. T. Stone of the Handicraft Department.

A special meeting was held on July 18 when two candidates were interviewed for the post of Deputy Headmaster. The third candidate, Mr. R. Bristow was unable to attend as he had suddenly been taken seriously ill. It was decided not to make an appointment until Mr. Bristow could be interviewed.

Mr. J.B. Maudsley resigned from the Governing Body and was succeeded by Mrs. M.E. Griffin.

Members of staff attended courses on:-

Organising a Department in a Secondary School
Certificate of Secondary Education
Teaching of Science
Secondary Girls' Gymnastics
Use and Effects of Nuclear Energy
Mrs. M.J. McQue – a vacation course on Domestic Science

Re-open September 11 with:-
Mr. J.H. Miller (Head of Mathematics Department)
Mrs. E.N.C. Pinnegar (English & French) – one term only
Miss J.C. Howe (P.E.)
Miss M.C. Evans – temporary
Mrs. J.D. Brown (Needlecraft) to take charge of Department in January 1963 following retirement of Mrs. F.P. Blay
Mrs. P.A. Mills (P.T. & Maths) – one term only
Mrs. B.J. Evans (temp. – further year extension)
Mrs. D.M. Wilson had a year's leave of absence to take an advanced Mathematics course. N.O.R. 708. Admissions from Primary Schools 172. Leavers summer 88.

Mr. Bristow was interviewed and promoted to the post of Deputy Headmaster and Mrs. G. John resigned on September 30.

Flying Officer J.A. Judd, W.R.A.F. Liaison Officer visited on October 2. Mr. Barnes attended a one week Science course at Maiden Erlegh School from October 26–31 and Miss Howe and Mrs. Milne a Gymnastic course on November 9. Prize Day was on November 14 when the Principal Guest was Air Marshal Sir Douglas Macfadyen. Youth employment interviews was on the 22nd, talks to Summer Term leavers (1963) December 6.

During the month parties attended performances of Hamlet and Henry V and carol services were held at St. Luke's and Methodist Churches. The last day of term (December 20) saw the retirement of Mrs. F.P. Blay after twenty years service and also the music master Mr. L.H. Piercey's resignation. Leavers 36. 524 meals were now being served daily in five shifts, three at the main school, two at the annexe. The two Grade I Posts of Responsibility were filled – Mrs. J.D.Brown (Needlecraft), Mr. I. Severn (Geography).

1963

The new term commenced January 8 with Mr. M.S. Carmack (Music), Mr. P. Mulliner (General Subjects) and Miss E. Williams (Needlecraft). On the 11th the school contributed £50 to the Ockenden Venture mainly for the upkeep of a girl formerly living in a displaced person's camp. From the 29th medical inspections took place on Tuesdays and Fridays for a period of four weeks.

A very useful discussion took place between Head Teachers of Charters (Sunningdale), Edgbarrow (Crowthorne), Cove (Farnborough), Gordon (Maidenhead) and Heads of Departments of English, Mathematics, Needlecraft and Handicraft in connection with the Certificate of Secondary Education. Syllabuses were prepared and sample questions drawn up. To gain experience certain groups of children would be unofficially examined next term and their work marked or assessed by panels of teachers from the four schools. The staff concerned spoke enthusiastically of the value of their meetings. Mr. Bristow had been chosen to be a member of the Modern Languages Subject Panel for the Southern Region.

Nine members of the fifth year had asked to be considered for transfer to the sixth forms of the Grammar School in order to undertake 'A' level work. Two former pupils had been accepted by Teacher Training Colleges this year and one other would complete her course in July.

Members of staff again attended courses on 'O' Level English Literature, Use of English and Handicraft at Slough, Reading and Maiden Erlegh respectively.

For some years considerable use had been made of the Domestic Science rooms by evening school groups. A request that the East Berks. College be asked to consider alternative accommodation for these groups or share the facilities available at the four secondary schools when preparations for their Autumn programme was made was suggested.

Youth employment interviews took place on February 13, March 19, 20 and 22. N.O.R. 664 (boys 351, girls 313).

March appeared a busy month. A visit by a theatre group on the 6th, the Simplicity Fashion Show on the 8th, a group visited the

Ideal Homes Exhibition on the 14th, Mr. Bristow and the Headmaster attended Windsor Grammar School exhibition of teaching machines on the 21st, a party attended the International Folk Dance Festival at the Albert Hall on the 23rd and a member of the B.B.C staff observed a class receiving a 'Listening and Writing' broadcast on the 29th.

The school presented a programme of Drama and Music at the Methodist Church Hall, High Street on April 2 and 3. This included scenes from Oliver Twist and New World Folk Songs. Easter holidays began on the 5th the last day for Mrs. McQue (Domestic Science), Mrs. Milne (P.E.) and Mrs. Clarke (part-time Domestic Science) although she did return on Monday morning and Wednesday for the Summer Term.

A party of thirty-six left on April 8 for a 12-day most successful school journey to Zell am See in Austria. They travelled via Ostend, Cologne, Munich and Worgl. Staying in excellent accommodation in a delightful guest house the most favourable weather contributed to the attractions of the area. An excursion via two cable railways took them to the Glacier area of the high Alps where ski-ing was in full swing. A visit to the great Kaprun Alpine Power Station was most impressive. A full day in Salzburg was followed by a short visit to Berchtesgaden. The guest-house proprietor commented favourably on the behaviour and deportment of the pupils. Miss K.M. Taylor, former Health Visitor and Mr. K. Turner, Youth Employment Officer, accompanied the group.

Another party of eight girls and nine boys accompanied by Miss Cook and Mr. Bristow commenced the journey to Paris on April 17. This was the most enjoyable of the three trips the school had arranged for Paris. Travelling by Skyways Coach/Air the coach service did much to make the journey less tiring and easier for organising. Highlights of the visit included the ascent of the Eiffel Tower, a day's visit to Fontainebleau, a boat trip on the Seine and a conducted tour of the illuminations.

When the Summer Term commenced on April 23 Miss C. Bloomfield became the Domestic Science teacher. On the 26th Mrs. Joan Gerlach, a former pupil visited after thirty years. She was undergoing a course of training for teaching and had gained the major award at her College.

The D.E.O. reported that at a recent survey of all schools, teaching staff establishments had been carried out. It had been recommended that the staff establishment at Gordon should be reduced by one on the first resignation received after September 1963 and when a second resignation was received before an appointment could be made the Divisional Executive wished to consider the matter. This recommendation had been arrived at because of the recent opening of the new Furze Platt County Secondary Modern School.

B.C.G. vaccinations on May 7 and 14, French Oral G.C.E.'s began on the 9th, dental inspections 17th and 24th, six pupils attended the Mayor making ceremony on the 22nd and the District Athletics Championships were on the 29th.

Form IIA travelled to the Cotswold area to follow up a history project on June 13, a party visited the Aldershot Tattoo and Static Exhibition on the 14th, another group attended the College of Art Fashion Show on the 21st and Form VI visited the History Museum at Whiteknights, Reading on the 26th.

Fifth year boys visited the Morris Motors Works, Cowley, Oxford on July 1, IIA visited Shottesbrooke to take brass rubbings on the 2nd, an athletics contest versus Blackstone School, Wallingford took place on the 4th, a talk by Capt. Winder on Army Careers on the 5th, Form IIIB visited the Isle of Wight on the 9th the day Miss Coltham spoke about the Duke of Edinburgh Award Scheme, Inter-house Athletics on the 11th and the Inter-Schools Swimming Gala on the 17th. Gordon won the 100 yards championship for boys and girls, the boys team race and were second in points total. The Inter-house Swimming Gala was on the 22nd. Open Day from 3.00pm–8.30pm was on the 18th, when an excellent attendance of parents took the opportunity for discussing the progress of their children with the staff. On the 23rd parties visited the Science Museum, Stock Exchange and House of Commons. School closed on the 25th the last day for Miss P.E. Cook and Mrs. B.J. Evans (both English and French), Mr. P. Mulliner (English and R.E.), Mrs. P. Pethybridge (English and History), Miss M.C. Evans (General Subjects), Mrs. J.M. Clark and Mrs. J. Jones. Leavers 99.

In this year's G.C.E.'s twenty-two pupils gained certificates and following particular successes eight were offered transfers to Grammar Schools. A special feature was the number of Grade I passes (Distinction level):-

K. Gwilym	Physics, Mathematics, Machine Drawing
- O'Hara	Mathematics, Machine Drawing
P. Kimberley	History
K. Blundell	Art
D. Morris	Art
P. Wilson	French

The first pupils to gain transfer to the Grammar Schools following G.C.E 'O' Level passes were leaving college after following teacher training courses. Passes were gained in Pitman Typewriting Examinations at Elementary Level and 1st and 2nd passes in Intermediate Level.

Mr. Stone, the Woodcraft Master attended a course at St. John's College, York from August 3–17. He was awarded first prize in the design and construction of a chair. Other staff attended courses on 'Use of English' (continuation), 'O' Level English', 'O' Level Physics', 'Handicraft' and 'Adding Machines'. Several staff were actively engaged in the preparation of syllabuses and examination papers for the Certificate of Secondary Education. Mr. Bristow and Mrs. Brown were representing the County on the Southern Region Subject Panels for French and Needlecraft.

As the Annexe would shortly cease to be available it was suggested that additional staff accommodation must be provided. This could be done by use of the existing stock room and the conversion of an old section of the senior boys lobby into a stock room (provision of doors and shelves in old section). Projects put forward included:-

1. Adaptation of school to Three Form Entry size (Major Building Programme 1965/66)
2. Provision of fourth lobby and demolition of antiquated toilet accommodation (Minor Building Programme 1964/65)
3. Alterations in metalcraft room (Minor Improvements Programme 1964/65).

The new term commenced on September 10 with Miss B.J. Williams (Domestic Subjects), Mr. J. Sheppard (History and English), Miss D.B. Critchlow (History and Games), Miss D. Moss (French and English), Miss F.M. Thornton (English) and Miss M. Waldron (English and Games – one term only). 106 children were admitted from Primary Schools. Miss Britnell, a Nursing Officer, spoke to senior girls on the 25th.

Groups attended at the Empire Pool and International Stadium at Wembley for the Festival of Movement and Dance.

John Cook, a former pupil, was top to qualify at H.M.S. Excellent in the various courses of Chief Ordnance Artificer and qualified for the Prendergast Prize.

Inter-House Cross Country was on October 16, an Education Officer from the B.B.C. visited to observe a broadcast lesson on the 22nd and a Youth Officer spoke to senior pupils on the 30th.

Mr. J. Dimmick, Principal of Reading Technical College was the guest at Prize Day on November 6. His friendly word with every individual prize winner was a feature of this year's event. Although it prolonged the programme it was very worth while from the pupil's point of view. Gratitude was expressed to the Governors for so generously supporting the Prize Fund.

Youth employment interviews on November 19 and 20, a talk to fifth year leavers on the 26th and further interviews on December 4 and 5. G.C.E. examinations for High School candidates was on December 5. Groups attended a performance of Macbeth and a Folk Dance party at Earley on the 6th and a Carol Service at St. Luke's Church on the 18th. The gymnasium was now ready for use making it possible to dispense with the Pearce Hall and bring to an end a considerable amount of movement in all weathers.

On the last day of term (December 20) Miss M.M. Claydon, Senior Mistress, completed her duties on retirement after nearly thirty years service at the school. Her work in connection with History and Folk Dancing had been of a very high standard. She was interviewed by the Governors and wished a happy retirement. Because of falling numbers the staffing establishment was being reduced by one, this being done by not replacing Miss Claydon. It was Mr. Carmack's last day too.

It was interesting to note the effect of the new school leaving regulations. There would be no Christmas leavers and those born after February 1 would be unable to leave until July, the difference in roll would decrease as the year progresses. As a comparison with 1962–63:-

1st term a difference of 84
2nd term a difference of 43 (664–621)

3rd term a difference of 27 (616–589)

Although for the first time there was a significant drop in the number of admissions at the beginning of the school year, the number staying on for a fifth year increased to 60.

Appreciation was recorded of the kindness of Miss E.B. Marsh over a long period of years and to express regret that she had ceased to be a Governor following her removal to Yorkshire. Mr. P. Murray also resigned.

1964

Re-assemble January 7 with Mr. D.E. Healey as Music Specialist. Pitman Typewriting Elementary Examination results on the 10th, successes for Margaret Johns, Marilyn Voyt, Margaret Sampson, Barbara Poolman and Valerie Trim.

Medical inspections commenced on February 7 and was completed by March 6 with Youth Employment interviews being held on February 27 and 28th.

The Simplicity Fashion Show was on March 3, a member of the Duke of Edinburgh Award Scheme visited on the 9th and commenced work with the group on April 30, a Good Grooming Demonstration by Yardley together with a film and talk by Ercol, furniture manufacturers, was on the 10th, a well supported "Evening of Plays" at the Town Hall was on the 12th, a six-a-side tournament at Wokingham where the school team reached the final of a subsidiary tournament on the 14th, a party visited the Festival of Dance at the Albert Hall and a small group attended the Hockey International at Wembley also on the 14th, thirty-six attended the Ideal Homes Exhibition at Olympia on the 16th. Thirty-one pupils and five adults paid a return visit to Stadt Wien, Zell am See, Austria during the Easter vacation. They travelled by air to Basle and thence by train via Zurich, Leichtenstein and Innsbrook through the high Alps. Two girls from the Ockenden Venture were guests of the school.

Miss M. Jackson returned to join the staff after two years in Cyprus on April 7. Miss Hope and Miss Williams commenced teaching practice on the 22nd. On the 23rd a party visited the Comedy Theatre while another group attended a quiz at the

Public Library. A commercial group visited I.C.I. on the 24th.

It had been suggested that the existing practical block which houses the Science, Metalcraft and Homecraft rooms should become a Science Department and that a new practical block should be built to provide for Art and allied crafts, Needlecraft, Woodcraft, Metalcraft and Technical Drawing. 1966/7 could be a possible date for commencement. It was admitted though that after September it was unlikely that numbers would justify four full-time teachers in Domestic Subjects.

A former pupil, Alan Whitbread had passed his final Accountancy Examinations.

B.C.G. injections on May 5 and 12, Youth Employment interviews on the 7th and 8th, G.C.E. French Oral on the 11th, Careers Convention on the 13th (the Headmaster, Mrs. Wilson and Mr. Miller attended a Careers Conference at Maiden Erlegh School on June 11), a C.S.E. Conference on the 15th.

A group attended the Comedy Theatre for a performance of Macbeth on June 2, Form III visited Bray Church for brass rubbings on the 5th, Mrs. Roberts and Miss Williams took a party

Hockey Team in the 1960's.

from IVA and IV to a cake decorations demonstration on the 18th, Jacqueline Caswell's performance at the Berkshire Athletics Championships held at the Braywick Track on the 20th was quite outstanding. She won the 100 yards and 150 yards events for girls and was a member of the winning relay team. She gained her County badge and was chosen to represent Berkshire at the All-England Championships at Hendon. From the 29th two French boys were working with classes for the remainder of the term.

Mrs. Roberts and Miss Williams attended a Domestic Science course at Abingdon on July 2, the Certificate of Proficiency in Arithmetic Examination was the following day. Fifteen pupils visited the Public Library on the 15th. Open Day on the 16th attracted a very pleasing number of parents and friends especially in the evening. The new gymnasium provided the opportunity for a dress show and displays of physical education to be added to the programme. A group attended the All-England Athletic Championships at Hendon on the 17th and Form VI visited the Stock Exchange and Houses of Parliament on the 22nd.

At the District Swimming Championships Ann Thompson won the 100 yards event and Susan Woodhams was placed first in the diving. Certificates awarded:- Beginners 44, Elementary 45, Intermediate 31, Advanced 6.

On the last day of term, July 24, Miss K.E.F. Phillips, Senior Mistress, retired after forty years devoted service. In addition to her outstanding work as teacher of Biology she initiated and developed the Pre-Nursing Course. The Governors interviewed and thanked her for her loyalty. Other resignations included Miss Williams through staff reduction, Miss Hibberd, Mr. Reynolds, Mr. Richards, Mr. Shadbolt, and Miss Moss and Miss Thornton who were leaving the area to be married.

It was recorded that Gordon was possibly the only school not scheduled for re-building which had no hard tennis courts.

G.C.E. statistics:-

No. of Subjects	*No. of Candidates*
7	3
6	10
5	14
4	10

3	8
2	5
1	3
	53

Subjects	*Candidates*
English Language	47
English Literature	36
French	19
Geography	23
History	18
Cookery	2
Human Biology	18
Physics	12
Mathematics	31
Engineering Workshop Theory & Practical	1
Art	21
Total no. of papers	228

City of Guilds Certificate of Proficiency – No. of Candidates 10.

Re-assemble on September 8 with the following new staff:- Miss J. Blight (French and English), Miss D.E. Cook (English and Games), Mr. D.A.E. Lawrence (History and Religious Education), Mrs. G.B. Nielson (History and English) and Miss T. Weeks (Biology). New admissions 104. It was interesting to note that the Summer leavers were the last of the record 1959 entry of 210 pupils and that this year's entry was almost exactly half of the 1959 total. The school will gradually become more balanced. Present position:-

1st year	104
2nd year	105
3rd year	156
4th year	139
5th year	54

Posts of Special Responsibility

Mr. R. Bristow	Deputy Head and Head of English and French Departments
Mrs. D. Wilson	Senior Mistress

Heads of Department	
Mr. E. Lacy	Art and Crafts
Mr. J. Miller	Mathematics
Mr. H.E. Jones	Science
Mr. I. Severn	Geography
Mr. D.A.E. Lawrence	History and Religious Education
Graded Posts	
Mr. C.E. Jeavons	Head of Handicraft
Mr. M. Organ	English and Drama
Miss M. Jackson	Girls' Welfare
Mrs. J. Brown	Needlecraft
Mrs. C. Roberts	Homecraft
Miss J. Howe	P.E.
Mr. D.C. Williams	P.E.
Mr. D. Healey	Music
Mr. T. Stone	Woodcraft

The month of September ended with dental inspections on the 21st and 28th, youth employment talks on the 24th and the school closing for the Reading Conference on the 25th.

A talk and film by R.A.F. Officers on October 6 and by Major Paget Clarke on the 21st. A party visited Morris Motors and toured Oxford Colleges on November 3.

Prize Day on November 11 was held at the Town Hall. Being in the evening a larger number of parents were able to attend and appreciated the more pleasant amenities. On the other hand a majority of the pupils were not present. The principal guest was Mr. H.G. Herrington, Managing Director of High Duty Alloys.

Films and demonstrations of electric typewriters took place on November 13 and Naval Careers films on the 16th. Mrs. P. Kennedy commenced part-time needlecraft duties on that day. With Youth Employment interviews on the 23rd and 24th, Inter-House Cross Country on the 25th the school closed for the Prize Day holiday on the 27th.

Miss P.R. Croxford was re-appointed Co-optative Governor for three years and Miss J.G. Claxton and Mr. J.C. Powell new Governors.

A Carol Service was held at St. Luke's Church on December 16 Christmas holidays beginning on the 18th. It was the last day for Mrs. J. Brown (Needlecraft), Mrs. P. East (General Subjects) and

Mrs. Lancaster-Jones (General Subjects, part-time).

Numbers had dropped from 714 in 1961 to 557 at the present time so, because of the greatly reduced entry, the candidates sitting for G.C.E. 'O' level subjects would ever again approach this year's total.

Adaptations recommended had not been included in the 1965/66 Minor Building Programme and it was considered as a long term policy a major project should be pressed for in the 1967/68. Concern was expressed about the lack of hot water for washing in one of the cloakrooms with a request that a water heater be provided.

1965

The new term commenced on January 7 with Mr. M. Klimaytys (Mathematics and Technical Drawing), Mrs J. Docker (General Subjects), Mrs. J. Nalder (4/5-English) and Mrs. Kelly and Mrs. Kennedy (1/2 time Needlecraft) for one term only. Medical inspections on the 12th and 14th. A party of twelve boys were entertained by J.M. Jones Ltd (builders) and given informative talks and a tour of the sites on the 19th. A representative from Optical Measuring Tools also gave a talk to senior boys. The following passed the Pitman Elementary Typewriting Examination:- Joan Bristow, Linda Forster, Jill Phillips, Janice Dean, Jennifer Bailey and Hazel Jefferies. A careers talk given by a member of staff at Dynatron Radio was on the 27th and Youth Employment interviews on the 28th and 29th.

Follow-up visits to Optical Measuring Tools, February 3 and 26 and Dynatron Radio February 9 and March 2. March was also a month for visits – Maidenhead Laundry on the 1st; Beecham Toiletry on the 3rd; Metal Vents on the 8th; Ideal Homes Exhibition on the 9th; a talk on 'Crusaders' on the 23rd. Youth employment interviews, 9th and 10th. A very interesting illustrated lecture on climbing activities in South America was given on the 4th by Robin Brooks a former pupil and one of the first to gain the Duke of Edinburgh Gold Award. Staff courses on Calculating Machines ran from the 17th–19th and Human Relationships from the 24–26th.

The Divisional Executive's Staffing Section met on March 17 to consider the staffing establishment of all schools in the Division. Taking into account the fact that Gordon was situated on two sites, the Section decided that the establishment should remain at Head plus 29 plus 4 part-time teachers. It was also noted that the school was one of three selected by the Authority for conversion of its existing boilers to enable bituminous coal to be used instead of coke which, at that time, was in short supply. A sum of £1,325 had been included in the estimates for that purpose.

An evening of Drama, Music and Mime took place at the Town Hall on April 12. Close for Easter holidays on the 13th. It was the last day for Miss Williams. Number of leavers 31. During the holidays four boys spent a complete week on an Insight into Industry Course. They visited six different firms in Slough and the College of Further Education. Some of the girls attended a Windsor Group Hospital course.

Gifts to the school included an electric print machine together with material and accessories installed by British Ermeto, a Mr. Knight gave a Citroen engine and a Mr. Barnes a car for the use of the Science and Handicraft Departments.

A Special Meeting was held on May 4 to consider the organisation of secondary education. The memo prepared by the Divisional Officer together with diagrams of various alternative forms of organisation had been circulated and a long discussion took place. A large majority was in favour of the introduction of a West Riding type of organisation and minority views were expressed in favour of (a) a Croydon type of organisation but with an age range for the High School of 12 to 16 years, (b) a West Riding organisation but with all single sex schools. It was thought that Gordon should become a middle school under the West Riding type of organisation.

Re-assemble on May 3 with Mrs. M. Davis (Needlecraft). A party of girls visited Hurley Farm Institute on the 11th and a party of boys the Slough factory of G.D. Peters. The Southern Electricity Board gave a demonstration on the 20th. At the District Athletics on the 31st the school won the cup newly presented by the Mayor for the 12–14 girls section. The following set up new records:-

100 yards girls under 16	J. Caswell*
Long Jump boys under 16	C. Franklin*
Long Jump girls under 16	J. Caswell (Broke County Record)
Shot girls under 16	R. Stickley
High Jump girls under 12	P. Edwards: C. Bull
Shot girls under 14	M. Owen

*chosen to represent Berkshire at the All-England Championships. Georgette Richards was placed first in the javelin event.

A party of girls visited Cadbury's factory on June 4, a visit to Hewen's Garage on the 15th, a demonstration by the Gas Company's Cookery expert on the 17th and visits to Cliffords Dairies and Metal Vents Ltd on the 22nd. The Headmaster, Mrs. Wilson and Mr. Miller attended a Careers Conference at Wick Hill on the 16th. The staffing establishment was reduced on June 15 from Head plus 29 plus 2/5 to Head plus 28.

July 1. The first Headmaster of Gordon, Mr. E.A. Bell, completed 29 years service from 1907–1936. Today, the second Headmaster, Mr. L.E.J. Adderson also completed 29 years service. Visits to H.M.S. Vernon at Portsmouth and the Stock Exchange and Houses of Parliament also on the 1st. On the 7th to the Road Research Laboratory, Fords on the 9th, Formica Ltd. on the 15th, All-England Championships at Watford on the 16th and the Commonwealth Institute Conference at Earley on the 17th. A well attended Open Day on the 21st.

Close for summer vacation on July 23, the following ceased their duties:- Mr. J.W. Barnes and Mr. R.N. Stallwood (promotions), Miss B. Critchlow (marriage), Mrs. G.B. Nielson and Mrs. C. Roberts (both to Slough), Mrs. Nalder (maternity). Mr. Cartland had served the school as caretaker for twenty-five years and was due to retire at the end of September. He requested to be allowed to work during August instead of taking leave so that he could have the school in good condition to hand over to his successor.

In the G.C.E. 'O' Level Examinations seventy subjects were taken:- Physics (6), Human Biology (17), Art (16), English (4), Geography (5), History (6), Mathematics (11), French (5). Eighteen boys and five girls gained certificates. A feature of this year's results was the success of all pupils entered for mathematics.

In the Certificate of Secondary Education one hundred and ninety nine subjects were taken:- Art (13), Typewriting (12), Domestic Science (12), English (47), Geography (25), Woodwork (7), Metalwork (8), History (16), Mathematics (25), French (18), Needlecraft (11), Religious Education (5). Thirty boys and twenty girls gained certificates. Thirteen members of staff had been involved in sixteen C.S.E. Subject Panel and Consortium meetings mostly in the evenings during the term.

Re-open September 7 with Mr. R. Atherton (retarded Pupils), Mr. P.D. Mountford (History), Mr. P.W. Proffitt (Science), Miss S.M. Pyatt (History and Religious Education), Mrs. M. Wiseman (4/5-Homecraft) and Mrs. R. Philpott (2/5-Music). Mr. D.E. Healey would be working three days only in future in order to spend more time composing.

A visit to the Meteorological Office at Bracknell on September 23 and a County Netball Coaching Session on the 27th.

Pitman's Typewriting Examinations showed:-

Business Stage, three 1st Class passes
Business Stage, three 2nd Class passes
Intermediate Stage one 1st Class pass
Intermediate Stage two 2nd Class passes
Elementary Stage sixteen passes

Of the group who transferred to Grammar Schools in 1963, four pupils gained admission to training colleges and one to Great Ormond Street Hospital Training School.

October 12 saw the 50th meeting of Governors since its formation under the Education Act 1944. Of the original board of Governors only Mrs. P. Flew now remained. For the first time the number of leavers in July (110) had exceeded the number of entrants for September (from Division Primary Schools 88, from outside the district 13). Fifth year pupils numbered 58.

The Band of the 3rd Green Jackets performed on October 20 and youth employment talks on the 21st. Prize Day awards were distributed by the Mayor at the Town Hall on November 10, the School Cross Country Race was on the 24th and a party of thirty-six boys visited the motor works at Abingdon on the 25th.

With Youth Employment interviews on November 17 and

December 16, carol services at the Methodist and St. Mary's Churches, 16th and 17th, school closed for Christmas vacation on the 21st the last day for Mr. Lawrence.

The first ski-ing holiday at Oberwald was greatly enjoyed by forty pupils. Fourteen gained proficiency badges. A motion film was made and shown at the Governors meeting on February 8, 1966.

1966

Re-open January 6. Talks on the 19th (to senior boys) on Army recruiting by the Nursing Recruitment Officer on the 27th and a representative from Lever Bros. on the washing of materials on the 31st. Medical inspections on the 14th, 18th, 25th and completed on February 4. A visit to Westwell Works Ltd on the 28th. Twelve pupils attended a week-end residential course at Thamesfield, Henley on the 26th and 27th. The programme included wider aspects of life – talks and discussions on social behaviour, personal relationships, uses of leisure and learning to budget.

A party of boys visited Furze Platt School to see a demonstration of physical activities by an Army Unit on February 3, a talk by the Manager of the National Provincial Bank on money matters on the 7th, a visit to Art Print Productions on the 16th. Youth Employment interviews, 22nd and 24th. Fifteen pupils led by Mr. Lacy and Miss Howe participated in an Outdoor Pursuit Course at Lakeside on the shores of Windermere during the month. Groups from Woodley County, Fitzharry's Abingdon and John O'Gaunt, Hungerford also took part.

A visit to Optical Measuring Tools on March 17, the Vicar of Macclesfield attended assembly and addressed pupils on the 23rd and a programme of Music and Drama presented at the Town Hall on the 30th.

It was felt that the uncertainty of the future of Gordon could have an unsettling effect upon parents, staff and pupils and a statement indicating that a change is unlikely to occur before 1968 would be helpful. A special meeting of Governors held on April 19 discussed the Working Party proposals that the new Cox Green Comprehensive School would first open as a joint comprehensive school with the existing Gordon County Secondary School. One Headmaster would take charge of both schools. The Working Party was anxious to preserve the work and traditions of Gordon and it was intended these would not be lost but enabled to expand in larger and better equipped premises. On May 24 the Divisional Executive Officer stated that the County Education Committee had been asked to agree to the reconstitution of the Governing Body in view of the fact that the Governing Body of Gordon would have to act as the Governing Body of the joint Gordon-Cox Green Comprehensive School. This was subject to the plans for the introduction of Orthodox Comprehensive Schools in the Maidenhead Division being approved by the County Council.

Mr. Bristow and Miss Blight left with a group for Paris on April 4 returning on the 14th. Visits to Shalibane Engineering took place on April 27 and May 24.

May and a party visited the Army Apprentices School at Arborfield on the 18th, a meeting of parents at Furze Platt School to hear a talk on the re-organisation on the 23rd, a group visits Hewen's Garages on the 24th and dental inspections on the 25th and 26th.

June and a month of visits. Dynatron Radio (2nd), Vandervells (8th), Victoria and Albert Museum (23rd), Chelsea College of P.E. (29th) and a concert at Kneller Hall while juniors go to Blenheim Palace (30th).

A group visits Berkshire Farm Institute, Hurley on July 1; Sports Day (5th); talk on banking (7th); a group at the Marlow Exhibition and a party of VI Formers at Vandervells (7th); swimming gala (11th) and a well attended Open Day especially in the evening when the programme included (1) Orchestra and Choir (2) Dress Show (3) P.E. Display (13th). Close for summer vacation July 15. The following staff ceased their duties:- Miss Pyatt and Miss Weeks (marriage), Miss Blight and Mrs. Davis (leaving area), Miss Howe (to Bedford College of P.E.), Mr. Williams (changing to junior work) and Mrs. Wiseman who was part-time. School leavers 119.

Now that the Certificate of Secondary Education was established a different pattern of subject entry was evident. Fewer pupils sat for G.C.E 'O' level the majority offer subjects at more appropriate C.S.E. level. Grade I C.S.E. was considered equivalent to a pass at 'O' level.

	G.C.E.	C.S.E.
English	4	48
French	7	16
Mathematics	16	28
Art and Craft	13	14
Geography	5	22
History	5	17
Household Cookery	4	8
Human Biology	5	11
Physics	4	16
Dress	3	7
Geometrical Drawing	5	7
Engineering Workshop Theory & Practice	3	-
General Science	-	13
Woodcraft	-	9
Metalcraft	-	7
Religious Education	-	6
Typewriting	-	15
	74	244

G.C.E. certificates gained –	Girls 10	Boys 12	
C.S.E. certificates gained –	Girls 21	Boys 28	
Pitman's Typewriting Examinations –	Business Grade		2nd Class 5
	Intermediate Grade		1st Class 8
			2nd Class 3
	Elementary Grade		Passes 11

Four girls were transferred to High School and a very pleasing number of pupils went on to Colleges of Further Education.

At the beginning of the Autumn Term admissions were again lower than leavers. New staff:- Mr. A.C. Durran (P.E. – Head of Department), Mrs. L.M. Fairbrother (P.E.), Mrs. P. Buchan (Homecraft), Mrs. J. Mairs (Biology and Religious Education), Mrs. J.R. Sulley (French and English). A film and talk on the Royal Navy, September 22; the Headmaster on a Residential Course at St. Heda's College, Oxford on the 23rd and, with Mr. Miller, a conference at the Junior Leaders' Establishment, Bovingdon on the 29th.

Prize Day was held at the Town Hall on November 3 the principal guest being the Director of Education Mr. T.D.W. Whitfield. The Mayor, a former pupil, was also present. A group visited Warner Bros. Brick and Tile Works on the 9th; the Army Apprentices School at Arborfield on the 16th; a performance of Richard III at the Windsor Cinema on the 23rd; Fairey Survey Ltd on the 25th; the Folk Dance Festival at the Albert Hall on the 26th and Beecham's Toiletries on the 30th. A 'Good Grooming' lecture and demonstration by Chesebrough-Pond was on the 18th.

Mr. R. Atherton requested two days leave of absence to attend a competition in France in connection with the career he intended following in the future as a 'pop' singer. He was granted one day's pay but not for the second.

In accordance with the recent amendment to the School's Instrument of Government Mr. W. Burrough and Mrs. J. Steel (Authority Representatives) and Mrs. J. Hobson and the Rev. T.W. Morcom-Harnies (Divisional Executive Representatives) were appointed to the Governing Body.

A Commonwealth lecture took place on December 6; a Carol Service at St. Mary's Church on the 14th; a programme of films and the prefects party on the 15th, school closing for the Christmas vacation on the 16th, Mr. Atherton's last day. During the holidays a sound projector and tape recorder was stolen from a locked cupboard in the Science room. The mode of entry was not established.

1967

The Divisional Executive Staffing Section decided at their meeting on November 23, 1966 that the establishment be reduced to Head plus 24 from January 1.

The new term commenced on January 4 but Mr. Miller and Mr. Jones were absent with a ski-ing party of twenty-eight in Austria returning on the 6th.

January appeared a month of meetings – with the Drama Organiser on the 10th who was commencing a series of six weekly demonstrations from February 8; with Head Teachers on the 12th; a special Governors meeting to consider sketch plans of the Cox Green new buildings on the 16th; Heads of Departments at the High School on the 18th and Governors discussed the Department of Education and Science recommendation that in

September 1967 the establishment of separate autonomous secondary modern schools in each of two buildings (Raymond Road and Highfield Lane, Cox Green) and that Acting Heads (from existing staff at Gordon without national advertisement) should be appointed for each of the two schools until September 1970 when a Head would be appointed to take overall charge of the two tier comprehensive school. The two tier system means that Gordon would cater for an age range of 11–13 years, Cox Green 14–18 years. When amalgamated to form a single mixed comprehensive school catering for age range 11–18 years.

A visit was made to Vauxhall Motors on January 17 – Youth Employment interviews on the 19th and 20th.

On February 4 a party of fifteen in the care of Mr. Jones left for the Lakeland Centre on the shores of Windermere for two weeks in company with similar numbers from Charters Sunningdale, Edgbarrow Crowthorne and Blackstone Wallingford. At the Berkshire County Cross Country Championships held in Maidenhead on February 25, 31 secondary schools entered teams with 150 competitors. Mervyn Evans won the under fourteen championship. Pupils modelled garments at the Simplicity Patterns Dress Show on the 28th.

A talk by a member of Messrs. J.M. Jones Ltd. on March 1 was followed by an all-day visit on the 6th. The London Theatre Group presented 'The Discoverers' by Brian Way on the 7th; a party to the Ideal Homes Exhibition on the 8th; a lecture by the Flour Advisory Bureau Ltd on the 9th; B.C.G. vaccinations on the 10th (also April 21 and 28); forty senior pupils attended the Civic Reception at the Town Hall on the 16th: Easter holidays commencing on the 22nd. Mr. Richards the Art Specialist ceased duties.

The school presented a very successful evening of music and drama with mime at the Town Hall on March 15. A very large cast received very good support. Music for the presentation of the 'Three Thieves' from Chaucer's the Pardoner's Tale had been written by Mr. Healey and the dance-mime arranged by Mrs. Fairbrother. Mr. Organ had written an adaptation of Around the World in Eighty Days. As producer he was assisted by Mrs. Sulley, Miss Cook and Mr. Sheppard.

A party of twenty-five left for the Holiday Fellowship Hostel,

Malhamdale, Yorkshire on March 24, led by Mr. Mountford, Miss Cook, Mr. Sheppard and Mr. Proffitt returning on the 31st.

Numerous week-end and evening courses were attended by members of staff:-

Certificate of Secondary Education – Consortia and Moderation
Creative Drama in Secondary Schools
Aids in Language Teaching
English Study Group
Methods and Aims in Primary School Language Teaching
Comparative Education
Modern Mathematics

Re-open April 10 with Mrs. S. Hardie as the new Art teacher. Senior boys visited the Science Museum on the 12th and forty girls a cookery lecture and demonstration at the Town Hall, Reading on the 13th. The film 'Lord of the Flies' was shown on the 19th. Members of the school took part in the Orchestral Concert at the Grammar School on the 25th.

Mr. E. Lacy a member of staff for fourteen years and present Head of the Art Department was appointed Headmaster of the new Cox Green School. Mr. R. Bristow, Deputy Head and also a member of staff for fourteen years was appointed Headmaster of Gordon as from September 1. It was worthy to note that there had been no outside appointment since the first Headmaster took up his duties in 1907.

C.S.E. examinations commenced May 1; a party to Vandervells on the 8th; a visit to Dynatron Radio on the 17th.

The following successes were recorded at the District Athletics on May 18:-

Mile	1st M. Evans (new record)
880 yards	1st M. Evans (new record)
Junior High Jump	1st Jacqueline Stevenson (new record)
Junior Long Jump	Maureen Peat

Intermediate Events

100 yards	1st Linda Hewitt (new record)
150 yards	1st Linda Hewitt (new record)
Long Jump	1st Linda Hewitt
High Jump	1st Philippa May

Shot Put	1st Pamela Edwards
Discus	1st Brenda Gee

The girls won the cup for the highest aggregate of points. All the above were chosen to represent the District at the County Sports at Bracknell Stadium. Also chosen H. Speed (100 yards), J. Wheeler (150 yards) and J. Cadle (mile).

In a triangular match against the High School and Furze Platt School Gordon were first with 131 points, Furze Platt second (106 points) and the High School third (91 points).

The school was entered on May 19, the second time in twelve months when a stop watch, a starting pistol and a 200′ measuring tape was stolen from the Headmaster's room. As the windows of this room had been barred it was considered that access via the outside windows was not possible.

A small group attended an orchestral concert at the Grammar School on May 28. The school orchestra was developing well and several pupils were members of the successful Schools Orchestra which was led by one of the senior Grammar School pupils. A generous grant of £75 by the Spoore Trust for the purchase of instruments had been a great encouragement.

A visit to the Berkshire College of Agriculture in connection with a G.C.E. History project took place on June 1, exams commencing on the 4th.

The Maidenhead and District Schools Swimming Championships were held on June 7. It was pleasing that the new cup (Thomas Cup) presented by His Worship the Mayor, himself a former pupil, should be awarded for the first time to the school whose boys gained the highest aggregate of points. Other successes:-

100 yards championship for the Association Cup (Boys) K Sinden
Senior Boys Team Race – Curtis Shield – Gordon School 1st
Junior Boys Team Race – 1st in new record time.
The Girls team was placed 2nd to the High School.

A first year group visited Hampton Court and London Airport on June 15 (a second party on the 22nd) and a third year group the Old Bailey on the 20th.

June 26 and a presentation to mark the retirement of the

Headmaster, Mr. L.E.J. Adderson. Among those present was the Mayor and Mayoress, Mrs. E. Sheasby, the Director of Education and Mrs. Whitfield, the Divisional Education Officer and Mrs. Wain, the Chairman of Governors and Mrs. Wheeler, Governors of the School, Members of the Old Gordonians Association, parents and colleagues. Tribute was paid to the long and outstanding service given and it was unanimously agreed that the name of Mrs. Adderson be associated with this tribute.

A group attended a dress making display at the College of Art on June 27; Sports Day the 28th; advanced swimming tests on July 3 and a party from the fifth forms visited the Houses of Parliament and shown a computer in action at a London Bank on the 4th. A well supported Open Day was on the 6th with an exhibition of work, the choir and orchestra performed accompanied with a dress show and P.E. displays.

The Inter-House Swimming Gala was held on July 10, school closing for the summer vacation on the 14th. It was the last day for:-

Mr. L.E.J. Adderson, Headmaster retirement after 36 years
Mr. E. Lacy, Head of Art Department after 14 years to become Headmaster at Cox Green
Mr. M. Organ, Head of English Department after 8 years on transfer to Cox Green
Miss M. Jackson on transfer to Cox Green
Mrs. S. Hardie, part-time Art on leaving the district
Mrs. J. Mairs, resignation for family reasons.

The Annexe ceased to be part of the school after being in use for 8 years. Much of the furniture and equipment was transferred to the main school or to Cox Green. This brought to an end the many problems faced during those years.

Mr. Adderson's last entry in the Log Book reads 'August 31, Today I ceased my duties after 31 years as Headmaster of this School'.

Examination entries and results for 1967:	*C.S.E.*	*successes*	*G.C.E.*	*successes*
English	48	48	9	6
French	23	23	8	4
Mathematics	48	47	15	12
Physics	18	18	2	2

General Science	13	10	–	
Human Biology	17	17	2	1
Machine Drawing	30	26	–	
Metalcraft	10	9	–	
Woodcraft	12	12	–	
Art and Craft	16	16	9	4
Geography	22	21	5	4
History	19	19	5	1
Domestic Science	13	11	–	
Needlecraft	2	2	5	5
Typewriting	11	10	–	
Music	–		1	1
Religious Knowledge	1	1	–	
Pitman's Typewriting Examinations: Intermediate Grade				7
Elementary Grade				8

Two girls and three boys transferred to local Grammar Schools to take 'A' level courses.

Re-open September 5. N.O.R. 462. Number of pupils beyond statutory age 65.

Establishment:-
Headmaster: Mr. R. Bristow (formerly Deputy Head)
Deputy Headmaster; Head of Mathematics Dept. Mr. J.H. Miller
Senior Mistress; Mathematics, Mrs. D.M. Wilson
*Mr. M.J.R. Bright, Art
Mrs. P.N. Buchan, Homecraft
Miss D.E. Cook, English
Mrs. M. Davis, Needlecraft
Mr. A.C. Durran, P.E. Head of Dept. (one day at Cox Green)
Mrs. L. Fairbrother, P.E. (one day at Cox Green)
*Mr. M.M. Gulliford, Geography & English
*Mrs. M.E. Grover, Science (temp)
Mr. D.E. Healey, Music (four days each week)
Mr. C.E. Jeavons, Metalcraft Head of Dept.
Mr. H.E. Jones, Science Head of Dept. (seconded for one year)
*Mrs. H.P. King, English Head of Dept.
Mr. M. Klimaytys, Machine Drawing
*Mrs. M.L. May, Mathematics (temp to be made permanent)
Mr. P.D. Mountford, History & English
Mr. P.W. Proffitt, to be in charge of Science for one year during secondment of Mr. H.E. Jones (advance study of Education at University of Reading)

Mrs. M. Smets, Homecraft
Mr. J. Sheppard, History
Mr. I. Severn, Geography Head of Dept.
Mr. T. Stone, Woodcraft
Mrs. J.R. Sulley, French
*Mrs. J.M. Wardhaugh, part-time History and Games.
*New appointment September 1967.

Youth employment and careers talks on September 13, 18 and interviews on October 2. A representative from Lever Bros spoke on 'Care of Modern Fabrics' on September 25 the day when twenty-five pupils visited the Town Hall to see the work of the various departments. Harvest Festival was celebrated on October 4, children's gifts of food being distributed to old people in the town. A party of 4th and 5th year pupils visited the A.B.C. Cinema to see Richard III on the 5th and 5th year girls visited the Victoria and Albert Museum on the 12th. Ten boys were at Optical Measuring Tools on the 30th, 5th year boys on November 2nd. Prize Day was at the Town Hall on the 31st, principal guest, the Mayor.

A careers talk on November 6 by a staff member of the G.P.O. was followed by three groups of boys and girls visiting the various departments on the 14th. Mr. Severn and fifteen pupils departed for the Outdoor Pursuits Course, Lakeside on the 11th returning on the 25th. Mr. Jeavons and ten 4th year boys visited the Army Apprentices College, Arborfield on the 15th. Prize Day visits for the Headmaster – Blackstone School, Wallingford on the 8th and Furze Platt and Boyne Hill Girls on the 16th. At the North East Berkshire Schools Netball on the 18th the under 14 team were placed 1st. A careers talk by the Berkshire College of Agriculture on the 27th and two pupils attended the presentation ceremony for Mr. Rippon the retiring Head of Courthouse Primary School on the 30th.

Youth employment interviews for 4th years on December 1; careers talk on the Royal Navy, 4th year boys on the 4th; senior party held in the Hall on the 12th; Carol services for children in the afternoon at St. Mary's Church, parents in the evening of the 14th; last day of term on the 15th. Mrs. Wardhaugh resigned.

Thirty-seven pupils led by Mr. Miller and Mr. Jones left for Reith-Bei-Seefeld, Austrian Tyrol on December 27 returning January 5. Although the weather conditions were not ideal the journey was very successful. The Director of Education commented favourably on the childrens' conduct.

Christmas food parcels collected and distributed by children were delivered to old people living near the school. An interesting feature of the Christmas activities was the sale of charity Christmas cards organised by 4th year girls during dinner hour. Orders totalled £24. Enquiries were also being made about the possibility of senior girls helping in local hospitals. A collection was also made for Dr. Barnardo's Homes. Five members of staff attended courses ranging from Mathematics, French, English and Technical Subjects.

1968

Re-open January 9 with Mrs. Close commencing part-time teaching of History and Games. Mrs. J. Squire commenced on the 15th working with children who had real language problems. Boys visited Vauxhall Motors at Luton on the 19th; medical examinations on the 23rd; youth employment interviews for summer leavers on February 1; school exams starting on the 5th.

At the Berkshire Cross Country Championships on February 3 the school was placed 5th in the under sixteen section. At the District Championships on the 17th the under sixteen team was placed 1st and the under fourteen team 6th.

Brian Cox visited the school on the 16th. He had just completed training in the Royal Marines and was the only one of his section to be awarded the King's Badge. Visiting speakers for the 4th year careers programme included the Merchant Navy and Hairdressing and visits to W.H. Smith and Marks & Spencer.

Second year children went to Reading on March 4; the Band of the Green Jackets from Winchester performed in the Hall on the 13th; the 4th year to the Ideal Homes Exhibition on the 19th and the girls won the North East Berkshire Netball Rally on the 22nd.

The school was informed at the morning assembly of the sad death of Mr. W.A. Roberts a Governor and former Chairman. Easter holidays April 5–30. N.O.R. 464. Leavers 13.

Football Team 1968–69.

Rugby Team 1968–69.

Mr. C.A. Harrop became the Authority Representative Governor. Mr. Durran was invited to attend the Amateur Swimming Association Training Course at Loughborough College for two weeks during April but only received support for one week. It was however agreed to second Mr. Klimaytys during 1968/69 to attend a Mathematics Course at Worcester College of Education.

A visit was made to Lullingstone (Hertfordshire) Silk Farm on May 9; at the Slough Arts Festival (Gymnastics) on the 13th the boys team won the group entry and in the solo performances J. Rimmer was 1st and N. Baldwin 3rd. Girls also competed in team and solo events. A Summer Fair in spite of bad weather raised £143 on the 25th. District Athletics (Field Events) was on the 27th and Track Events on the 29th. The Headmaster was at the Junior Speech Day at Maidenhead Grammar School on the 30th.

A party of third year children visited the Commonwealth Institute, Kensington on June 11; third and fourth years visited a Bible Exhibition at Desborough Hall on the 14th. At the County Athletics meeting at Bracknell Sports Centre on the 15th twelve children represented the school and gave outstanding performances. In the:-

880 yards M. Evans was 2nd in 2 mins 2.5 secs
100 yards L. Hewitt was 2nd in 11.9 secs
150 yards L. Hewitt was 1st in 17.6 secs (new record).

A party of fifth year visited the Palace of Westminster and the Stock Exchange on June 18 and fourth year girls a North Thames Gas Demonstration; thirty-six boys H.M.S. Vincent at Gosport on the 25th and a group to the College of Agriculture at Burchetts Green on the 27th. A film was shown to third year pupils by the Youth Employment Officer on the 28th the day a member of the Society for the Mentally Handicapped spoke to fourth years.

July 2 and third year visited Hampton Court, fourth year girls to the Berkshire College of Art Fashion Display; Inter-House Athletics Championships on the 3rd; first year to Whipsnade Zoo on the 4th. Conferences had been arranged for fifth year pupils on July 4, 5, 11 and 12. A number of speakers visited the school and topics covered included 'The Money You Earn', 'Leisure

John Rimmer top gymnast.

Time Activities', 'Religion', 'The Trade Union Movement' and 'Good Grooming'. All fifth year saw the display of work at Maidenhead Borough Council Town Hall on the 10th. Open Day on the 18th was well attended with performances of Beggar's Opera, Boys and Girls P.E. Displays, a dress display and the practical rooms in operation. The Headmaster visited the new St. Luke's C.E. Secondary School on the 19th, Inter-House swimming on the 22nd, summer holidays commencing on the 24th. Resignations from Mr. H.E. Jones (Head of Science Dept.), Mrs.

M.E. Grover (Science) and Mrs. J. Close (part-time). A party led by Mrs. Sulley and the Headmaster left for Brive, Central France on July 29 returning on August 5.

Examination results became available during the holidays and showed:-

G.C.E. passes in 52 subjects
C.S.E. passes in 282 subjects

In more detail:-

G.C.E.	*Subject*	*Passes*	*Highest Grades*
	Mathematics	16	2
	English Language	12	1
	History	5	1
	Geography	3	1
	French	6	5
	Physics	5	1
	Dress	5	2

C.S.E.	*Subject*	*Number*	*Grade I Passes*	*Others*
	Art & Craft	17	3	14
	Typewriting	8		
	Home Economics	9	–	9
	English	58	11	43
	Geography	25	–	22
	Metalwork	1		
	History	44	6	38
	Mathematics	50	7	39
	French	20	2	18
	Needlework	10	2	6
	Technical Drawing	34	–	25
	Physics	20	5	14
	Human Biology & Hygiene	18	1	14

Former pupils success:-
Keith Gwilym 1st Class Honours Degree in Science, Goldsmith's College
Robin Brooks gained University entrance British Columbia.
Four girls and two boys applied for transfer into sixth forms of local Grammar Schools.

Re-open September 10 with Mrs. S.M. Casement (Science) and Mr. R.E. Kennedy (Mathematics & Technical Drawing) replacing

Mr. Klimaytys seconded for one year. Mr. C. Ward became a new Governor and allocation of special allowances were awarded to Mr. P.W. Proffitt, Head of Science Dept., Mr. J. Sheppard, Head of History and Integrated Studies Dept. and Mr. P. Mountford for work in connection with the Duke of Edinburgh Award Scheme. N.O.R. 455. Number beyond statutory leaving age 69.

Youth employment talks to 4th and 5th year took place on September 24 and twelve boys visited the Army Apprentices College, Arborfield on the 25th. The Simplicity Fashion Show was on October 8, Harvest Festival Service conducted by the Rev. R. Wareing on the 11th, the school took part in an Education Sunday Service at St. Mark's Methodist Church on the 13th, the Headmaster attended Boyne Hill Girls School Prize Day on the 24th while Gordon's was held in the Desborough Hall on the 29th. Principal Guest, Dr. G.N. Westgarth, Principal of Shoreditch College.

November – a 'Careers' month. October 31/November 1 Youth employment interviews for 5th years, two G.P.O. representatives from Engineering Dept. and Postal services together with a member of staff from McGraw Hill Publishing who spoke about office work generally on the 4th followed by visits of boys to G.P.O. and girls to McGraw Hill on the 11th, a visiting speaker from the East Berks. College Catering and Hairdressing Depts on the 25th, the Home Economics Group visited St. Mark's Hospital and Boyn Grove Old Peoples Home on the 26th and a cinema visit 'Far from the Madding Crowd' on the 27th. In the evening senior pupils attended a meeting in the Town Hall to discuss ways of raising funds for the new Youth Centre. Youth employment interviews for Easter leavers on the 28th.

4th year pupils visited Slough College of Technology on December 2, a talk to 1st year boys by a Police Liaison Officer on the 12th, a careers talk to 4th year boys and girls by Royal Navy representatives on the 16th, junior and senior Carol Services 17th and 18th, a Christmas film 'Monsieur Hullot's Holiday' on the 19th, school closing on the 20th. Miss P.J. Weeks became an additional teacher to help with 39 immigrant children and Mr. R.H. Abell became a Governor.

1969

Re-open January 7. 5th year girls travelled to the Victoria & Albert Museum on the 13th when careers talks by J.M. Jones Ltd. builders and Maidenhead & District Laundry Co. was followed up by visits on the 20th. Youth employment interviews for summer leavers on the 30th.

The County Cross Country Championships took place at Windsor on February 1; a talk on the 'Retail Trade' by the Head of Dept. East Berks. College was on the 3rd followed by a visit to Windsor on the 10th; girls and their parents attended the Butterick/Vogue Fashion Display Dress Show on the 6th; the District Cross Country Championships were on the 8th, the Senior Team came 1st Junior Team 2nd; third year pupils and a group of musicians attended a Folk Dancing afternoon organised by the County Music Advisor on the 19th and a fifth year party went to the Playhouse Theatre to see a production by the Oxford University Dramatic Society of 'Romeo and Juliet' on the 20th.

Fourth year boys visited the Army Junior Leaders' Course at Nuneaton on March 4; nine boys, six girls accompanied by Mr. Durran left for the Outdoor Pursuits Course at Lakeside on the 8th. (A film was made with colour slides of activities and shown to parents on April 30.) Talk on Army careers for girls (10th) and by the Tutor, Heatherwood Hospital (13th), a visit to the Berkshire College of Agriculture (13th) with, as a follow up, the film 'Red Sky at Night' (17th), Ideal Homes Exhibition (same day), 'Technology Today' an exhibition at the East Berks. College (21st) and a careers talk on the Royal Navy for both boys and girls (24th).

The Governors of Cox Green County Secondary School agreed that when Gordon closed and pupils transferred to the Cox Green building consideration should be given to the incorporation of the word 'Gordon' into the name of the combined schools.

Mr. D. Healey was granted leave of absence from April 11–29 to take part in a music festival in Canada. In addition to other activities he had been invited to take part in a performance of one of his own compositions which was to be recorded for broadcasting. He was also to be interviewed for a post at the University of Ontario.

The Headmaster attended the Open Evening at the new Youth Centre on May 5; an R.S.P.C.A. talk to 2nd years on the 7th. District Athletics Championships on the 19th when the girls gained 2nd place in the under 14 events and 1st place in the under 16. Nine boys and five girls were selected to represent the District in the County Championships. A film and careers talk on 'Banking' also took place.

4th years visited the Royal Navy, Portsmouth on June 12; 3rd years the Commonwealth Institute; 5th years the Palace of Westminster and Stock Exchange on the 19th and a talk by Barclays Bank (24th) followed by a visit to their Training Centre at Teddington on the 26th. Mrs Fairbrother left on June 28 to attend the World Gymnaestrada in Basle, Switzerland as one of the team coaches. Two girls from Gordon had been selected for the Slough team.

An Open Evening and Evening of Drama for parents and friends took place on July 2. Practical and classroom work was exhibited and there were Physical Education and Fashion Displays. The District Swimming Gala was on the 3rd; 5th year group travelled to Reading to see the French film "Les Enfants du Paradis" on the 4th; performances of "Mr. Punch", a children's opera written by Mr. Healey and "Sunday Costs Five Pesos", a one-act play on the 8th and 9th; a 5th year visit to the Town Hall also on the 9th; 3rd year children to the Berkshire College of Agriculture; the All-England Athletics Championships at Motspur Park, Surrey, on the 10th when Linda Hewitt and Mervyn Evans represented Berkshire; Inter House Athletics and Swimming 11th and 14th; summer holidays commenced on the 16th. Mr. A.C. Durran transferred to Cox Green, Mr. I.R. Severn had been appointed Head of Lower School at Grange County Secondary, Aylesbury and Mr. M. Klimaytys resigned. Mr. Healey resigned on August 31.

The school journey to Jony-en-Josas near Paris was from July 23–31. Accompanied by Mrs. Sulley, Mr. Sheppard and the Headmaster forty children were accommodated in a private school which stood in its own grounds of 50 acres. Being able to use the swimming pool and playing areas it had the advantage of rural community life beside easy access to Paris.

Number of candidates taking G.C.E. 'O' levels 41. Subjects:- English Language, English Literature, Mathematics, History,

Geography, French, Home Economics, Dress, Physics, Human Biology, Art and Music. Two gained six subjects. Number of candidates taking C.S.E. 63. In addition to the above subjects:- General Science, Technical Drawing, Woodwork and Metalwork. Forty three gained Grade I Passes.

Re-open September 9 with Miss Clark (Home Economics), Miss Guest (Geography, Craft) and Mr. Griffiths (Physical Education). Mr. Kennedy's appointment became permanent. Other changes:-

Miss D.E. Cook Head of Department for Remedial Work
Mr. J.H. Sheppard Head of Department for History and Integrated Humanities
Mr. P.W. Proffitt Head of Department for Science
Mr. M.M. Gulliford Graded post for Geography.
Mrs. M.M. Smets Graded post (recommendation)

2nd year girls visited the Silk Farm at Lullingstone on September 25; Youth Employment talks to 5th year (26th); a little over £200 was raised at the Autumn Fair (27th) and 4th years visited British Ermeto and McGraw Hill (29th). Mrs. J. Rose became the new music teacher.

4th years to Gregory's Garage and Beecham's Products on October 6; the Simplicity Fashion Show (9th); careers talks by the Royal Navy and Royal Marines (13th); a performance in hall by the Band of the Royal Green Jackets (16th); a Lever Bros. Demonstration and talk to 4th year girls (17th) and a visit to the Army Apprentices Centre, Arborfield (22nd). Miss R. Givens, Community Service Volunteer commenced on the 31st.

The principal guest at Prize Day in Desborough Hall on November 9 was Miss H. Bussell one of the first women engineers to be appointed to the staff of British Railways. A careers talk on the Retail Trade (Heelas) was on the 17th.

2nd year forms visited the Transport Museum, Clapham on December 4; Christmas services and the senior party was on the 17th, school closing on the 19th. Resignations were received from Mrs. Fairbrother and Miss Cook. Thirty four children travelled overland to enjoy an extremely successful winter sports in Switzerland during the Christmas holiday.

1970

Times of the morning session had been changed from 8.55am–12.00 to 9.10–12.15. It was recommended that Mrs. J.E. Sulley should become Head of Department as from January 1. The new term commenced January 6. Medical examinations on the 13th; a Police careers talk on the 16th; a visit to Vauxhall Motors, Luton on the 21st; a G.P.O. talk on the 26th (followed by a visit to Slough on February 2) and a visit to Boots and Woolworths also on the 26th.

A party of fifteen led by Mr. Proffitt spent two weeks at the Outdoor Pursuits Centre, Lakeside from February 21 to March 6.

Careers visits to a J.M. Jones building site, Transitron, East Berks College and Ideal Homes Exhibition during March. Road Safety Talks to 1st and 2nd years on March 17. The death was announced of one of the Governors, Dr. E.M. Bell. Three members of staff, Mrs. Davis, Mrs. Sulley and Mrs. Smets were members of subject panels for C.S.E. and met to discuss the planning and control of C.S.E. examinations.

4th year pupils visited Boyn Grove Old Peoples Home on April 27 and St. Mark's Hospital on the 30th.

Proposals were agreed for the re-organisation of secondary education which would mean Gordon would become a comprehensive secondary school whose pupils were in the age range 11–13 years. It was hoped that this would take place about 1972 or 1973 and the need for the interim arrangements would continue until it was possible to accommodate all pupils at Cox Green. The appointment of Mr. R. Bristow as Headteacher would be extended for as long as the school remains a secondary modern school and that he be recognised as Headteacher Designate of the school during its interim stage of re-organisation. Mr J.H. Miller would be recognised as Deputy Headteacher Designate.

On May 1 Mr. M.J.R. Bright, Art Master, was invited to attend the Royal Academy having had a painting accepted for showing this year. A parents meeting of 4th and 5th years on the 5th when the film 'When They Leave School' was shown. A group of thirteen 4th year spent a two day residential course for leavers at the Thamesfield Centre, Henley. A visit to Barclays Bank Training Centre, Teddington on June 23 and a 5th year visit to the Palace of Westminster on the 30th.

A 2nd year visit to the Berkshire College of Agriculture on July 8; Inter-House Athletics on the 10th when Linda Hewitt left for Solihull to represent N.E. Berkshire in the All-England Athletics, an Open Evening on the 15th; school closed on the 17th. Resignations during year:- Mr. P.D. Mountford, Mr. T. Stone, Mr. M.M. Gulliford, Mr. M.J.R. Bright, Mr. P.W. Proffitt, Mr. R. Kennedy and Miss M.R. Callaghan (one term only). Examination Results:- 44 passes in G.C.E. subjects (11 in Mathematics, 9 in English Language, 7 in English Literature). 263 passes in C.S.E. subjects, 35 at Grade I, (14 in Mathematics, 7 in English and 4 each in History and Technical Drawing).

The Headmaster was admitted to hospital on July 18 and would be unable to return until November.

The new term commenced on September 7 Mr. Miller acting as Headmaster. The following members of staff took up their appointments:- Mrs. C. Alterskye, Mr. T. Hayes, Mr R.J. Sibley, Mr. C.V. Wellard, Miss R. Bolton, Mr. J.H. Rinnick, Mr. C. Jowett, Mrs. G. Larche and Miss V.A. Lucas, Community Service Volunteer helping with the teaching of small groups of immigrant children. N.O.R. 466. Approximately £250 was raised at the Autumn Fair on September 26 funds going to reclaim ground at the end of the garden and for a display cabinet for the assembly hall.

A group attended a special film programme at the A.B.C. Cinema in connection with St. Mary's Church Centenary Year on October 1; a Simplicity Fashion Display on the 5th; a careers visit to the Royal Navy at Portsmouth on the 14th; Mr. Streams resigned as caretaker on the 25th as he and his wife were flying to Australia to join their family. His successor was Mr. G. Pickard.

A joint meeting of Representative Governors of Cox Green and Gordon was held on October 20. It was proposed and seconded that Mr. L.E.J. Adderson, Miss M.M. Claydon, Miss P. Croxford, Mr. H. Edwards (declined) be appointed Co-optative Governors for the triennial period ending August 31, 1973. (Mr. A.G. Hacker vice Mr. Edwards).

November 14–28 a group at the Outdoor Pursuits Centre on Lake Windemere with Mrs. Sulley, a day trip to Calais on December 10 again organised by Mrs. Sulley, term ending on the 18th. Resignation Miss Clark (Homecraft).

1971

Re-open January 5. New appointments Mr. R.J. Temple (English/Mathematics), Mrs. K. Wenninger (English). 4th and 5th years paid a visit to the Victoria and Albert Museum on the 11th, 4th years to R.A.F. Odiham on the 19th and there was a Dylon demonstration on home dyeing on the 21st. Brian Way Drama Group Performances presented 'Children of the Sun' to years 1–3 on February 15.

Many children had to be sent home on February 24 as one section of the boiler which provides heating for the main block was cracked. Those kept in school:-

February 24	5th and 4th years
February 25	5th and 3rd years
February 26	5th and 2nd years.

5th years paid a visit to the various departments at Maidenhead Town Hall on March 10, 5th year boys attended an Open Evening at Barclays Bank on the 25th and twelve 4th year leavers attended a two day 'Leavers Course' at Thamesfield Centre, Henley-on-Thames on the 26th.

School closed at 3pm on March 19 to allow a meeting of Departmental Heads and teachers in charge of subjects to discuss the re-organisation of secondary education.

It was reported that the Education Authority approved September 1973 as the date for the introduction of comprehensive education in secondary schools in the Maidenhead area. Proposals were made by the Schools Management Committee for the alternative arrangements of the transfers of pupils to other secondary schools and the conversion at an early date of Gordon School to a primary school to serve the centre of the town.

Thirty-five children, three staff and three parents took part in a one day excursion to Boulogne on April 2nd.

Mr. Bristow wrote in the School Log Book on April 7 'This is the last day of term and my last normal school day as Headmaster. My original appointment as assistant was in July 1953. Mr. J.H. Miller has been appointed Acting Head for the Summer Term, a permanent appointment will be made in the near future'. Mr. Bristow had been congratulated by the Governors on his new appointment in the Careers Service of the Inner London Education Authority. Resignations:- Mr. Griffiths and Mrs. Rose.

Summer term opened on April 27 with three members of staff short – Mr. Bristow, Mrs. Rose and Mr. Rinnick. New appointment:- Mr. R. Holland (P.E.). A member of the St. John's Ambulance spoke to some 2nd and 3rd year boys on May 7; 4th and 5th year visited a Slough cinema on the 24th to see 'Jane Eyre'. Careers visits included the Fire Station and Reading Telephone Exchange.

Three candidates were interviewed at a special meeting on May 20 for the appointment of Headmaster. Mr. Miller the Deputy Head was successful.

Following on from a talk by a visiting speaker 4th year visited the Berkshire College of Agriculture on June 7. Other places included Hewens Garage, Hacker Radio and London Airport (Engineering) on the 28th and 29th.

A talk and demonstration on 'Make-up' for 4th year girls on July 5; approximately 180 attended and observed 'normal' lessons at the Open Day on the 7th; the Swimming Gala on the 12th; careers visits to the 'Maidenhead Advertiser' and Taplow Paper Mill; 4th year went on a Geography Fieldwork to Kingsclere near Basingstoke on the 13th; Sports Day 14th; summer holidays began on the 16th. Mr. Sheppard took ten boys to the Royal Navy, H.M.S. Fearless, Southampton, Cherbourg, Avonmouth returning on the 23rd and Mrs. Sulley took thirty children on holiday to Brive, France on the 20th. Staff resignations:- Miss Bolton (P.E.), Miss Guest (Geography), Mrs. Wenninger (English), Miss Iles (temp. Home Economics), Miss Lucas (C.S.V.) and Mr. Goodman (temp. Music). Examination results, G.C.E. subjects:- Mathematics 14; Geography 10; English Language 9; History 9; English Literature 7; Physics 6; Engineering Drawing 6; Grade I passes 5. C.S.E. 234 passes; 36 Grade I. Ten boys in the 4th year leavers group attended an Engineering Course at the East Berks. College, Maidenhead one day each week. Courses were available in Agriculture/ Horticulture and Building at other Colleges. Discussions were taking place about the possibility of extending Gordon's participation in these courses next year.

Public notices had been issued under Section 13 of the Education Act 1944 on August 20 of the Education Authority's intention to close Gordon and to establish in the premises a two-form entry County Junior School and a two-form entry County Infant School.

The Autumn Term commenced on September 7 with 85 new entrants. N.O.R. 456. Staff appointments:- Mr. E. Smith (Head of Science Department), Mr. J.C. Bradbury-Williams (Mathematics), Mrs. E. Porter (Girls' P.E.), Mr. E.T. Hosken (Geography), Miss W.J. Reed (Home Economics), Mr. P.K. Newman (Craftwork), Mrs. C. Hawes (Music), Mr. N.W. Fenton (temp. English) and Miss A. Cassidy (Community Service Volunteer). The Autumn Fair on the 25th raised over £250 the money buying a trampoline for use in the P.E. Dept. Mr. Holland the boys' P.E. Master had represented Great Britain in trampolining. The popularity of school meals was declining the numbers dropping from 230 to 130.

Thirty-five boys visited the Royal Navy at Portsmouth on October 19.

The Bishop of Buckingham, the Rt. Rev. G.C.C. Pepys, presented the prizes on Prize Day November 4. Mr. Holland took a group of fifteen to the Outdoor Pursuits Centre, Lake Windermere from the 6th–20th. November 9 was the 'French Holiday Evening' when parents were invited to see photographs and slides of the holiday at Brive earlier in the year. Mr. Hayes attended a Strand Glass (Model Boat Building) Course on the 29th.

December events:- an evening of Music and Drama in the school hall (9th); forty pupils at a Careers Exhibition in London (10th); the McCall's Dress Show (14th); film 'Khartoum' (15th); Carol Service St. Mary's Church, 4th/5th year party in evening (16th); holidays commence (17th).

As we approach the final years of the school it would seem appropriate to record the senior staff and their responsibilities.

Headmaster	Mr. J.H. Miller
Deputy Head	Mrs. D.M. Wilson
Senior Master	Mr. C.E. Jeavons
Head of History-Integrated Humanities Dept. (organisation of History throughout school-co-ordination of Geography/History in 1st and 2nd year-careers)	Mr. J. Sheppard

Head of Science Dept. (responsible for organisation of Science throughout school)	Mr. E.F. Smith
Head of English Dept. (responsible for organisation of English throughout school)	Mrs. H.P. King
Head of French Dept. (responsible for organisation of French throughout school)	Mrs. J.R. Sulley
Geography (organisation of Geography-co-ordination of Geography/History in1st and 2nd year)	Mr. C. Wellard
Home Economics (responsible for Home Economics Dept. and co-ordination of girls' craftwork)	Mrs. M. Smets
Library and English (responsible for organisation of Library/English examination work)	Mrs. C. Alterskye
Needlecraft (organisation of Needlecraft throughout school and other craft activities for girls')	Mrs. M. Davis
Remedial (organisation of remedial teaching programme throughout school)	Mrs. G. Larche
Physical Education (organisation of boys P.E. and Games Activities)	Mr. R. Holland
Physical Education (organisation of girls P.E. and Games Activities)	Miss R. Bolton
Woodcraft (responsible for Woodcraft/Out of School Activities)	Mr. T. Hayes
Recommendation	
Art (responsible for Art Dept.)	Mr. R. Sibley
Head of Mathematics Dept. (organisation of Mathematics teaching throughout school).	New appointment

1972

The new term commenced January 4, Mr. Bradbury-Williams attending a Computer Course. 4th/5th year girls visited the Victoria and Albert Museum on the 10th and thirteen pupils were on a three-day School Leavers Conference at Thamesfield House, Henley from the 31st.

The P.E. Dept were enthusiastic to extend the range of games/leisure activities they offered to 4th/5th year children. To help provide these extra activities contact had been made with the Army Youth Team who visited the school on February 10 to consider introducing 0.22 shooting, orienteering and a five-day camp. Mr. Hayes attended Boyne Hill (Art Fibre Glass Work) Course on the 22nd and 23rd. The Boys' Inter-House Cross Country Race was on the 11th.

At a fire drill on March 21 the school was cleared in under two minutes. Forty-five children attended the Science Fair at Paddington Technical College on the 28th.

Mr. and Mrs. Wellard and Mr. Hosken took thirty-four 4th/5th year children on a Geographical Fieldwork Expedition to Fairbourne, Merioneth, North Wales on March 24. They studied Ro Wen sand-spit, visited Harlech Castle, Barmouth, Dolgellan and surveyed the Blaenau-Ffestiniog Hydro-Electric Power Station and a State Quarry. They climbed Cader Idris and walked on a mountain Nature Trail to the north of Dolgellan. This type of study is an important feature of the C.S.E. Geography Course. They returned on the 30th. Mr. Newman resigned at Easter to take an appointment in Northern Ireland and Mr. Fenton's appointment was made permanent from May 1.

A letter of congratulations was sent from the Governors to former pupil Robert Lamb on obtaining a scholarship to Cambridge University.

Careers and general interest visits included:- Maidenhead Nursery School, Boyn Grove Old People's Home, Slough College (Catering Dept.), East Berks. College (Business Studies Dept.), Computer Centre Dept. of Health and Social Security Reading, B.E.A. Engineering Base, Careers Exhibition Olympia, Vandervells, Taylowes Ltd., A. Fabb (embroidery), Richmond Ice Rink, Albert Hall (England v. W. Germany Basketball), Wexham Park Hospital.

4th year to Barclays Bank Training Centre, Teddington on May 8, 3rd/4th year Parents Evening (9th), £40 raised at a jumble sale for the Guide Dogs for the Blind Fund on the 13th. A follow-up talk took place on the 27th June.

From June 26–30 some of the fifth year were in camp at the Y.M.C.A. Outdoor Pursuits Centre, Padworth with the Army Youth

Team. Activities planned included canoeing, horse-riding, orienteering and local visits. Second year paid a visit to the Silk Farm on the 27th.

Open Evening was on July 6, 5th year visited Tilbury Caves (7th), Inter House Swimming Gala (10th), Inter House Athletics (12th), 4th/5th year end-of-year dance (13th). Safety week was held July 10–14. Organised by Mr. Smith, (Head of Science Dept.) this included a series of lectures and films by visiting speakers on various aspects of safety-Hill, Road, Water, Fire. Summer holidays began on the 14th. Resignation after six years of Mrs. Sulley (maternity), Mr. Bradbury-Williams temporary appointment ceased.

Re-open September 5 with Mrs. E. Dalley as Head of French Dept., Mr. P.J. May, Head of Mathematics Dept. (resigned December 15) and Mr. H.J. Waterman, temporary Head of History Dept. as replacement for Mr. Sheppard who had been seconded to attend a one-year course for a Diploma in Advanced Education at Bristol University. Mr. A.G. Brian joined the Boys Craft Dept. staff and Miss F. Mayhew became the C.S.V. for one term only. The final first year intake to the school was eighty-five. The Autumn Fair on September 23 raised approximately £240 for School Funds £80 going to Guide Dogs for the Blind.

The R.A.M.C. Band gave a concert on October 16 and thirteen pupils attended the Outdoor Pursuits Centre on Lake Windermere for two weeks commencing on the 21st. Mrs. Casement resigned on the 31st (maternity) and Mr. B. Ashmore began teaching Biology.

Mr. F. Bough of B.B.C. Television presented the awards on Prize Day November 16. The Mayor of Maidenhead, Councillor C.A.H. Nock attended. School closed for the 25th wedding anniversary of H.M. The Queen and the Duke of Edinburgh on the 20th.

First years visited London on December 11 as part of their work in Discovery, 4th/5th year dance (13th), Carol Service at St. Mary's Church (14th) and the film 'Kes' on the 15th. Term ended with the resignation of Miss Reed.

In planning for the final year (September 1973–July 1974) concern was expressed that a generous staffing ratio should be maintained to allow for academic courses and a full range of subjects. It was hoped that there would be no modification or removal of buildings until the school was closed. The confirmed allocation of Head plus 14.2 was disappointing for the continuation with fifth year Option Groups and the introduction of alternatives for R.O.S.L.A. children.

1973

Spring Term began on January 9 with Miss J. Farrar (Home Economics). Miss S. Hayward was the new Community Service Volunteer. Fifth year exams commenced. 4th/5th year girls visited London Museums and Fabric Sales on the 15th, the annual School Leavers Conference at Thamesfield, Henley being from the 29th–31st. Twenty-four pupils attended Barclays Bank Training Centre, Teddington on the 30th the day an Area Careers Convention was held in the school hall.

Thirty boys visited Vauxhall Motors, Luton on February 8, the same number of first years Windsor Castle on the 14th, twelve fifth year the Oxford Playhouse on the 15th and eighteen to 'Journey through Music' in London on the 16th. A film/talk on Road Safety was on the 26th.

1st/2nd year parents met on February 28, 3rd/4th year on March 6. Three 5th year boys, Andrew Prestt, Christopher Boini and Nicholas Olive took part in a Rotary Public Speaking Competition on March 7. Talking on 'Air Safety', although unplaced, the boys gave a creditable performance. A Birds Eye Food Demonstration for 4th year girls on the 8th; boys and girls Inter-House Cross Country Competition (9th); Mr. Holland attended the Crystal Palace Sports Centre to coach trampolining for one week from the 12th. Mr. Jeavons completed twenty-five years service on the 15th and was presented with a gold watch during assembly.

Arrangements were made for present third years to transfer to other secondary schools in the town, parents and pupils being given the school of their choice. Altwood 31, Cox Green 28, Furze Platt 44 and the High School 2.

April 2 and 4 demonstrations and displays by visiting speakers on 'Leisure'; end of term dance for 4th/5th years (4th); thirty-six 5th years on a one week Fieldwork Expedition to Penzance Youth Hostel, Cornwall from the 5th. Work included Town Study, the

Mr. Jeavons celebrates 25 years in 1973.

Fishing Industry, the Tourist Industry, Geology of the area and a visit to Lands End. Close for Easter on the 6th, Mrs. Larche resigning as Remedial and French teacher to take a similar position at Maidenhead Boys' Grammar School from May 1.

Summer Term began on May 1, Mrs. Easterbrook and Mrs. Morrison being given temporary appointments to help with Science, Mathematics and Remedial work. Mrs. May, because of illness, was only teaching half-time. A visit to the College of Art Fashion Show at the Esso Motor Hotel on the 8th and twenty-five boys to the R.A.F. Odiham on the 24th.

Fourteen boys were engaged on a Walking Expedition in the Chilterns, staying in Youth Hostels, from June 22–25, a presentation of the Guide Dogs for the Blind photograph and completion of payment of £250 on the 27th and thirty boys visited the Royal Navy at Portsmouth on the 29th. N.O.R. 423.

Twenty-nine 5th year pupils were in camp in Huntingdon from July 1–6, a programme of outdoor pursuits having been arranged, fifteen pupils to the Road Research Laboratory at Crowthorne on the 10th, Open Evening the 12th showing exhibitions of work and displays by children, Inter-House Swimming Gala on the 16th, Inter-House Athletics on the 18th. 'Health Week' – a series of talks and films on various aspects of health was from the 16th–20th.

July 20 was the final day of Gordon as a complete school. In addition to 5th year leavers the whole of the 3rd year were leaving to join other Maidenhead Secondary Schools in September. A number of staff were leaving and because of the reduction in the numbers of children, were not being replaced. Mrs. Alterskye, Mr. Temple, Mrs. Hawes, Mr. Waterman and Miss Hayward all resigned. Mr. Sheppard took an appointment at Cox Green and Mrs. Smets at Newlands (Maidenhead High School). Both would come to teach at Gordon one day a week. Mrs. May retired after many years of loyal service.

September 4, the beginning of the new term and final year with 17 full-time staff and 261 children on the roll. Part-time staff – Mrs. Binstead and Mrs. Wood. Arrangements were made for the interchange of staff with other secondary schools. Mrs. Davis Furze Platt for three mornings, in return, Mr. Hosken would teach eight periods at Cox Green, Mr. Brian eight periods, Mr. Holland four periods at Furze Platt.

3rd year visited Blenheim Palace on October 4; fifteen pupils at the Outdoor Pursuits Centre in the Lake District (13 to 27); eight pupils at a Maidenhead Council meeting at the Town Hall (16th). Refreshments were taken afterwards with the Mayor and Councillors.

Five immigrant pupils visited Windsor Safari Park on November 6; school closed for the wedding of H.R.H. Princess Anne to Capt. Mark Philips (14th); third years to Science Museum (22nd); School Leavers Conference at Henley (27 to 29); Prize Day awards presented by Mr. L.E.J. Adderson on the evening of the 29th; Mrs. R.M. Tyrrell appointed by the Education Authority to the Governing Body in place of Mrs. N. Bromley who had resigned in June.

It was suggested that schools in neighbouring areas of the

County should send details of vacancies to enable staff to be satisfactorily placed on the closure of the school.

N.O.R. 259. Thirty pupils and two staff were ski-ing in Austria December 15 to 22; Carol Service at St. Mary's Church (18th); close on the 19th with the film 'Those Magnificent Men in their Flying Machines'. Mr. Brian and Mrs. Binstead resigned from December 31. Careers visits:- Black & Decker; Police Station; Metal Vents Ltd; a printing firm.

1974

Beginning of the Spring Term January 8; start of internal exams (9th); the fifth year parents meeting was well attended on the 23rd.

Thirty children at the Richmond Ice Rink on the evening of March 1; careers talk and film – Barclays Bank – (22nd); Inter-House Cross Country and St. John First Aid exam for fifth years (27th); Mr. Hayes left to take an appointment at Waingels Copse School, Woodley, and Mr. Holland to Turn Pike School, Newbury on the 29th. School leavers 17.

Enquiries were made to other schools especially those who would be receiving Gordon pupils to see whether they would like any of the cups and trophies. It was felt that one cup should be offered to be added to the Town's Silver Collection. Cox Green Secondary School should be offered the memorial boards but should a suitable arrangement not be agreed, these boards should then be offered to one of the local churches. Log Books and other papers would go to the County Archivist.

Summer and the last term commenced on April 23. Third years enjoyed a trip along the Kennet and Avon Canal on the 24th.

A Governors Sub-Committee meeting to discuss an end of school function was held on May 7. Ten boys in the 5th year visited the Army at Aldershot on the 22nd. A careers talk by a Major from the Army took place on June 11.

Twenty-five fifth year visited the Tate Gallery on June 14. An instruction course on moped riding (five sessions each of two hours) also began for fifth years. This age group also took part in a Chiltern Hills walk on the 25th.

Staff of longstanding Mrs. D.M. Wilson and Mr. C.E. Jeavons.

The final meeting of Governors was held on June 25, membership from April 1974:-

Berkshire County Council (6)

Mrs. R.M. Tyrrell
Mr. W. Burrough
Miss J.G. Claxton
Mrs. J. Steel
Mr. A.E. Wheeler
vacancy

Windsor & Maidenhead District Council (6)

Miss P. Croxford
Mrs. J. Smith
Mrs. P. Flew
Mrs. M.E. Griffin
Mrs. J. Hobson
Mr. J.C. Powell

Co-opted Governors (4)

Mr. L.E.J. Adderson
Miss M.M. Claydon
Mr. A.G. Hacker
vacancy

Cups and trophies were gladly received by other secondary schools in the area but the memorial boards still had to be settled.

The Governors moved a vote of thanks to the Headmaster and staff for the satisfactory way in which the school had been run. A copy of the Headmaster's final report was not in the file.

160 pupils and 16 staff enjoyed a one day visit to Boulogne on July 1. The remaining children went to Windsor Safari Park.

Because their school building had been declared unsafe Furze Platt second year pupils (approx 180 children and staff) used Gordon premises and would do so until the necessary repairs had been carried out. Gordon School would cease to be maintained by the Authority at the end of the current term, furniture not being removed for the time being.

A fifth year group cleared litter from Maidenhead Thicket on July 8. Approximately 400 people attended an informal gathering of Governors, present and past staff and former pupils and friends to mark the School's closure on July 12. Mr. A.E. Wheeler, Chairman of Governors and himself an old pupil, made a very appropriate speech. The swimming gala had to be cancelled on the 15th due to rain, third years visited Coventry Cathedral on the 16th, Sports Day on the 17th.

July 19 and the Log Book reads:- 'The final day in the 67 year history of Gordon School. Although this is a sad occasion all associated with the School can look back with pride on the fine achievements of the School and its contribution to education in Maidenhead'.

(signed) J.H. Miller
Headmaster
19.7.74.

A.E. Wheeler
19/7/74.

G.C.E. and C.S.E. Examination entries for 1974

G.C.E. 50 candidates taking 159 subjects with the Associated Examining Board.
3 candidates entered for Portuguese with the London University Board.

C.S.E. 87 candidates taking 451 subjects.

Transfer of pupils	*2nd Year*	*3rd Year*
Altwood	16	35
Cox Green	23	23
Furze Platt	37	23
Newlands	2	

Again it was possible to give parents and pupils the school of their choice.

Staff appointments for September
Mr. J.H. Miller's secondment was approved (taking course at Reading University leading to a Diploma in Advance Education)
Mrs. Wilson – Desborough School
Mr. Jeavons – Cox Green
Mr. Hosken – Cox Green
Mrs. Davis – awaiting result of secondment for a one-year course
Mrs. Porter – maternity leave.

9
The Berkshire School of Art and Design

Incorporated as an independent Further Education Institution on April 1, 1993 when the site assets were transferred from the Local Authority to the College as a result of the Further and Higher Education Act 1992 the buildings are currently occupied by the Berkshire School of Art and Design which was formerly known as Berkshire College of Art and Design prior to its merger on January 6, 1997 with Reading College of Arts and Technology.

The Berkshire School of Art and Design now forms one of four divisions of the merged College.

I am indebted to Mr. John Aston, Principal of Berkshire College of Art and Design from January 1992 to January 1997 and Associate Director (Overseas Programmes) of Reading College of Arts & Technology from January to July 1997 for personally conducting me around the buildings and grounds and explaining the work of the School. To see over my 'old secondary school' after fifty five years and compare then with now proved both interesting and nostalgic.

May 1997

Index